Discovering Nature

Robert Weller's richly documented account describes the extraordinary transformations which have taken place in Chinese and Taiwanese responses to the environment across the twentieth century. Indeed, as the author points out, within a relatively short time both places can be said to have "discovered" a new concept of nature. The book focuses on nature tourism, anti-pollution movements, and policy implementation to show how the global spread of Western ideas about nature has interacted with Chinese traditions. Inevitably these interactions have been reworked and reconstituted within the local context, and differences of understanding across groups have caused problems in administering environmental reforms. These differences will have to be resolved if the dynamic transformations of the 1980s and 1990s are to be maintained in the twenty-first century. In spite of a more than a century of independent political development, a comparison between China and Taiwan reveals surprising similarities, showing how globalization and shared cultural traditions have outweighed political differences in shaping their environments. The book will appeal to a broad readership from scholars of Asia, to environmentalists, and anthropologists.

ROBERT P. WELLER is Professor of Anthropology and Research Associate of the Institute on Culture, Religion, and World Affairs at Boston University. His numerous books and articles on China and Taiwan range from religion to political change, including most recently *Civil Life, Political Change, and Globalization in Asia* (editor, 2005).

Discovering Nature

Globalization and Environmental Culture in China and Taiwan

Robert P. Weller

Boston University

CAMBRIDGE UNIVERSITY PRESS
Cambridge, New York, Melbourne, Madrid, Cape Town, Singapore, São Paulo

Cambridge University Press
The Edinburgh Building, Cambridge CB2 2RU, UK

Published in the United States of America by Cambridge University Press, New York

www.cambridge.org
Information on this title: www.cambridge.org/9780521548410

First published 2006

Printed in the United Kingdom at the University Press, Cambridge

A catalogue record for this publication is available from the British Library

ISBN-13 978-0-521-83959-4 hardback
ISBN-10 0-521-83959-9 hardback
ISBN-13 978-0-521-54841-0 paperback
ISBN-10 0-521-54841-1 paperback

Contents

Illustrations

Acknowledgments

I have played with this project long enough that my debts are too great to list properly. Foremost among them is the help I have received over the years from Peter L. Berger and my other colleagues at Boston University's Institute on Culture, Religion, and World Affairs, and at its predecessor, the Institute for the Study of Economic Culture. The Institute provided the funding for the first few years of research through a grant from the Bradley Foundation, and its intellectual greenhouse has allowed my ideas to grow. Thanks also to my many other colleagues, especially in the Department of Anthropology at Boston University and the Fairbank Center for East Asian Research at Harvard University, who have been both personally supportive and intellectually challenging.

Much of the work in China took place in cooperation with the Harvard University Committee on the Environment. Most of the research in the People's Republic was funded through them, with grants from the V. Kann Rasmussen Foundation and the United States Department of Energy. I am grateful for the help and support of William Alford, Leslyn Hall, Chris Nielsen, Karen Polenske, Yuanyuan Shen, and David Zweig on that project. Jiansheng Li was invaluable as a postdoctoral researcher.

The Committee on the Environment also funded some of the research on earlier Chinese ideas about nature. For that part of the book, I especially want to thank Peter Bol, who shared responsibility for that first phase of the project with me, and who is one of the people who got me started on the topic over lunch many years ago. Thanks also to Ping-tzu Chu and Andrew Meyer, both graduate students at the time, who helped so much.

In Taiwan I am grateful above all to Hsin-Huang Michael Hsiao, who expedited much of the work, and shared his ideas, time, and contacts so generously. Julia Huang was a wonderful research assistant both there and in Boston for several years. Funding for some of the Taiwan research came from the Wenner-Gren Foundation for Anthropological Research, whose help I gratefully acknowledge.

I have presented portions of this material at many talks over the years. The most important to me in shaping the final form of the book was the Hume Memorial Lecture at Yale University, and I am grateful to the organizers for giving me the opportunity. Many thanks also to those who have helped me, often by challenging me, in presentations at the China Environment Forum at the Woodrow Wilson Center, the Institute of Chinese Studies at Oxford, the Department of Anthropology at Cornell University, and East Asian studies programs at Bard, Skidmore, and Stanford, and on many occasions at Harvard.

I gratefully acknowledge the permission of Chiang Hsun and Chu Ko to reproduce their paintings here, and I hope my admiration of their work is clear in the text. I also want to thank the Administrative Offices of Taroko National Park and Kending National Park in Taiwan for permission to use their visual materials. Every effort has been made to secure necessary permissions to reproduce copyright material in this work, though in some cases it has proved impossible to trace copyright holders. If any omissions are brought to my notice, I will be happy to include appropriate acknowledgments in any subsequent printing.

Finally, I am especially grateful to the people who have read and commented on parts of the manuscript for this book: Steve Harrell, Richard Louis Edmonds, Thomas Moran, Eugene Anderson, and Wen-hsin Yeh. I learned a great deal from each of them, and many of their comments helped shape the way this book turned out. Any acknowledgment here is inadequate repayment of the labor they put in, but at least it is a token.

1 Discovering nature

The notes from my first period of fieldwork in Taiwan, in the late 1970s, reveal no sign of nature beyond the immediate demands of farming. Almost two years in a village just outside the small town of Sanxia produced no reference to complaints about pollution, for example, even though two decades of rapid economic growth had caused serious environmental deterioration.[1] One study found that thirteen of sixteen major Taiwanese rivers and streams (including Sanxia's largest river) were seriously polluted in their lower reaches; the others were moderately polluted. Only 1 percent of sewage water received even primary waste treatment.[2] With the exception of a large noise meter that appeared in the busiest part of Taipei during that time, there was also little visible environmental activity from the government. Nor did anyone seem very interested in the appreciation of nature for its own sake. One friend raised orchids, and his adult children sometimes accompanied me on walks in the hills. We rarely saw anyone else on those walks though, with the exception of a very few of the more exciting mountain paths that attracted Sunday groups of college students from Taipei, a bumpy hour and a half away by bus or motorcycle.

In part, the absence of nature in my notes reflects my own interests, which were in religion at the time. Yet it also reflects local priorities and conceptions. Most people in Sanxia were either farmers or farmers' children who had newly entered Taiwan's rapidly developing industrial economy. They were just too close to their daily toil with the environment to feel much affection or nostalgia for it. Those years of the late 1970s had not been easy for farming. Families typically no longer had enough labor to harvest their crops, and soldiers had to come help out. This period also marked the beginning of the end for the tangerine farmers who occupied some of the higher hills in Sanxia. A terrible glut of tangerines in 1978 drove the price down beyond what most farmers could bear. Like everyone else in town, I ate dirt-cheap tangerines until I could not stand to look at another one. Country roads stank with piles of rotting fruit that farmers had just abandoned. The industry never recovered. As a sign of the gradual decline of this old rural way of life, the last of the working water buffaloes disappeared from the local area at roughly this same period.

I would never have attended to the absence of nature in my data if I had not returned to find a complete contrast in Taiwan a decade later. Taiwan had discovered "nature" sometime in the mid-1980s. I could hardly pick up a newspaper without seeing reports of environmental demonstrations, although I had never heard about one in the 1970s. Some cities had enormous, ongoing movements against factory construction. In the most famous case, the multinational giant Dupont had been forced to cancel plans for a titanium dioxide plant in Lugang in 1986.[3] Smaller skirmishes popped up all over the island, and fights over landfills were so numerous that the newspapers dubbed them the "garbage wars." These even affected Sanxia, as I discovered when I visited only to find the streets smelling awful again – this time because a blockade of the town dump meant that trash had gone uncollected for weeks in Taiwan's tropical summer heat.[4] The government also gingerly began to face its environmental problems at this time. Several important environmental laws were passed in 1987, and the government created a separate Environmental Protection Administration that year.

Just as astonishing to me, the island suddenly boasted four national parks, having had none before. They were impressive, too, rivaling anything in the United States. They had excellent roads and facilities, and state-of-the-art exhibits and interpretations. These parks had a broad appeal as well; all four were among the top ten domestic tourism destinations in 1988 and 1990, and they accounted for three of the top five.[5] As further evidence of this strong new domestic market for nature tourism, hundreds of private sites had opened up, and were booming. In some cases, rural farmers had bought their old water buffaloes back to feed a new market in farm tourism. Even some of the old tangerine farms got new life from pick-your-own arrangements. Others let the hills grow wild, built a pagoda near a waterfall, and charged admission. Still other mountain backwaters received heavy investment to develop into full-scale resorts.

Magazine racks in bookstores confirmed this new consciousness of nature with a wealth of new offerings. The most spectacular was probably *Nature* (*Da Ziran*), with its large format and gorgeous color photography, but there were many others focusing on gardening, fishing, environmental protection, exotic travel destinations, and much more.[6] Just a decade after my initial experience there, many Taiwanese had apparently rethought their ideas about their relationships to the environment. Notions of nature itself were transformed.

Related changes are happening in the People's Republic of China (PRC) right now, although not entirely in the same way. Local environmental protest has become common when people feel that some nearby factory has directly damaged their health or economy, although it is politically impossible for them to organize on the scale of Taiwan's demonstrations. The environmental protection bureaucracy also receives massive numbers of letters of complaint, and acts on at least some of them.[7] This is a remarkable change in a country that had dedicated itself to utter environmental transformation in the cause of socialist revolution, denying any possible negative consequences.[8] Vaclav Smil has documented the results of this in depressing detail, from unsustainable agriculture to undrinkable water.[9] An airplane ride over even sparsely settled rural areas of north China on a cloudless day provides enough casual proof in the coating of smog that obscures the ground everywhere.

As in Taiwan a decade earlier, environmental protection has been upgraded within the national bureaucracy, with the State Environmental Protection Administration receiving ministerial status in 1998. Many new environmental laws have been passed, and there have been extensive propaganda campaigns about the environment. Actually implementing these laws is a more serious problem (as I will discuss in chapter 6), but the effort has had a dramatic effect in a few cases. Major cities, for example, have stopped selling leaded gasoline. They have also successfully converted large numbers of urban residents to using gas instead of coal for heating and cooking.

The domestic market for nature tourism remains smaller in the People's Republic than in Taiwan. Nevertheless there is strong evidence for the beginnings of new attitudes, especially among urban people. City residents typically rank the environment high on their list of important problems, and show some significant knowledge of issues like global warming or the ozone layer.[10] Many imperial-era scenic sites remain popular and some areas are now developing new tourist sites as an economic strategy.

These changes have been more government-led in the PRC than in Taiwan, where popular protest was a stronger driving force. Still, they do translate into behaviors that go beyond any government campaigns. Tianjin and some other very large cities, for example, had a fad for "oxygen bars" (*yangqi ba*) in the mid-1990s. These were small businesses where people could pay to breathe pure oxygen from tanks for a few minutes. The primary clients were mothers bringing their children in for relief from the pollution. A shift in both government and popular (or at least urban) attitudes is under way, comparable in part to what happened in Taiwan a decade earlier.

This book explores the causes and consequences of these changes in the ways people understand the environment and in the concept of nature itself. Both "nature" and "environment" entered the Chinese vocabulary in their modern forms only early in the twentieth century, but both terms also resonated broadly with earlier ways of thinking about how humanity relates to the physical world around it. My focus is the interplay between the older and newer concepts, and in what the results mean for actual environmental behavior.

In particular, I will concentrate on two broad and intertwined mechanisms. The first is the influence of globalization, both directly through influential carriers of new ideas about the environment, and indirectly through reactions to the vastly increased industrialization and commercialization that occurred over the twentieth century. The second is the influence of different forms of state power, which the contrasting political histories of Taiwan and China allow us to explore in some detail.

The globalization of nature

Taiwan and the People's Republic of China are not, of course, the first places to show these signs of a new consciousness of nature. In modern times, nature tourism initially took off in western Europe and North America over the course of the nineteenth century, beginning as the Alps became a defining Romantic experience of elite Grand Tours, and ending with John Muir's quasi-religious paeans to wilderness that ultimately helped to create the first national parks. This was a stunning change from an older view of wilderness as chaos to be made bountiful through human intervention. Colonial North America, for example, had lived much closer to God's words to Noah after the flood: "The fear of you and the dread of you shall be upon every beast of the earth, and upon every bird of the air, upon everything that creeps on the ground and all the fish of the sea; into your hand they are delivered. Every moving thing that lives shall be food for you; and as I gave you the green plants, I give you everything."[11] This was the general view of nature, common throughout Western civilization at the time, that Keith Thomas characterized as "breathtakingly anthropocentric."[12]

Environmental policy changes in the West began most strongly early in the twentieth century, especially with the sanitation and conservation movements. This was already several decades later than the first popularization of new forms of nature tourism. Environmental protest and a broader environmental politics became regularized even later, especially in the decades after important crises like the Love Canal protests or the nuclear accident at Three Mile Island. By the end of the twentieth century environmental politics loomed as large in eastern Europe as in western Europe or North America, and was one of the important factors in the political transformations of 1989. At this point environmental politics is important around the world, and nature tourism (at least for an international market) is equally widespread.

The rapid changes in Taiwan and the People's Republic thus appear to be facets of changes that have swept the entire world. We can understand some aspects of the global spread of environmental concern as responses to the prior spread of modernity, and to the exploitative environmental thinking that went with early industrialization. Some of the new concern grew directly out of reactions against the environmental degradation that has accompanied industrialization. More broadly, though, new ways of thinking about nature – both environmentalist and exploitative – simultaneously responded to and resulted from the general cultural and moral experiences of modernity, including the drive to ever more efficient and rationalized production, increased bureaucracy, and the transformation of many social relationships to market ones.

I will expand on the significance of those processes in chapter 3, but for now let me simply note that many explanations for the rise of environmental consciousness in North America and western Europe are versions of this approach. They focus on how some of the core experiences of modernity encouraged new ways of thinking about nature that became increasingly important beginning in the nineteenth century. This was the period when the proportion of the population in agriculture began its historic decline, as the industrial revolution and its related infrastructure attracted people to the cities.

Nature began to take on a new meaning for these urban people in several rather different ways. Some embraced the power and progress that modernity promised. Both socialist and capitalist states reveled in their new control over nature, trumpeting every new and more technologically sophisticated dam, canal, and railroad line as another victory for humanity. Genres ranging from oil painting to children's books celebrated the power of steam shovels, locomotives, and airplanes. While this attitude faded to an extent toward the end of the twentieth century, we continue to see it clearly in projects like China's colossal Three Gorges dam.

Others, however, were far less content with the new world of modernity. Some looked for an untamed contrast to the artificial world of the city, the wilderness ideal that had attracted the Romantics and helped encourage the national park movement. Others developed a nostalgia for an imagined, but now lost rural world of bucolic peasants.[13] Both versions react to the broad discontents of modernity – the new disciplines of an increasingly rationalized work world, the pervasion of political and social bureaucracies, the reduction of all values to market price, and the shifts in personal identity.[14] These pressures are part of modernity everywhere, not just in Europe and North America. We should thus not be surprised when people in newly successful market economies like Taiwan and increasingly China imagine similar natures as an idealized alternative to urban, industrial life.

Related to this is the simple increase in wealth that the middle class enjoyed during this same period when new attitudes about nature were developing. Nature tourism, for example, could only thrive when people had leisure time to take such trips, had the cash to afford them, and had a transportation infrastructure that could get them there. One of the most influential explanations of the rise of environmental consciousness around the world focuses on these new characteristics of the middle class. Ronald Inglehart, for example, correlates wealth and education with the global rise of what he calls "postmaterialist values," including environmental consciousness.[15] Urban-based professionals in fact dominate environmentalist organizations (as opposed to anti-pollution demonstrations) in many countries. People in the "new" middle class – lawyers, teachers, doctors, and others in the knowledge sector – tend to be particularly active environmentalists. García, for example, argues that just these kinds of people form the heart of Venezuela's environmental movement.[16] I will return more critically to this issue of class and nature consciousness in later chapters (especially chapter 5), but the cross-cultural evidence does suggest that these new class positions are one important factor in explaining new attitudes toward the environment.

This kind of explanation – based on how people around the world react to the economic and cultural experience of modernity – has some important limitations. It explains global similarities as parallel adaptations to a set of shared underlying conditions, the way very different animals may evolve to look similar because they adapt to similar niches – marsupial and mammalian mice or wolves, for instance. In this case, the underlying pressure is an implied necessity of adapting to modernity in ways that reproduce the earlier experience of the West. In fact, however, the situation is more complicated because, among other reasons, North American and western European views of nature are themselves globalizing, creating a broad and direct diffusion of ideas through various colonial and postcolonial mechanisms of transmission to the rest of the world.[17] These ideas sometimes clash directly with the market globalization that spreads at the same time. The West exports both land reclamation programs and wetland protection schemes, both broader markets for new foods and attempts to protect endangered species.

In this view, the market may have been a crucial driver of culture in the first cases of capitalism. After that, however, the new economic system and its associated culture spread throughout the world. There is thus only a single case – the entire world system – instead of many separate cases that can be treated as if they were independent. The creation of this world culture has not been just a matter of benign diffusion for many of these theorists. They see it instead as an act of domination, historically rooted in colonialism, with an economic division of labor in which the core capitalist countries profit from the peripheral position of the rest of the world. Such a view animates the anti-globalization demonstrations that have accompanied important international economic meetings in recent years. Protesters oppose the ability of global rule-makers like the International Monetary Fund to impose social policy or the power of multinational capital flight (or just its threat) to influence local labor. McDonald's – as both economic actor and cultural icon – represents this process for many; others like to cite Hollywood or MTV.

For the environment we can see this in the spread of specifically Western ways of conceptualizing nature and human interactions with it, carried through development programs, the worldwide spread of environmental nongovernmental organizations (NGOs) based in the West, education, and the media. Specifically Western forms of nature tourism also spread widely, initially through the creation of preserves under colonialism and more recently through the international ecotourism market. Many African national parks, for example, began as colonial hunting preserves and evolved into conservation areas to protect wildlife from the native peoples. In the unequal contest between colonial and indigenous views of how people should relate to the environment, the colonial view of a preserved, wild nature largely ousted local people from the land on which they had made a living for centuries.[18]

All of these approaches, whether they focus on the shared experience of market modernities or on a more direct kind of cultural imperialism, suggest that the world today has an increasingly homogenized and universalized view of how humans and the environment interrelate. As a result, they also share some problems. The first is that the case for global convergence tends to be made too forcefully. People have met globalization everywhere by embracing it, but also by reworking it and rejecting it. We typically see reassertions of local or regional culture, identity, and economy even as globalization creates a pressure toward international homogeneity. Japanese pop and anime, for example, show this kind of reworking in a way so successful that they have created their own globalizing flow.

Several authors see a threatening tension between globalization and local culture. Anthony Giddens, for example, writes that

In a globalising world, where information and images are routinely transmitted across the globe, we are all regularly in contact with others who think differently, and live differently, from ourselves. Cosmopolitans welcome and embrace this cultural complexity. Fundamentalists find it disturbing and dangerous. Whether in the areas of religion, ethnic identity or nationalism, they take refuge in a renewed and purified tradition – and, quite often, violence.[19]

Others, and I include myself, see less Manichean drama in the interaction between local and global. Empirically, it seems more fruitful to examine the long interaction where the local and the global change each other, and where some kind of dualistic struggle is only one, rather extreme, possible result.

One of the questions this approach opens up is the way indigenous categories of knowledge may reshape globalizing culture. In chapter 2 I take this problem up for the concept of "nature" itself. For the sake of semantic convenience, I will be using the word "environment" to indicate the broadest physical world in which humans live, and "nature" to indicate social constructions of that environment. Nature, in this sense, has particular histories. As I will discuss in the following chapter, the modern term "nature" (in English or in contemporary Chinese) had no real equivalent in classical Chinese, although it has now achieved a dominant position in Chinese discourse. Nevertheless, earlier ways of thinking about humanity and the environment in China did not wash away when Western ideas about nature became entrenched in the early twentieth century. Instead they remain in a lively and evolving dialogue with the global concepts, and they continue to influence a broad range of environmental behavior in China and Taiwan. One of the problems in massive statistical surveys like Inglehart's study of "postmaterialist values" is whether people in different contexts actually understand the same things by "nature" or "environment." Cross-cultural surveys of that kind assume a prior globalization of categories, and leave little room for the influence of indigenous ideas.

Taking a closer, empirical look at the local side of globalization also complicates the issue of just what the local is. In loose opposition to the idea of global homogeneity, the concept of the local can point to everything from a small village on a remote mountain, to regional agglomerations of millions of people (Cantonese speakers, for instance), to nation-states. The complexities of local social structures can also be lost when locality becomes a simple shorthand for opposition to globalization. Even the most local communities include a range of social and power dynamics based on gender, age, wealth, and many other factors. Much of this book will spell out the very different ways people in different social positions in Taiwan and the People's Republic of China relate to their environment through nature tourism, environmental protest, and environmental policy implementation. The local is not a simple opposite to the global.

A second kind of problem is that discussions of globalization tend to treat the globalizing forces themselves as homogeneous and unitary. This ignores the enormous disagreements that exist within the areas that are said to be the primary emitters of global ideas. American society, for example, promotes a global neoliberal market ideology, but it is also a major source of ideas opposed to that ideology. It exports both cigarettes and antismoking campaigns, big dam construction and tree-hugging protestors. A wide range of people carry globalizing messages – intellectuals, business executives, development consultants, tourists (old and well-heeled, young and at loose ends), missionaries, the media, and more. Some are more powerful than others, but all have globalizing influence and all may carry different messages.[20]

Nor is globalization simply a diffusion from a single core to the rest of the world. While the United States, followed by western Europe, plays a dominant role, other areas and other kinds of geographies rework globalizing ideas and create new global forces of their own. In East Asia, Japan has played an especially important role because of its economic clout and its colonial history. Pop music and fashion, which had obvious Western origins, have taken on distinctive East Asian styles as they are reworked in Japan and often Hong Kong, followed by the rest of the region. Uniquely Japanese models of nature tourism (and golf, which is related) have played an important role in Taiwan, as I will discuss in chapter 4. In some cases, East Asia itself is the primary emitter for globalizing forces. Zen Buddhism and Japanese corporate management styles, in their very different ways, have had periods where they swept the world.

Other kinds of globalization have no clear geographical center. Arjun Appadurai has argued effectively that the combination of extensive migration and easier communication is fostering new kinds of transnational communities.[21] These often claim a common place of origin, but in practice exist across all lines of nation and geography. Such transnational connections are as important for East Asia – especially mainland China and Taiwan – as for the Indian cases that Appadurai documents. All these multiple, overlapping, and sometimes conflicting forms of globalization shape environmental attitudes in China and Taiwan.

Comparing political contexts

The combination of global influences and indigenous social and cultural resources has altered the entire spectrum of daily life in the environment – changing fuel costs, protest movements, the labor requirements of cooking, government regulations, education, leisure activities, and more. Both Taiwan and the People's Republic have been transformed, in spite of their differences. At heart, these changes imply a genuine innovation in how people conceptualize the relationship between humanity and environment, as I will argue in chapter 2. China and Taiwan share most of their history, but have also taken separate political and social paths since 1895 (except for the brief and unhappy unity of 1945–9). This makes them a fruitful way to compare how similar global influences and a largely joint cultural tradition may (or may not) lead to divergent results in different contexts. As much of this book will discuss, the differences turn out to be less salient than we might expect from the contrast between capitalist and communist paths of development.

Both Taiwan and the People's Republic had powerful authoritarian governments for most of the twentieth century. Nevertheless, they took sharply different political and economic roads over the last century. The mainland spent the first half of the century struggling with warlords and later enduring a corrupt but more unified rule by the Nationalist Party (Guomindang, GMD) until the Japanese invasion of World War II and the Communist revolution tore through the country. The Communist state that took over in 1949 completely reorganized social and political life under a centrally planned economy. The reform period that began in the late 1970s gradually opened up a market economy and created more social space for people, but the underlying political system remains intact.

Meanwhile, Taiwan spent the fifty years between 1895 and 1945 as a Japanese colony, molded to serve primarily as a rice basket to feed Japan's industrialization. It spent most of the next fifty years under the very tight authoritarian control of the Nationalist Party, which moved its governing apparatus there after losing the civil war on the mainland. Taiwan's market-based economy grew steadily, but its politics changed only after 1987 when the forty-year state of emergency stemming from the "Communist bandit" insurgency – martial law in all but name – was finally lifted and the island quickly democratized.

In spite of these differences, Taiwan and the People's Republic share some features that may help explain changing environmental attitudes. The most obvious is that both places are severely polluted as a result of decades of government encouragement of economic growth regardless of the economic consequences – one of the indirect results of the globalizing industrial economy. Rivers and urban air suffer from serious industrial and agricultural pollution, exacerbated in northern China by extensive burning of coal and biomass for winter heat, and by the dusty winds that blow eroded soils through the region. A recent World Bank study, for example, estimates that urban air and water pollution in the mid-1990s cost the People's Republic US $32.3 billion (over 9 percent of the Gross National Product).[22] Water of any quality is in short supply throughout the northern half of China.

Taiwan is hardly better. I was driving down the east coast once with a local friend, admiring the heart-stoppingly steep cliffs overlooking the Pacific Ocean. We paused to admire a place called the "yin-yang sea," a small, rounded inlet with the water sharply divided into two different colors. As a young student, my friend recalled, she had been shown this spot as a kind of scenic wonder. Now it was known to be the result of heavy metal runoff from a former factory on the site. The currents in the inlet kept the polluted water from dispersing. Such stories are unfortunately common – I heard tales of irrigation water in fields near refineries that would ignite at the touch of a match; children evacuated from schools when local factories made the air unbreathable; and garbage dumps alight with fires that could not be quenched and whose stench pervaded whole neighborhoods. These problems seem even more severe when we recall that Taiwan has a much better ability to cleanse its environment than most places in China, thanks to its high rainfall.

Problems like this may provide an important encouragement for people to rethink their ideas about the environment, but pollution alone cannot be a sufficient explanation. This is because people can view pollution simply as a normal part of life, as indeed it has been since sedentary agriculture first posed serious problems of human and animal waste disposal, made far worse with the beginnings of urbanization. London's deadly smogs of the nineteenth century provide a fairly recent European example. Much the same is still true in places like rural Anhui Province, where a study I took part in found people completely unconcerned with the possible health effects of burning rice stalks in the fields after the harvest, even though the resulting pollution had closed the local airport at the time we conducted the interviews.[23] In addition, people often have no way of making a direct connection between pollution and effects that may be quite distant in space (like acid rain) or time (like the burial of hazardous wastes). Taiwan's water pollution, for example, was worst in the late 1970s, when there was hardly any environmental movement.[24] Finally, while pollution has an obvious relationship to environmental protest, it has no direct or obvious relationship to other developments like nature tourism or fishing magazines.

Both Taiwan and the People's Republic experienced periods of rapid economic growth, which began a few years before we see much evidence for new environmental consciousness. Taiwan's economy grew strongly under the Nationalist regime, but it began mired in poverty, with much of the Japanese colonial infrastructure in ruins after the Allied bombings of World War II. Only in the late 1980s did Taiwan join the ranks of the newly developed countries. It currently has a per capita GNP of over $12,000 (from under $200 in 1952 and under $2,000 in 1979), a life expectancy just behind Denmark, and an infant mortality rate only slightly worse than the United States.

In the People's Republic, the snail's-pace growth of the Cultural Revolution gave way to some of the highest growth rates in the world after the market-based reforms that began in agriculture in 1978 and spread to the urban economy in the 1980s. The overall standard of living in the People's Republic is still far lower than in Taiwan, although some coastal regions are no longer far behind. Some very large rural areas in the PRC remain mired in poverty, and the slow demise of many state-owned enterprises is creating a worrisome degree of urban unemployment. Nevertheless, an enormous population – especially in the coastal cities and their surrounding areas – recognizes that it is much better off now than it was one or two decades ago.[25]

In addition, both places have undergone rapid and significant political change. This has been quite fundamental in Taiwan, where a true democracy has evolved. This change was impossible for me to imagine when I first lived there, and was capped by the startling election of the Democratic People's Party, which had seemed like a permanent opposition party, to the Presidency in 2000. Nothing so stunning has happened to politics in the People's Republic, but there has been a systematic attempt to shrink the power of government over every aspect of life, and to create a real (if limited) social sphere. The old totalitarian project that animated the Cultural Revolution – the dissolution of society into the state and total commitment from each individual – has been abandoned.[26] People now have much more space to create a social world, as long as they stay away from politics.

The different modern histories of Taiwan and China focus our attention on what difference they might make for environmental attitudes and behavior. Many of the theories of globalization I discussed earlier have declared the imminent death of the nation-state, but surely they have been hasty in reaching that conclusion. There are pressures on the nation-state, of course. The great mobility of capital influences and sometimes undermines national economies. Global migrations, both legal and illegal, have forced rethinking of the concept of citizenship. The international human rights movement encouraged the idea that the rights of individuals might supersede the rights of citizens.[27] The Internet and other breakthroughs in communication also help to dissolve national boundaries.

The mid-1990s thus saw two different books published under the title *The End of the Nation-State*.[28] Saskia Sassen writes regularly about what she terms "denationalization," and Arjun Appadurai speaks of an "emergent postnational order."[29]

Yet the nation-state is clearly not dead yet. The most powerful global bodies – the United Nations, World Trade Organization, International Monetary Fund, and the rest – are structurally tied to the system of nation-states. Multinational corporations and international NGOs are ultimately grounded in the legal frameworks of one particular state. Many crucial aspects of the nation-state remain unchallenged, including core functions like taxation and control of armed force. Even the boldest predictions of its demise recognize that we are still in the early stages of this transformation, and that their arguments are as much hypothetical as empirical. The following chapters will show how much the state in both Taiwan and the People's Republic of China has contributed to the understanding of nature. This occurs directly through each government's control over policy and education, and indirectly through the new spaces opened up by the political transformations of both places over the last two decades. Each of the substantive case studies that follow – on nature tourism, environmental movements, and policy implementation – will compare the two sides of the Taiwan Strait.

Sorting through issues

My goal in the rest of this book is to sort through these factors that may influence current environmental behavior – those indigenous repertoires of cultural and social resources that remain relevant, the multiple globalizations that have shaped both the environment and how we understand it everywhere, and the specific roles of the different states we see in China and Taiwan. Each of the chapters that follows works its way through some part of these issues. I begin in chapter 2 with the ways people in China and Taiwan thought about the relationship between humanity and environment before the major globalization of Western ideas in the nineteenth and twentieth centuries. There was no word really equivalent to "nature" in its modern use until *ziran* became the accepted translation for the Western term in the early twentieth century. There were, however, various other ways of thinking about the environment and how we should live in it. Looking both at more philosophical versions of this and at practical behavior in the environment, I will explore some of the environmental ideas that were available to Chinese as they entered the twentieth century, emphasizing the ones that continue to have the most influence. These were quite diverse, but none was the same as the new thinking about nature that would enter from the West in the twentieth century. Looking at these ideas as they still influence behavior helps to clarify the "local" side of global/local debates. These views offer potential alternatives to globalizing nature, and I will return to them at the end of the book.

Chapter 3 turns to the process of globalization of nature, particularly in the twentieth century. There were of course earlier globalizations that affected China, including ties to the Roman Empire, the Buddhist entry through the Silk Road, the later Arab trading networks, and extensive Chinese trade with Southeast Asia. Western ideas about nature also entered before the twentieth century in some limited ways. Jesuits had brought perspective to landscape painting and Western science to astronomy, although the influence of both was limited to a small elite. The second half of the nineteenth century also saw a strong missionary push, which brought Christian concepts of nature to a broader group. Only in the twentieth century, though, did the vocabulary for talking about the environment change, and only then did the new ideas have a pervasive influence through the education system. This chapter follows the various streams of ideas about nature and the environment as they had flowed from the West and into China. These include both the idea of the triumph of progress and human achievement as a conquering of nature, and the contrary idea that nature and wilderness should be appreciated for their own sake. Chapter 2 complicates the issue of the local; chapter 3 does the same thing for the global side of the equation.

The remaining chapters look at specific contemporary examples where these issues play out, keeping an eye on both the dynamics of globalization and the political comparison between China and Taiwan. Chapter 4 explores the origins and rise of nature tourism. This developed earlier in Taiwan and is currently much more established there. Nevertheless, the last few years have also brought very significant changes in the People's Republic. Nature tourism in Taiwan arose out of a complex set of forces. It has roots in religious pilgrimage, in government campaigns to create a healthy and patriotic youth, and in bird watching groups begun by members of the United States armed forces. The national park system was directly modeled on the United States, but the provincial park system looked instead to Japan. China too felt the influence of diverse forces, from bird watching groups of their own to sending youths to the countryside. The global models, though, have come much more from the United Nations than from the United States. Spinning out the example of the treatment of rocks in painting, at nature parks, and in popular worship, I will show the intertwining of local and global forces from the very beginnings of nature tourism in both places, as well as the crucial intermediary role of the state.

Chapter 5 looks at environmental actions, especially protest. Taiwan has a much stronger environmental movement than China, most obviously because of the political differences between the two places. Here I distinguish more clearly between local and national attitudes, which can be seen in different goals and methods of environmental protest. Indigenous environmental concepts are primarily important at the most local level. They have much less salience among either academic or political elites, or among environmentalist NGOs, all of whom attune more closely to global trends. I look, for instance, at the use of temples in local Taiwanese protests, and at the grassroots politics of the "garbage wars" there. It is much more difficult to get field data on protest in the People's Republic, but I analyze some survey data and expand on several specific cases. This is especially revealing on the role of official propaganda in creating an environmental consciousness that can lead to action. Overall, however, environmental movements in Taiwan and China show remarkably similar patterns of a split between NGO and popular goals and methods of environmental action, and in the degree of global influence on their thinking.

The final substantive section, chapter 6, turns to the problems of environmental policy implementation. Both the Chinese and the Taiwanese governments have actively tried to change environmental behavior through new policies, driven partly by their severe pollution problems and partly by global pressure. The problem is how to translate these policies into effective local behavior. Rural data from China so far tend to show a lack of environmental awareness, and little effect from sometimes extensive government campaigning. In contrast, work in Tianjin shows rapid change, comparable to what happened in Taiwan. Both Taiwan and China, however, show a regular slippage between policy and practice, partly growing out of different understandings of nature between policy-makers and policy-users. The chapter concludes with a reconsideration of the potential contribution of indigenous ideas about the environment, both to Chinese policy and to Western understandings of nature.

NOTES

1. For the sake of consistency, I will use *pinyin* to romanize all Mandarin Chinese words, with the exception of a very few words or names that are far better known in English with other spellings (e.g., Taipei, Chiang Kai-shek). I will mark the occasional term in Taiwan's Hoklo dialect (Southern Min) with an H. A character list is appended.

2. Steering Committee, Taiwan 2000 Study, *Taiwan 2000: Balancing Economic Growth and Environmental Protection* (Taipei, 1989), iv, 152.
3. See James Reardon-Anderson, *Pollution, Politics, and Foreign Investment in Taiwan: The Lukang Rebellion* (Armonk, NY: M. E. Sharpe, 1992).
4. I discuss this in some detail in chapter 5.
5. Republic of China Ministry of Transportation, Tourism Bureau, *Zhonghua Minguo 77 Nian Taiwan Diqu Guomin Lüyou Zhuangkuang Diaocha Baogao (Investigative Report on the Condition of Citizens' Travel in the Taiwan Region, Republic of China, 1988)* (1989); Republic of China Ministry of Transportation, Tourism Bureau, *Zhonghua Minguo 80 Nian Taiwan Diqu Guomin Lüyou Zhuangkuang Diaocha Baogao (Investigative Report on the Condition of Citizens' Travel in the Taiwan Region, Republic of China, 1991)* (1991).
6. My unsystematic and extremely incomplete collection of this new genre also includes *The Earth* (*Da Di*, which looks rather like an oversized *National Geographic*), numerous fishing magazines (*Taiwan Diaoyu* (*Taiwan Fishing Magazine*), *Diaoyu Ren* (*Fisherman*), *Diaoyu Shijie* (*Fishing World*)), gardening magazines (*Zaoyuanjia* (*Gardener*), *Zaoyuan* (*Garden*), *Lü* (*Green Life*)), and environmentalist magazines (*Huanjing yu Shenghuo* (*Living Environment Protection*), *Guojia Huanjing* (*National Environment*)).
7. See Jun Jing, "Environmental Protests in Rural China," in *Chinese Society: Change, Conflict and Resistance*, ed. Mark Selden and Elizabeth J. Perry (New York: Routledge, 2000).
8. Judith Shapiro, *Mao's War against Nature: Politics and the Environment in Revolutionary China* (New York: Cambridge University Press, 2001).
9. Vaclav Smil, *China's Environmental Crisis: An Inquiry into the Limits of National Development* (Armonk, NY: M. E. Sharpe, 1993).
10. Yuan Fang, "The Environmental Awareness of Chinese Citizens: A Sociological Analysis," in *Environmental Awareness in Developing Countries: The Case of China and Thailand* (Tokyo: Japan/Asia Economic Development Institute, 1997); Holger Blasum, *Report on Environmental Awareness of Middle School and University Students*, n.d., accessed 21 July 2001, http://www.blasum.net/holger/wri/environ/china/studenv.htm. Environmental awareness in the countryside, however, is significantly lower (see William P. Alford *et al.*, "The Human Dimensions of Pollution Policy Implementation: Air Quality in Rural China," *Journal of Contemporary China* 11 (2002): 495–513).
11. Genesis 9:2–3.
12. Keith Thomas, *Man and the Natural World: A History of the Modern Sensibility* (New York: Pantheon, 1983), 18. See also William Cronon, *Changes in the Land: Indians, Colonists and the Ecology of New England* (New York: Hill and Wang, 1983).
13. For more on this, see Thomas, *Man and the Natural World*, 242–87; Simon Schama, *Landscape and Memory* (New York: A. A. Knopf, 1995).
14. Peter Berger, Brigitte Berger, and Hansfried Kellner, *The Homeless Mind: Modernization and Consciousness* (New York: Vintage, 1973); Robert N. Bellah *et al.*, *Habits of the Heart: Individualism and Commitment in American Life* (Berkeley: University of California Press, 1996).

15. Ronald Inglehart, *Culture Shift in Advanced Industrial Society* (Princeton: Princeton University Press, 1990).
16. María Pilar García, "The Venezuelan Ecology Movement: Symbolic Effectiveness, Social Practices, and Political Strategies," in *The Making of Social Movements in Latin America: Identity, Strategy and Democracy*, ed. Arturo Escobar and Sonia E. Alvarez (Boulder, CO: Westview, 1992), 150–70. See also Michael Redclift, *Sustainable Development: Exploring the Contradictions* (London: Methuen, 1987); Robert P. Weller and Hsin-Huang Michael Hsiao, "Culture, Gender and Community in Taiwan's Environmental Movement," in *Environmental Movements in Asia*, ed. Arne Kalland and Gerard Persoon (Surrey: Curzon, 1998), 83–109.
17. The first version of this argument about whether globalization was a set of independent reactions to shared economic problems or the result of direct power relations in a single system occurred over the spread of the market economy. See, for example, Walter W. Rostow, *The Stages of Economic Growth: A Non-Communist Manifesto* (Cambridge: Cambridge University Press, 1960); Immanuel Wallerstein, *The Modern World-System: Capitalist Agriculture and the Origins of the European World-Economy in the Sixteenth Century*, Studies in Social Discontinuity (New York: Academic Press, 1974).
18. On the colonial and postcolonial history of national parks in Africa, see John M. MacKenzie, *The Empire of Nature: Hunting, Conservation and British Imperialism* (Manchester: Manchester University Press, 1988); Jonathon S. Adams and Thomas O. McShane, *The Myth of Wild Africa: Conservation without Illusion* (Berkeley: University of California Press, 1996).
19. Anthony Giddens, *Runaway World: How Globalization Is Reshaping Our Lives* (New York: Routledge, 2000), 22–3. For similar views, see Benjamin R. Barber, *Jihad vs. McWorld* (New York: Times Books, 1995); Thomas L. Friedman, *The Lexus and the Olive Tree: Understanding Globalization* (New York: Anchor Books, 2000).
20. See Peter L. Berger and Samuel Huntington, eds., *Many Globalizations: Cultural Diversity in the Contemporary World* (New York: Oxford University Press, 2002).
21. Arjun Appadurai, "Global Ethnoscapes: Notes and Queries for a Transnational Anthropology," in *Recapturing Anthropology*, ed. Richard G. Fox (Santa Fe: School of American Research, 1991), 191–210.
22. Todd M. Johnson, Feng Liu, and Richard Newfarmer, *Clear Water, Blue Skies: China's Environment in the New Century* (Washington, DC: The World Bank, 1997). These estimates are notoriously difficult. Another study estimates losses equivalent to about 4 percent of Gross National Product in 1992; Guang Xia, "An Estimate of the Economic Consequences of Environmental Pollution in China," in *Project on Environmental Scarcities, State Capacity, and Civil Violence*, ed. Vaclav Smil and Yushi Mao (Cambridge, MA: Committee on International Security Studies, American Academy of Arts and Sciences, 1997), 41–59.
23. Alford *et al.*, "The Human Dimensions of Pollution Policy Implementation."
24. Steering Committee, *Taiwan 2000: Balancing Economic Growth and Environmental Protection*, 138–52.

25. I will explore some of the significance of income disparity in chapter 6, through a comparison of a relatively poor rural area with a major city on the eastern coast.
26. The most important exception is political control over reproduction, which has increased under the reforms.
27. See Saskia Sassen, *Losing Control? Sovereignty in an Age of Globalization* (New York: Columbia University Press, 1996).
28. Kenichi Ohmae, *The End of the Nation-State: The Rise of Regional Economies* (New York: Free Press, 1995); Jean-Marie Guehenno, *The End of the Nation-State* (Minneapolis: University of Minnesota Press, 1996).
29. Saskia Sassen, *Globalization and Its Discontents* (New York: New Press, 1998); Arjun Appadurai, *Modernity at Large: Cultural Dimensions of Globalization* (Minneapolis: University of Minnesota Press, 1996).

2 Night of the living dead fish

Anthropologists make it a point of pride to eat anything, although Chinese banquets can sometimes challenge the ethic. I have eaten camel's paws and toad's toes, caterpillars and snakes, and even a few dogs. The one meal that lingered in my mind for years afterwards, however, was the night of the living dead fish. The "living dead fish" itself was no greater a challenge to my gastronomic relativism than the others – I have hesitated longer over lima beans – but the event left me puzzled.

The meal took place in the foreigners' dining hall at Nanjing University, where I was living at the time. It was a banquet to celebrate the end of a study abroad program, and I was seated at a table with some of the American students and some of the Chinese administrators and faculty involved in the program. The hosts proudly explained that they had ordered the highest-quality available menu, featuring the chef's signature dish, his claim to fame, "living fish" (*huoyu*). They seemed quite excited, and described it for me in some detail.

I have asked people about this dish in the intervening years. Some have never heard of it, and others know quite different versions. As this chef prepared it, the result was a large, whole fish with the meat nicely cooked and the nervous system still sufficiently alive to have it twitch and squirm on the platter. The trick is apparently to gut the live fish, wrap its head and tail in cold, wet towels, and cook the rest of it very quickly in hot oil – a living dead fish.

As it turned out, the American students did not share either their hosts' enthusiasm for the dish or an anthropologist's compulsion to eat it anyway. Several of them were visibly upset. One tried to still the twitching corpse by severing the spinal cord with a knife. This turned out to be more difficult in practice than in theory, unfortunately, and the young woman next to me burst into loud sobs and fled the room during the surgery. Everyone else forged on, but the evening ended with both the Chinese and the Americans baffled and upset by the incomprehensible culinary taste of the other side.

The event posed two puzzles. The first was how to understand the aesthetic behind eating "living fish." At the time, our hosts explained that it proved the consummate skill of the chef. This is true, of course, although Chinese chefs also have innumerable other ways of showing their skills. Then they explained that the twitching fish was proof of absolute freshness. This is also true, but there are many other, easier ways to make the case. Chinese seafood restaurants, for example, typically allow patrons to choose their meal while it still swims in a tank. This particular dish does more though. It mobilizes enormous skill and effort to serve the fish at the moment when it has been caught between fundamental categories of thought, at once alive and dead, raw and cooked. I will expand on this in the following sections, and just note here that the puzzle started me thinking about what a living dead fish says about how people relate to the environment. Food, after all, provides one of the most intimate links between humanity and nature.

The second puzzle was the depth of the American students' reactions. Whatever aesthetic resonated so strongly for our Chinese hosts clearly had no appeal to the Americans. If I was right that the living dead fish said something broadly about how people understood nature, then the enormous mismatch of expectations implied that at least for these individuals, very different categories of knowledge were at work. The living dead fish is an unimportant corner of Chinese culture, but it is the sort of experience that prods us to reconsider variations in how people think about relations between human and environment.

Words for "nature"

Any modern dictionary will tell you that the Chinese word for the English "nature" is *ziran* or *da* ("great") *ziran*. This easy equivalent, however, masks the difficulty of the terms in both English and Chinese. Raymond Williams called the English term "perhaps the most complex word in the language."[1] The Chinese *ziran* became the accepted translation only in the twentieth century, superimposing the historical complexities of the English "nature" (and other Western equivalents) onto indigenous understandings of nature. This chapter explores some of those indigenous understandings, especially those that continue to influence behavior today. The following chapter examines the entry of the Western concept into China.

Unlike many of the terms that entered Chinese in the late nineteenth and early twentieth centuries to translate Western social science and philosophy, *ziran* was not newly coined. Instead, it was wrenched from its earlier meanings to serve its new purpose. Its two characters mean something like "self-evidently" or "spontaneously." It appeared frequently in the combination *ziran er ran*, "as a matter of course." This overlaps with some secondary meanings of the English "nature," as when we say that something happens "naturally," meaning spontaneously or because of its inner makeup. Nevertheless, *ziran* does not touch on much of what "nature" has come to mean in the West: the essential quality of something; the inherent force directing the world or humanity; the material world itself.[2] Nor does it capture the opposition between nature and culture that has been so important in Western uses, especially since the Enlightenment.

Was there an equivalent to the English word "nature" in Chinese before the twentieth century? The monosyllabic answer is no, as we might expect for concepts carrying such a heavy cultural and historical load. There are, however, some terms beyond *ziran* that overlap in interesting ways with "nature" and that help shed light on some Chinese views. Most important of these is surely *tian* and its various combinations. English translators in fact often render *tian* as "nature," although several decades ago they more often used "heaven" instead. This alone should alert us to the differences between the Chinese and English concepts.

Tian comes closest to the meaning of nature as an inherent force directing the world. Etymologically, the word initially referred to the sky, but it quickly took on broader connotations of heavenly power. In some cases, *tian* was anthropomorphized as a deity (*Tiandi*, the Emperor of Heaven), but in many others it is an abstract force. Emperors ruled by dint of their heavenly mandate (*tianming*), and worshipers honored heaven by burning incense in large pots that stand in front of every major temple. Early Catholic missionaries used the term to translate God as the Lord of Heaven (*Tianzhu*).

There are some combinations of characters where a translation as "nature" seems especially tempting. Some texts write of a world divided into three broad spheres: heaven, earth, and mankind (*tian di ren*). The characters heaven and earth (*tiandi*) are often used as a unit, meaning all aspects of the world apart from humanity. This is reminiscent of the modern Western distinction between nature and culture, or of the opposition we often make between the natural and the man-made. Philosophical texts often expressed an ideal of "the unity of heaven/nature and mankind" (*tian ren he yi*), which again seems compatible with some Western environmentalist thought. Nevertheless, *tian* retains fundamentally Chinese characteristics. Even at its most abstractly philosophical, *tian* draws as much on notions of proper ethical order as of the natural world. When it was anthropomorphized into a heaven that spoke of these ethics through divinities, it stood even farther from the natural environment.

One other initial possibility to capture some of the meaning of English "nature" is *shanshui* (literally "mountains and water"), which was the term for a painted landscape. While both the Chinese and Western landscape genres featured natural scenery, they also had crucial differences that help reveal different conceptions of nature and humanity. Most obviously, the great majority of Chinese "landscapes" include humans or their artifacts, quite unlike the majority of European landscapes. Mountains, rivers, and waterfalls may dominate the scene, but a close look almost always reveals some tiny farmers, a mountain hermit, some small houses, or other bits of humanity. Unlike a Western tradition that tried to capture a pure nature apart from human beings, people form an inevitable part of the Chinese landscape.[3]

Rather than showing a natural world apart from human interference, these paintings tend to depict a flow of energy that runs through both humans and environment. This cosmic energy – *qi* in Chinese – characterizes everything in the world, constantly changing its character and altering its manifestations through yin and yang, and through the five elements of wood, fire, earth, metal, and water. It runs through complex paths in our bodies, creating health and illness. It runs through mountains and streams, creating areas of stronger and weaker power. It connects kinsmen to each other, and all of us to the broader environment. It is the chief concern of Chinese medicine, meditation, and *fengshui* (the beneficial geotemporal placement of buildings and tombs).

The aesthetics of *qi* run through paintings of the bizarre karst mountains of Guangxi, sticking up like so many trees in a gargantuan stone forest, and through the peculiar nooks and crannies of the "strange rocks" (*qishi*) that decorate Chinese gardens. This is not a force of "nature" as opposed to humanity, but instead an energy available to all. The painter thus does not simply imitate the flow of *qi* in the environment; he or she creates it anew through the flow of ink on paper. In the same way, even a miniaturized garden that intends to evoke a larger landscape requires the human creation of a new flow of *qi*.

We see the same comfort with human input in the nearly constant inclusion of poetry or other calligraphy in paintings. These poems further the sharing of the subjective state of the poet, in addition to supplying an opportunity to show the flow of energy through the calligrapher's brush. The stone seals ("chops") that nearly all artists and many owners use (including, most ostentatiously and famously, the Qianlong Emperor) provide yet another human input into the landscape, and yet another flow of energy through carver, stone, ink, and paper.

It would not be difficult to add many more Chinese terms to this list of partial translations of "nature." There is *wanwu*, for instance, the "ten thousand things" created out of the interaction of yin and yang. Or *benxing*, the inherent quality of something, which touches on quite a different quality of the English "nature." Perhaps this is already enough, though, to illustrate the simple point that Chinese and Europeans had very different cultural constructions of the relation between humanity and environment.

Rather than continue this exercise in translation, let me turn in more detail to some of the most important ways that Chinese constructed this relationship. There were in fact a great many different ways of conceptualizing relations to the environment, not always consistent with each other. As Mark Elvin argued,

> A systematic study of Chinese views of nature, however – at least in late-imperial times for which materials are abundant – reveals almost the entire spectrum of attitudes. There were Qing-dynasty enthusiasts for gigantic engineering projects . . . There were those who believed that nature should be attacked in military fashion. Others argued that humans should accommodate themselves to the pattern of natural processes without forcing matters. Others again saw nature as savage towards humankind, or indifferent . . . Others again saw nature as benevolent, or immersed themselves in it, beyond morality, in a kind of nature mysticism.[4]

Here I will take up just three of the most important views that still influence people today: anthropocosmic resonance, Buddhist compassion, and an image of power that radiated from margins as well as centers.

Anthropocosmic resonance

The role of the painter or gardener in shaping cosmic energy is just like the spontaneous (*ziran* again) flow of energy that creates all things in the world. This understanding is consistent with a worldview that the modern Confucian philosopher Tu Weiming has characterized as anthropocosmic. It is a fundamentally humanist view, comfortable with human use of the natural world and its energies, but one whose ultimate concerns are the establishment of a mutual relationship between humanity and the cosmic order of heaven, in which each of the parts resonates sympathetically with all the others.[5]

Texts spelling out ideas of a resonance (*ganying*) among the forces of the universe come to us from the second and third centuries BCE.[6] For example:

When the magnet seeks iron, something pulls it, when trees planted close together [lean] apart, something pushes them. When the sage faces south and stands with a mind bent on loving and benefiting the people, and before his orders have been issued, the [people of the world] all crane their necks and stand on tip-toe; it is because he has communicated with the people via the Vital Essence.[7]

Vital essence (*jing*) here is the most refined form of *qi* energy, and animates all living things. Like strings vibrating sympathetically, it places everything in a mutual relationship of complex interaction, with no simple cause and effect.

The idea of anthropocosmic resonance understands human beings to be in a position of mutual dependence on the broader world. In fact, concepts like *qi*, vital essence, or resonance do not really differentiate humanity from the rest of the natural world. Typically, however, these early texts bend their views of cosmic resonance to a humanist purpose. For example, the *Huainanzi*, written at the height of popularity of resonance theory in the Han Dynasty, shows how rulers should create harmony within their kingdoms by reinforcing the proper resonances, for example by worshiping in the south during the summer months, wearing red, and playing the proper music. It warns of the consequences of acting against these cosmic principles:

If in the first month of spring the ordinances of summer were carried out, then there would be unseasonable winds and rain; plants and trees would wither early, and the state would suffer anxiety. If the ordinances of autumn were carried out, the people would suffer epidemics; briars and overgrowth would spring up together. If the ordinances of winter were carried out, floods would create ruin; there would be rain, frost and great hailstones.[8]

The ruler must thus act within the appropriate cosmic principles, because he has great power to change the world through his own energies. Ultimately, though, his primary concerns are to rule well.

Daoists shared many of the ideas that resonance theorists spelled out, yet they departed from the Confucianists' concentration on political power and social order. They were more interested in individual cultivation to achieve a mystical union with the *dao*, the eternal "path." "Do nothing," writes Laozi, "and nothing is left undone."[9] Doing nothing (*wuwei*) is a constant theme in this earliest Daoist text, and means doing nothing that pushes against the flow of the *dao*. Zhuangzi illustrates this, as usual, with a tale:

Cook Ding was cutting up an ox for Lord Wenhui. At every touch of his hand, every lean of his shoulder, every move of his feet, every push of his knee – zip! zoop! He slithered the knife along with a zing, and all was in perfect rhythm, as though he were performing the dance of the Mulberry Grove or keeping time to the Ching-shou music. "Ah, this is marvelous!" said Lord Wenhui.[10]

I doubt that butchery has ever been described with such joy. When Lord Wenhui remarks on how sharp the knife must be, Cook Ding explains that lesser butchers must sharpen their knives every few days or weeks, although he has not sharpened his in years. His secret is that after years of cutting up carcasses, he no longer sees muscle, sinew, and bone. Instead he sees the vast empty spaces that make up the joints, lets his knife play there, and watches as the ox simply comes to pieces. He does nothing and accomplishes everything.

In spite of the long arguments between Daoism and Confucianism, both this story from Zhuangzi and the more Confucian versions of cosmic resonance show a concern with understanding and joining a broader cosmic order. This is not a nature apart from human culture, but the flow that underlies both nature and human life, a mutual resonance of all things. Both also have no qualms about using this flow for human benefit. Cook Ding, Lord Wenhui, and Zhuangzi himself, after all, seem perfectly comfortable with the death and butchery of the ox for human happiness.

Daoist meditational practice similarly offers a mystical unity with the cosmos, but in a way that also greatly empowers the Daoist himself. Michael Saso, for example, describes the meditation on the twelve earthly branches that some Zhengyi Daoists perform during the first spring thunderstorm. The point, however, is not simply unity with the Dao. It is internalizing the power of thunder to expel demons for the purposes of healing and combating heterodoxy.[11] The example illustrates a form of cosmic resonance (between the macrocosmic power of the storm and the microcosmic structure of the body), along with the general comfort about pursuing humanist ends through a unity with the broader forces of the world.

The limits on practical resonance: the rigors of time and space

Ideas about anthropocosmic resonance continue to inform many aspects of environmental understanding in China, but we also need to recall that they thrive most clearly in a specific textual tradition whose highest development came during the Han Dynasty, as part of an argument about the broad relationship of the Emperor to divinity.[12] If we look beyond the philosophical traditions to actual behavior in the environment, however, we begin to see the social and physical limits to resonance theory. In this section I will discuss these limits through concepts of ritual and agricultural time and through the related practice of *fengshui*. These practices show an awareness of the kinds of cosmological forces that the philosophical traditions also addressed, along with the same kind of comfort with manipulating those forces appropriately for human ends. There are also hints, however, of some new complexities in the understanding of the environment implied by these behaviors. In part, these come from the practical requirements of things like agriculture or the human diet. In part, though, they also stem from ideas about the sources of natural power that do not appear as clearly in the early philosophical sources, which were primarily guides to court ritual.

Maurice Bloch has suggested that practical activity, especially productive work, creates a different and more universal kind of cognition than ritual.[13] He was arguing in particular that agricultural work tends to foster a view of linear time, while ritual contexts produce the cyclical conceptions of time that anthropologists like to identify – a changeless time that enhances claims to ritual authority. This contrast between the cognitive consequences of practical life and ritual life is surely too strong, but it does suggest that the physics and biology of action in the world have consequences that must be addressed more in some arenas than others.

In fact, China concretized several quite different conceptions of time through calendars, and they are consistent with Bloch's claim. The best known is the lunar calendar. The lunar calendar determines nearly every important calendrical ritual, from the Chinese New Year to gods' birthdays. The hours, days, months, and years of the lunar cycle further proceed through finer cycles of ten heavenly stems (*tiangan*) and twelve earthly branches (*dizhi*). These stems and branches create particular characteristics for every time of day, and they repeat only every sixty years. The system as a whole, with its interlocking cycles within cycles, interdigitates with the theoretical apparatus of anthropocosmic resonance. Each particular combination of stems and branches thus correlates with yin and yang, the five elements, the twenty-eight asterisms that define the celestial equator, and so on. Traditional calendars are filled with information based on these characteristics – divinations of the coming year based on time of birth, or the appropriateness of each day (and sometimes each hour) for activities like getting married, traveling, or opening a business (see Figure 2.1). They are practical guides to the application of resonance theory.

A lunar system is not much use for agriculture, however – plants respond far more to the sun than to the moon. The Chinese adjusted the mismatch between the lunar and solar years by adding leap months to the lunar calendar every few years, but a farmer still could not plant or harvest crops according to the lunar date. Instead, the Chinese also developed a secondary calendar based on a division of the solar year into twenty-four periods of fifteen or sixteen days each. The names of the periods make the close ties to agriculture clear: they consist almost entirely

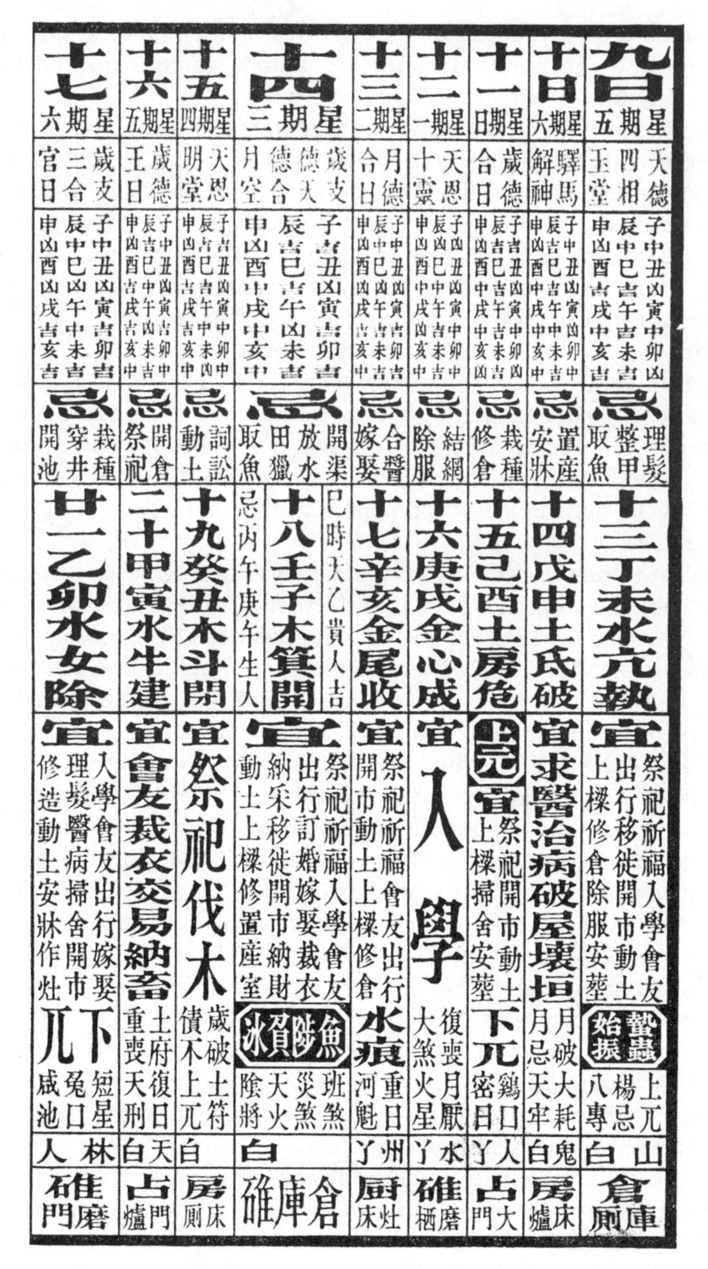

Figure 2.1 Almanac page showing divinatory information for February 9–17, 1979. The 14th was good for ceremonies but bad for fishing.

of standard solar markers like the solstices and equinoxes, and of agricultural or weather-related names like "Rain" (*yushui*), "Excited Insects" (*jingzhe*), and "Grain in Ear" (*mangzhong*).[14]

Agriculture requires both an understanding of broad environmental processes and a willingness to alter them for human benefit. The agricultural orientation of the solar periods is just a minor reflection of the enormous environmental change that Chinese civilization induced. The rice paddy, that prototypical Chinese rural environment, is essentially a man-made structure. It requires far more than just the obvious environmental necessities of agriculture – deforestation, plowing, and so on. The technical requirements of paddy agriculture demand an exquisite control over water flow, allowing farmers to raise and lower the level of water in the paddies as needed for the stage in the agricultural cycle and to adjust for rainfall. The field also had to be absolutely level, in order to maintain a constant water height. The result was an artificial but stable environment that utterly reshaped both land and water.

Over the centuries China also gradually deforested even upland areas unsuitable for wet rice agriculture. New crops (maize, potatoes, opium) sometimes encouraged deforestation for upland agriculture, and lowland market demand for charcoal and building materials furthered the process. This loss of tree cover encouraged erosion and eventually caused flooding downstream, at the same time as it transferred fertile soil from upland to lowland areas. The Chinese government was aware of many of these dynamics, and tried to use them. It sometimes invested in environmental change, for example by building dikes or helping reclaim land in areas that they felt needed rapid economic growth. Peter Perdue documents in some detail how this worked in the area around Dongting Lake in Hunan.[15] As the area prospered, private investors took over these functions, eventually going beyond what the environment could handle. Government attempts to halt this proved ineffective, leading to tragic flooding in the nineteenth and twentieth centuries.[16]

This glance at agriculture shows the difficulty of translating philosophy into action. Farmers undoubtedly shared some forms of resonance theory. They recognized cosmic principles through yin and yang and the five elements, and as anthropomophized in deities. They recognized the necessity for a proper relationship between those principles and human action in ideas like the mandate of heaven. Yet they also responded to other systems of meaning that could drive more exploitative environmental behavior – the need, for example, to create and recreate families. In the case of land speculators building illegal dikes to reclaim land from Dongting Lake, they responded to economic incentives quite familiar to us. The endless cycles of resonant time could give way to irreversible change.

Chinese *fengshui* offers a less strictly economic way of dealing with the landscape than agriculture, but shows many of the same dynamics. Like agriculture, it was also caught between the endless balances of anthropocosmic resonance and the need to meet immediate goals for the family. *Fengshui* specialists align the flow of *qi* through the landscape and the built environment with the *qi* of the people who live there. They play a crucial role at nearly all burials, lining up the coffin and the grave itself for the benefit of the descendants. Even in China after 1949, where the government has consistently denounced *fengshui* practitioners as extortionists and purveyors of feudal superstition, *fengshui* plays an important role in rural burials.[17] Large construction projects sometimes also bring in *fengshui* experts, and people may hire them for their homes if they are having problems. The most famous case in recent years, according to rumor anyway, was the Bank of China tower in Hong Kong, which people claim was constructed to cut the cosmic power of the British Governor's office.

It takes an expert to analyze *fengshui*. The system is an intricate combination of nearly every system of cosmic correlation ever devised in China, although most specialists in practice use only parts of it. The basic tool is a compass surrounded by concentric rings of stems, branches, hexagrams, asterisms, and every other possibility (see Figure 2.2). Many of the systems these compasses use ultimately reduce information to the five elements, which then must be balanced with each other through careful alignment of a grave or part of a building.

Like the lunar calendar, to which it is intimately related, *fengshui* reinforces the ideas of balanced interaction and harmony with a broader order of heaven/nature. Chinese have developed these ideals philosophically over the two millennia since cosmic resonance theory was first standardized, and their popular origins surely extend even further back. Once again, though, humanity is at the center of the scheme. *Fengshui* is less a matter of harmonizing people with a broader nature than of harnessing the energies of the universe for human benefit. The ability to benefit some at the expense of others explains why *fengshui* so often became involved in conflicts. It could, for example, benefit one brother or lineage branch over another, owing to their different *qi*. People also sometimes used it to attack construction by neighboring villages or factories.

As an example, we have historical records of stories of a local deity in Guangxi, called King Gan (*Gan Wang*), which explained his power as an even more egregious use of *fengshui*. A specialist told him that an ideal gravesite was available, which would surely guarantee his rise to high office. It was imperative that he use it right away, and so King Gan

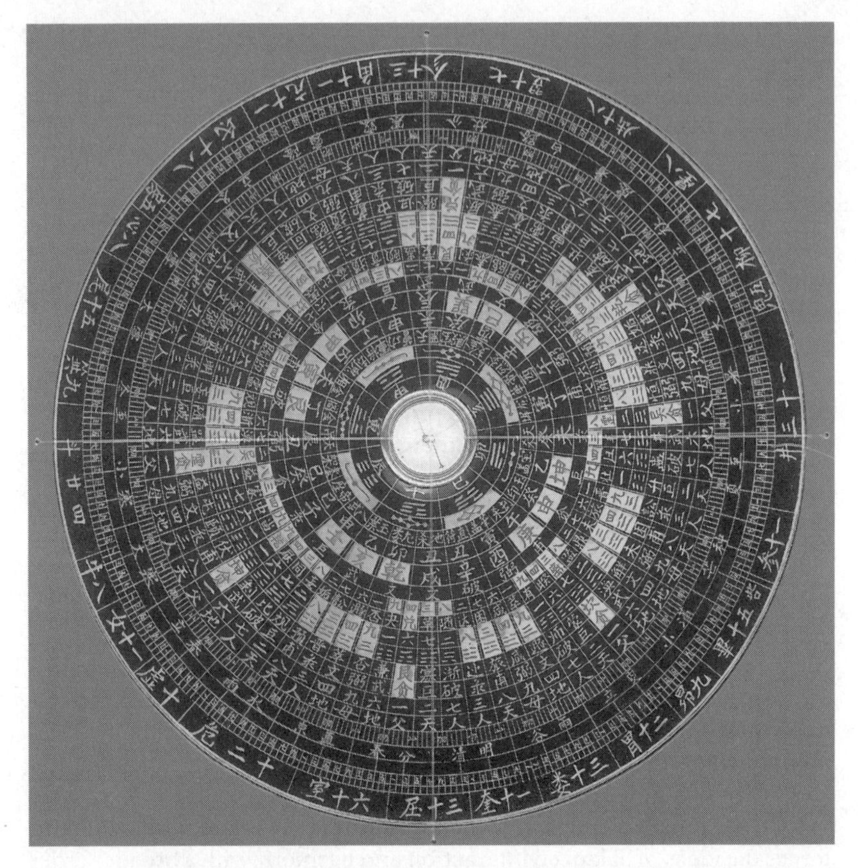

Figure 2.2 *Fengshui* compass in the author's collection. The rings of divinatory symbols can be aligned to face south using the small compass in the middle.

murdered his mother, buried her in the grave, and became a great success as an official and ultimately a god.[18] While much of *fengshui* addresses a Chinese view of the proper social order – balanced interaction with the cosmos in support of a human hierarchy that stems from family to state – stories like this remind us of its underside. Hierarchy and the balances of resonance theory were not the only sources of power, and the needs of daily life constantly put them in jeopardy.

A Buddhist view

Buddhism brought yet another stream of thought about humans and nature when it entered China along the Silk Road almost two millennia ago. In contrast to the Daoist embracing of the Way of the world or the Confucian concern with the proper ordering of society, most versions of Buddhism renounce the world as a place of dust and illusion, and life as a constant grasping after falsehood. They seek escape from the four bitternesses that make up life: birth, old age, sickness, and death.

In practice, however, this did not imply a total disregard for the welfare of the world. Buddhism contained several ideas with implications for how people related to the environment. Most obviously, the interrelated ideas of karma and reincarnation meant that every other living being – from insects to deities – is fundamentally connected to us as a possible past or future human being. Our treatment of these other beings affects our own karma, and thus our future reincarnations.

In addition, every being has a potential to transcend this world of suffering by becoming a Buddha. The Buddha-nature exists in everything, like a mirror that needs to be cleaned through dedicated self-cultivation in order to shine brightly. At a fundamental level, then, all living things are the same and humanity has no special privileges. For both these reasons, Buddhism forbids killing, and committed Buddhists in China take vows not to eat meat.

Finally, especially as Buddhism evolved in China, the ideal of the bodhisattva provided a justification to act for the benefit of the secular world. A bodhisattva is a being who could leave the world, achieving nirvana as a Buddha. Instead, however, the bodhisattva chooses to remain in this world until all beings have been saved. Little research has been done on the environmental consequences of this view in imperial China, but these ideas sprouted into the beginnings of new environmental thought in the twentieth century. The goal of compassion for all things has been especially important for the humanistic Buddhism that has developed over the last few decades, as I will discuss further in later chapters.

Still, we should not mistake Buddhist attitudes for a biocentrism in the style of some Western thought. Humans have by far the best chance of attaining nirvana – gods are far too comfortable and the other beings are far too miserable. Buddhist sutras speak to us above all about humanity, about our desires and needs, and about our potentials. In addition, given an irresolvable conflict between human interests and those of other beings, the humans have priority. We can kill vermin, for example, if the only alternative is human starvation. For all this, however, Buddhism added something fundamentally new to Chinese views of their relationship to the environment. Zhuangzi's joyful description of Cook Ding butchering the ox, to give just a tiny example, would never be read the same way again after Buddhism became popular in China.

I cannot do justice to resonance theory or to Buddhism in these few pages. Each of them developed internal arguments over the centuries, and they argued with each other as well. This brief discussion is enough, I hope, to indicate how all these streams of thought contributed important ideas about how humanity and the environment relate to each other, and how each of them imagines the world quite differently from the meanings usually captured by words like "nature" or the modern *ziran*.

The power of the center and the margins

Resonance theory in China tied to notions of central power, especially imperial power. The Emperor was the crucial linchpin of the universe, and his proper performance of the annual ritual cycle kept the world in harmony. The Buddhist alternative undercut this form of hierarchy. Even without Buddhism, though, there were other notions of environment and power that affected behavior. Here I will discuss just one: the idea that marginal spaces held their own kind of alternative to the power of the center.

Let me begin by showing these competing notions of power through a discussion of food, that crucial mediator of humans and their environment. I will look first at the most common foods, but end with the more surprising preferences that some Chinese show for endangered species or things like living dead fish. For millennia a standard meal in China has consisted of a core of grain (*fan*) surrounded by side dishes (*cai*).[19] The grain – now usually rice in south China and wheat noodles or steamed bread in north China – is the defining feature of a meal. An exceptionally elaborate feast might skip the grain or reduce it to a late course, but even then someone will inevitably comment that they never feel full if they skip the grain.

As one might guess from China's intensive agricultural economy, grain also held a powerful symbolic role beyond the dining table. A mixture of the five grains (*wugu*), for example, often symbolizes fertility. The grains are sometimes mixed with coins and nails (*ding*), punning on a word referring to male descendants (*ding*). *Fengshui* experts throw this mixture on new graves to ensure the fertility of the descendants. Daoists can also conduct a ceremony for people called worshiping the peck (*bai dou*), whose key symbol is a traditional grain measure filled with the five grains and other symbolic objects. Grain in the form of bread or cakes also provides an important gift leading up to a wedding; these gifts tend to circulate in networks of the bride's kin. Liu Xin documents how married-out daughters and their mothers also exchange bread during the harvest season.[20]

In a careful analysis of food symbolism in funeral ritual (mostly in Taiwan), Stuart Thompson shows how rice "epitomizes the pure, regenerative aspects of the deceased which have been ritually winnowed."[21] It is the key food offering in the process of transforming a wandering soul into an ancestor. He interprets rice as an appropriate symbol for ancestors because it is the product of ancestral land, ideally inalienable outside the lineage. Rice is thus "the stuff of ancestors."[22] Grain, at a meal or at a funeral, shows the world as Confucians – or at least as the elderly lineage men who ran funerals – would like it to be. Land and lineage extend back and forward in time, together guaranteeing the success of the family on its land and thus the state in its territory. Each of us is embedded in the hierarchical and environmental relations that result, with fathers anchoring families as emperors anchored the state and rice or wheat anchored a meal. Fathers and emperors are ultimately responsible for the welfare of their people by maintaining nature/heaven in its proper course, as shown by the abundance of grain they produce.

Yet there is another side to food, and even to Taiwanese funeral offerings. Pork must be offered in addition to rice, and the most important offerings are a pig's head and tail provided by the families of married-out daughters of the deceased. Even a strictly Buddhist funeral I attended in northern Taiwan included these offerings, in the form of vegetarian models of pigs' heads. As Thompson analyzes it, pork in general is exchanged, while rice remains within the agnatic line. In the part of Taiwan where he worked, some informants strengthen this by saying that it is unfilial for lineal descendants to eat pork during the funeral period.

Just as rice needs the yin qualities of earth and rain to be fertile, lineages must have women from outside the lineage. As mothers, women are idealized as nurturers and sources of fertility. As outsiders, though, women sometimes appear dangerous. Men blame them for breaking up extended families by quarreling with their sisters-in-law, promoting the interests of their own children over those of the extended family. Their relatives can be useful, but also tend to interfere. Among deities, women appear in both forms: goddesses of fertility who appear embracing babies, and spirits of sexual predation who seduce and kill men. Here is another source of power then – not the hierarchy going up to the Emperor who epitomizes the ability to influence and adjust cosmic forces for human benefit, but a source of power from the outside, from the margins.

I do not want to wander far from food symbolism into gender issues here, but make the point only because it clarifies that there are alternative sources of power in food as well. Foods of every kind share in the *qi* energies of the world, and everything eaten thus alters the balance of the eater. Special foods nourish pregnant women or people with colds. Some should only be eaten in summer or winter. Most people are keenly aware of their diet, even at ordinary meals. Americans, I have been told, suffer from too much "fiery energy" (*huoqi*), because we eat too many hot foods like coffee, red meat, and chocolate.

Grain is pure and neutral in this scheme. The more varied and medically powerful energies come instead from the side dishes, which are as important for a meal as affines are to lineage reproduction. Like marriages, the more the meal serves the purpose of social exchange rather than family reproduction, the more it features side dishes. The ultimate expression of this is the banquet, which is only performed for guests, and in which grain either is not served or occupies only a very minor place. Rice or wheat provides instead the prototypical core of a family meal. Cooked rice is also the most fundamental offering to ancestors. Gods, who come from outside the family, receive meat and no rice.

Some foods concentrate considerably more power than others, and these foods generally differ radically from rice or wheat. Grain is grown on ancestral land in valleys long associated with the heights of Chinese civilization. People grow most side dishes, of course, in the same general areas. Yet really powerful dishes come instead from the periphery, both physically and mentally. That is, they often come from physically distant and inaccessible places, and they often confound standard categories of thought and experience.

Let me illustrate this with a few examples. The coach of China's powerful national swim team a few years ago allegedly had his swimmers eat a special diet, which helped explain their international success. One of the key ingredients was something called "winter insect summer grass" (*dongchong xiacao*). This became a highly valued and very expensive delicacy as a result. I ate it just once, at a banquet given by a provincial governor. There was considerable excitement at my table as people looked at the menu for the evening. When I asked just what it was, people said it was both a caterpillar and a grass. They also told me about the swim team and assured me that it was extraordinarily nourishing and fortifying (*bu*). Most of them had never eaten it either. We ate it as a soup, with each bowl containing what appeared to be a small worm. I learned later that it is in fact a caterpillar that has been parasitized by a fungus. When the caterpillar burrows underground for the winter, the fungus feeds off its body and sends up a grass-like shoot. These caterpillar-fungi come from some of China's least accessible areas, and are often found by nomadic Tibetans high on the Qinghai plateau. "Winter insect summer grasses" come from the cognitive periphery as well; both animal and vegetable, they dissolve the usual categories. Here is a natural power utterly different from rice. Its strength comes from breaking categories rather than defining them, and from the periphery rather than the core.

The pangolin (*chuanshanjia*) provides a second example. Pangolins live in the mountains of southwestern China, where I ate them at still more banquets, again with some excitement from my hosts and statements about how fortifying pangolin stew is. Quite unlike the caterpillar fungus, I already knew about pangolins, although I had never seen or eaten one. Most anthropologists know about them from Mary Douglas's descriptions of them in her analysis of purity and food categories among the Lele of central Africa.[23] The pangolin is an anteater that burrows in the ground but climbs trees; it has scales like a reptile but suckles its young like a mammal. Among the Lele, according to Douglas, this crossing of cognitive lines results in a heavy symbolic load for the pangolin.

The pangolin is not quite so highly charged in the Chinese case, but we can see some of the same dynamics at play. The powerful energies of its scales make them command high prices as Chinese medicine, which accounts for most of the killing of this endangered species. Its flesh – stewed for many hours in a spicy broth to remove the flavor of its insect diet – is extremely *bu*. Like the insect/grass, pangolins live in remote areas that are often associated with non-Han ethnic minorities in China, or with foreign lands. Birds' nests come from Southeast Asia, bear and camel paws from the remote north or northwest, rhinoceros horns from Africa, and shark's fins from the ocean depths. Many of these most prized foods also share a kind of anomalous texture. Bird's nest, shark's fin, sea cucumber, camel's (and I assume bear's) paw and other banquet foods have very little flavor of their own, a vaguely translucent color, and a texture that almost defies description – a sort of crunchy, rubbery, gelatinous munch. All of them come from unusual and exotic creatures in the Chinese context. As Eugene Anderson describes it, "the more strange a food, the more power is ascribed to it."[24] These foods often originate in the physical periphery of China, but also rise up from the cognitive periphery that lies between standard categories of thought and even taste.

The living dead fish is a variation on this theme. Unlike the other foods I have been discussing, the fish itself is not special. The cooking style is what frees the fish from ordinary categories of thought and brings it into the same realm as these other more extraordinary creatures. Both alive and dead, the cooked flesh of the writhing fish dissolves boundaries as effectively and powerfully as an insect/grass caterpillar or a reptile/mammal anteater.

This quick look at food suggests two views of "natural" power. One, rooted in grain, epitomizes the idea of the family with all its implications of Confucian social order. Grain is the ancestral land, the appropriate offering for ancestors, and the heart of a family meal. It is also a core symbol for Chinese civilization as a whole, the ultimate product of the irrigated valley agriculture that distinguishes the Han from most of the other groups around them. It is the power that emanates down from the center.

Yet meals need more than grain, just as families need more than patrilineal kin to reproduce. The rarest, most desired, and most potent banquet foods typify this alternate form of power. These are the foods that most clearly dismantle the usual hierarchies of place and thought. This distinction is by no means identical with what we find in the philosophical traditions, but does resonate with some of the ideas there. Confucius, after all, liked his food cut into symmetrical pieces just as he liked social relations kept in their proper order. Daoists, on the other hand, tended to enjoy the boundaries, like the empty spaces between the joints in which Cook Ding played his knife. Some Daoists appropriately also avoided eating all grains as part of their self-cultivation.

These two kinds of power are "natural" only in the sense that they stem from the workings of the cosmos, from the flow of *qi* through all things. Both subsume the human and the physical worlds equally. They are not "nature" in the modern Western sense of something beyond human culture. The centralized, ordered, neatly categorized power of rice describes an idealized human society and its environment as much as a foodstuff. In the same way, the power of the margins extends far beyond food.

We can also see it in the broad ordering of space. Nearly all of China's major pilgrimage sites, for example, lie in relatively inaccessible mountains distant from the largest cities. Gimello describes travel to Mount Wutai, one of the most important pilgrimage sites, as a trip "to the very edge of China's cultural world, there to risk awesome encounters with things genuinely, if not totally, 'other.'"[25] Travelers would describe the extraordinary events that proved the divine/natural power of such places, from golden lights to manifestations of deities. Not coincidentally, non-Han minority groups also often lived in such remote areas. They too partook of the alternate power of the periphery, in the Chinese view – often associated with both sexual fantasy and magical potency. This is power from the margins instead of from Heaven via the Emperor in the Forbidden City, but both forms of power intertwine the human and the physical worlds. The power of the margins appears once again in stories of mountain hermits with miraculous powers, from Daoist adepts to masters of martial arts.

Some of the same dynamic recurs in Chinese domestic architecture and landscape. The basic structure of a house reiterates the idea of centralized and hierarchical power.[26] By doing so, it also helps recreate the image for each generation growing up in this kind of space. Housing styles varied widely across China, but rural houses everywhere mark central space from more private spaces. Even if the house has only a single room, the bed and cooking area are thought of as separate spaces. The central area is for entertaining guests, with the highest position facing the door, and lower-ranking people in progressively more marginal spaces. Ancestors and deities occupy the highest position of all, sitting on a high table or shelf – often the most elaborate piece of furniture in the house – placed against the wall opposite the door in the main room. Even when the Cultural Revolution banned such symbols, many people placed posters of Chairman Mao and other leaders in the same spot.

Official buildings followed the same pattern. Both community temples and a magistrate's official buildings (the yamen) center around a main hall where the deity or magistrate sits facing the door. Various secondary and tertiary rooms and buildings can extend out to the right, left, and rear, with status correlated to closeness to the center.

The ultimate vision of this image was the Forbidden City itself, where the privileged few allowed past the gates faced an enormous empty space, with a single hall standing in the distance ahead. Those permitted even more access would pass through this hall and would see another huge expanse of empty space and a second hall looming ahead. Each move down this central path moved a person closer to the Emperor, who ruled from the apparent center of the complex. He was the Son of Heaven, the axis of divine and earthly power, and the crux of the proper flow of energy through the world.

Yet in practice all of these spaces also had other foci. The rear of the Forbidden City abandons the architecture of power receding from the center. This was the residence of the imperial household, and is a warren of buildings, rooms, and paths, quite unlike the centralized logic of the public area. This is the most inner area, the most female – both symbolically and in practice – and therefore also the one closer to the Daoist admiration of disordered, liminal powers.

Most temples had no residential function, which helped them maintain the purity of their logic, yet many temples also let this alternative power leak through their architecture. The temple I know best is an ornate rebuilding, using traditional stone and wood carving techniques, of a major temple to Zushi Gong in Sanxia, Taiwan. It has the usual basic architectural structure of a southern temple, but also fills every nook, cranny and crack with elaborate carvings of various traditional tales with no relation to the deity. Many of these are too tiny and distant to see clearly. They twine around each other in the dim recesses of the rafters, creating an alternate universe of stories away from the central motif of the deity. Layers of ornament refract through all the borders of the building – roofs, doorways, windows – as other divinities thrive off the central axis of worship.

Ordinary houses rarely had the possibility of such baroque flights of fancy. People really lived in them, after all, which constantly compromised centralized order with the daily trials of life. Even the most beautiful and expensive altar tables, for example, quite often harbor kitschy souvenirs of past tourism alongside august statues of deities and tablets for the ancestors. As people gain the wealth to decorate, some obtain objects in the style of the old elite. One popular genre in Taiwan, for example, is a thin sheet of marble on a wooden stand. The marble is always chosen because its natural grain appears to recreate a landscape, usually a mountain range – a natural object that mimics a human imitation of a natural object. I have sometimes seen the same effect displayed in central rooms through the natural grain of a sectioned tree trunk, whose odd growth created a pattern that also recalled landscape painting. This is another interweaving of the physical and human realms. It is all one *qi* after all.

These objects also typify a common fascination in China with the oddities of nature. The most prized objects are not symmetrical arrangements around a central core, nor representations of nested hierarchy, nor even shapely representatives of their kind. They are instead the prodigies of nature, the bizarre results of *qi* twisted into its ultimate convolutions. This is the aesthetic that values the intricate twists and holes of "strange rocks" (*qishi*), for instance, over the calmer stones that emulate mountains in Japanese gardens. More broadly, it is part of the same view that makes pangolin more powerful than pork.

Many elite gardens, especially by the Qing Dynasty (1644–1911), specialized in this view of nature. Chinese gardens typically stood apart from the central axis of power of a house, just as the imperial household's private area did in the Forbidden City. While garden designs and goals varied widely, many attempted to reproduce at human scale the sorts of landscapes in which Daoist immortals might play.[27] Larger gardens often featured a "false mountain" (*jiashan*), which was a man-made miniature of a mountain, still big enough to walk around on. The cleverest of these featured a maze of unexpected twists and turns designed to confound and amuse visitors to the garden. The proper path, for instance, might require finding a small set of stone steps hidden behind a boulder. While European garden mazes probably provided equal pleasure to elite owners watching their lost guests, the Chinese version had none of the rectilinear order of European mazes, or even of Confucian sitting rooms. The European maze confuses because every path looks the same; the Chinese version confuses because everything looks different, and nothing is what it seems. The European version may have recalled the underground passages of the Minotaur, but the Chinese version toyed instead with legends of people lost in the mountains as they attempted to follow immortals at play.

"Strange rocks" are a smaller version of the same idea. Deeply eroded by water, the most valuable of these rocks were deeply pierced with many holes, leaving just a kind of stone skeleton that clearly showed the underlying flow of *qi*. Like the false mountains, they offered a vision of cosmic energy twisting and gamboling through the stone. The effect could be miniaturized to any level, because it is all the same *qi*, no matter what the scale. Gardens of this kind almost always miniaturized larger landscapes. Like landscape painters or Daoists internalizing cosmic forces, these garden designers recreated the same kinds of energy that flowed through the larger world. As Rolf Stein described it in his work on miniature gardens: "Reducing the whole thing in size, making it manageable, accessible to handling – this raises it from the level of imitative reality and puts it in the domain of the only true reality: mythical space."[28] Humans did not imitate nature so much as they molded its greatest forces as partners.

These views of the world see humans as a part of the energy flow of the universe, and understand centers and margins as creating their own different forms of power and efficacy. As I will discuss, such understandings continue to influence environmental behavior, from encouraging the consumption of exotic and often endangered species to shaping patterns of nature tourism.

Conclusion

I began this chapter with a naive question: how did you say "nature" in Chinese before the twentieth century? The first answer is that you did not, at least not in any way that translates directly or comfortably to modern Western concepts of nature. The second answer is that China did not have a unitary way of thinking about nature, even on its own terms. Its natures were multiple, drawing on diverse intellectual and religious traditions and on varieties of experience with the physical world.

All the views I have discussed, though, share some underlying features. First, Chinese thinking about nature typically accepted some form of *qi* theory. The core texts of anthropocosmic resonance theory had the strongest influence during the Han Dynasty – about two millennia ago. Later scholars sometimes questioned the texts. Imperial Chinese scholars could be harsh critical readers, raising issues of accuracy and authenticity for even the most canonical texts. Nevertheless, a very broad and generalized version of the theory remained widespread and enormously influential, as it still does today. The core ideas are of a cosmic energy that vitalizes everything in the world, from human bodies to mountain ranges. In its various forms (yin and yang, five elements, and all the rest), this energy interacts in complex ways that ideally achieve a balanced flow.

Second, because this *qi* energy flows through everything, there is no fundamental distinction between the human and physical worlds, or between culture and nature. That is why a painting of bamboo, a miniature garden landscape in a bowl, or an act of internal meditation creates new flows of *qi*, just as authentic as those that make up the physical world. It is also why improper rule by an emperor in Beijing explains earthquakes or tiger maulings in distant provinces. Finally, most versions of Chinese nature are perfectly comfortable with manipulating natural forces for human benefit. The form this might take varies widely, from Confucius' ruler-sage to Zhuangzi's Cook Ding, from a farmer reclaiming wetlands to a hunter supplying pangolin scales.

These broad constants in the view of nature (or should I call it heaven?) still leave enormous room for variation. An anthropocosmic universe of *qi* energy can reinforce the Emperor's crucial role as the most powerful conduit connecting heaven, earth, and man. Yet it fits just as comfortably with Zhuangzi's Cook Ding and other Daoist images of people in unexpected social positions who truly understand how to flow with the Dao to achieve their ends. Iron Staff Li (Li Tieguai), for instance, appeared as a deformed beggar, even though he was one of the most beloved of the Daoist Eight Immortals. Sculptors sometimes carved images of him out of grotesque roots, depicting him as both immortal human and a natural concentration of twisting *qi*. Buddhists added still more to the mix, with ideas of the Buddha-nature in all life and compassion for all beings.

Less textual sources like food or gardens revealed further variations on these themes. These media show multiple sources of natural power, and I identified in particular one that descends down from the center much as Chinese political authority did, and another that rises up from the most liminal physical and mental spaces. We can thus see religious power in community temples, usually controlled by local elites, but also in pilgrimage sites on distant mountains. Domestic power flows down from the central room and its ancestral altar, but also curls playfully through gardens. Culinary power lies in the core foods of irrigated agriculture – rice and wheat above all – but also in the exotic foods like pangolins and insect/grasses at the cognitive opposite pole from rice.

This analysis could easily be broadened and made still more complex. This is enough, I hope, to provide background for the chapters that follow, and to make the point that Chinese tradition offered a very different set of cultural resources for thinking about nature than what developed in the West. These ideas led in practice to one of the most remarkable agriculture regimes in history. It was extraordinarily productive by any world standard, and allowed stable exploitation of resources like rice paddies over many centuries. On the other hand, it also encouraged deforestation, and continues to foster a huge demand to devour exotic species. When I once complained at a banquet that the pangolins were protected by China's endangered species list, I was simply told that they were vermin – they burrowed holes in people's houses – and that the market for their scales was very good.

The twentieth century brought many of these ideas into question, but it did not eradicate them. We continue to see them directly in the popularity of Chinese traditional medicine, the continuation of *fengshui*, or the fad for *qigong* exercises. As I will argue in the chapters that follow, we also see them indirectly in modern innovations like the environmental movement or nature tourism.

NOTES

1. Raymond Williams, *Keywords: A Vocabulary of Culture and Society*, revised edition (New York: Oxford University Press, 1983), 219.
2. This is paraphrased from Williams, *Keywords*, 219.
3. I am grateful to Jonathan Spence, who originally suggested this possibility to me. Some other genres of painting, not called *shanshui*, did not include these signs of humanity, but were close-up studies of bamboo, flowers, or birds.
4. Mark Elvin, "The Environmental Legacy of Imperial China," *China Quarterly* 156 (December 1998): 755.
5. Tu Weiming, "Beyond the Enlightenment Mentality," in *Confucianism and Ecology: The Interrelation of Heaven, Earth, and Humans*, ed. Mary Evelyn Tucker and John Berthrong (Cambridge, MA: Harvard University Center for the Study of World Religions, 1998), 17–19.
6. For more detail, see Robert P. Weller and Peter K. Bol, "From Heaven-and-Earth to Nature: Chinese Concepts of the Environment and Their Influence on Policy Implementation," in *Confucianism and Ecology: The Interrelation of Heaven, Earth, and Humans*, ed. Mary Evelyn Tucker and John Berthrong (Cambridge, MA: Harvard University Center for the Study of World Religions, 1998), 313–41.
7. *Lüshi Qunqiu*, Sibu Congkan edition (Shanghai: Shangwu Yinshuguan, 1929), 9/9a.
8. John Major, *Heaven and Earth in Early Han Thought: Chapters Three, Four, and Five of the Huainanzi* (Albany: State University of New York Press, 1993), 225.
9. *Daode Jing*, ch. 48.
10. *The Complete Works of Chuang Tzu*, trans. Burton Watson (New York: Columbia University Press, 1970), ch. 3.
11. Michael Saso, "Orthodoxy and Heterodoxy in Taoist Ritual," in *Religion and Ritual in Chinese Society*, ed. Arthur P. Wolf (Stanford: Stanford University Press, 1974), 325–36.

12. Michael J. Puett, *To Become a God: Cosmology, Sacrifice, and Self-Divinization in Early China* (Cambridge, MA: Harvard University Asia Center, 2002).
13. Maurice Bloch, "The Past and the Present in the Present," *Man* (N.S.) 12 (1977): 278–92.
14. For a detailed chart, see Liu Xin, *In One's Own Shadow: An Ethnographic Account of the Condition of Post-Reform China* (Berkeley: University of California Press, 2000), 88–9.
15. Peter C. Perdue, *Exhausting the Earth: State and Peasant in Hunan, 1500–1850* (Cambridge, MA: Council on East Asian Studies, Harvard University, 1987), 197–233. For a similar example elsewhere in China, see R. Keith Schoppa, *Xiang Lake – Nine Centuries of Chinese Life* (New Haven: Yale University Press, 1989).
16. Perdue, *Exhausting the Earth*, 233.
17. Ole Bruun, "The *Fengshui* Resurgence in China: Conflicting Cosmologies between State and Peasantry," *China Journal* 36 (1996): 47–65.
18. Robert P. Weller, "Matricidal Magistrates and Gambling Gods: Weak States and Strong Spirits in China," *Australian Journal of Chinese Affairs* 33 (1995): 107–24.
19. The distinction apparently goes back at least to the Zhou Dynasty. See K. C. Chang, *Early Chinese Civilization: Anthropological Perspectives* (Cambridge, MA: Harvard-Yenching Institute, 1976), 134.
20. Liu, *In One's Own Shadow*, 94, 96.
21. Stuart E. Thompson, "Death, Food, and Fertility," in *Death Ritual in Late Imperial and Modern China*, ed. James L. Watson and Evelyn S. Rawski (Berkeley: University of California Press, 1988), 95.
22. Thompson, "Death, Food, and Fertility," 93.
23. Mary Douglas, *Purity and Danger: An Analysis of Concepts of Pollution and Taboo* (London: Routledge and Kegan Paul, 1978 [1969]), 167–73.
24. Eugene N. Anderson, *Ecologies of the Heart: Emotion, Belief, and the Environment* (New York: Oxford University Press, 1996), 46.
25. Robert M. Gimello, "Chang Shang-Ying on Wu-T'ai Shan," in *Pilgrims and Sacred Sites in China*, ed. Susan Naquin and Yü Chün Fang (Berkeley: University of California Press, 1992), 99.
26. This is clearest for rural houses, and can be seen in a range of studies across China. For examples, see Liu, *In One's Own Shadow*, 42–51; Sulamith Heins Potter and Jack M. Potter, *China's Peasants: The Anthropology of a Revolution* (Cambridge: Cambridge University Press, 1990), 222–4.
27. On gardens in general, see Craig Clunas, *Fruitful Sites: Garden Culture in Ming Dynasty China* (Durham, NC: Duke University Press, 1996); Joanna F. Handlin Smith, "Gardens in Ch'i Piao-Chia's Social World: Wealth and Values in Late-Ming Kiangnan," *Journal of Asian Studies* 51, no. 1 (1992): 55–81.
28. Rolf A. Stein, *The World in Miniature: Container Gardens and Dwellings in Far Eastern Religious Thought*, trans. Phyllis Brooks (Stanford: Stanford University Press, 1990), 52.

3 New natures

It would have been a stunning coincidence if Chinese had a straightforward equivalent of "nature," partly because the term's European history is defiantly complex. Well before the middle of the twentieth century, however, this situation had changed. Anyone with passing knowledge of the languages can say without hesitation that the Chinese word for "nature" is *ziran*. It took some time to settle on this, of course. When Yan Fu – the late Qing social theorist and translator of Herbert Spencer and Thomas Huxley – summarized Darwin, he continued to use the language of heaven and earth to stand in for Darwin's nature. As Schwartz translates it: "Living things struggle among themselves in order to survive. Nature (lit., 'heaven') selects [among them] and preserves the superior species. It is his view that humans and living things are born within a given space and together feed on the environment (heaven and earth)."[1]

Ziran had become the ruling translation for something like the Western meaning of "nature" by the 1920s. As with so many other technical terms from the social and natural sciences, China picked up this new use of the term from Japan, which had spearheaded the translation of Western concepts. A Japanese dictionary of 1924, for example, defines the term as (1) the opposite of "civilization," "culture," and "skill," and (2) a totality of actual existence, as opposed to "spirit" and "history."[2] Both definitions push the term far from its classical Chinese meaning of spontaneity, although that is yet another meaning that the English "naturally" includes. Nature as the opposite of culture, now given as the primary definition, resonates far more clearly with post-Enlightenment thought in Europe and America than with anything earlier in Chinese history. Chinese dictionaries quickly picked up this language from Japan – the earliest I have seen is a dictionary of philosophy published in 1926 – and definitions like this continue in wide use today.

Saying that *ziran* has come to represent a globalized European and American concept of nature does not get us very far, however. Europeans and Americans differ greatly in their own uses of "nature," both among and within their various languages and local traditions. Just as a single example, Simon Schama sums up a complex and nuanced argument about landscape traditions as follows: "What the myths of one ancient forest mean for one European national tradition may translate into something entirely different in another. In Germany, for example, the forest primeval was the site of tribal self-assertion against the Roman empire of stone and law. In England the greenwood was the place where the king disported his power in the royal hunt yet redressed the injustices of his officers."[3]

The concept of nature has evolved over time, too, not so much changing meaning as adding ever more stratigraphic layers. As I will discuss in a little more detail in the following sections, a kind of extended eighteenth century – from the Enlightenment to the Romantics – was especially important in this evolution. The opposition between nature and culture developed most strongly at the beginning of the period, but a new and more positive evaluation of the nature side of the dichotomy gained influence by the end.[4] As Keith Thomas summarizes the changes in England:

> By 1800 the confident anthropocentrism of Tudor England had given way to an altogether more confused state of mind. The world could no longer be regarded as having been made for man alone, and the rigid barriers between humanity and other forms of life had been much weakened . . . Not everyone now believed that mankind was uniquely sacred. Some Romantics preferred the once-condemned mystical view that "each shrub is sacred, and each weed divine".[5]

Things had changed greatly since the period a century earlier, when the separation of nature and culture had seemed so obvious. Both the earlier and the later views continued in Europe and America, and both would eventually influence views of nature in China and Taiwan. In the sections that follow, I will look quickly at a few of the main threads of "nature." I am not trying to capture its entire complex pattern, but just to identify the themes that would prove most influential in Chinese societies, and to follow a bit of their Asian reweaving. Much of the early history of Western influences on Chinese thinking about nature has yet to be written, and what follows is no more than a preliminary sketch.

Nature and transcendence

The Jesuits brought the first wave of Western science to China at the end of the Ming Dynasty. While some of them were masters of new European knowledge in mathematics and astronomy, they still offered a decidedly pre-Enlightenment view of the world. Alphonso Vagnoni, for example, presented Aristotle's theory of four elements (earth, air, wind, and fire) to the Chinese in 1633, and argued for its superiority to the Chinese five elements (*wuxing*: wood, fire, earth, metal, and water). Above all, Jesuit *scientia* provided them with a way of finding God through the workings of His creation, and of encouraging Chinese to do so as well.[6]

It was the newer, Renaissance-based ideas of the Jesuits, however, that had the greater impact on Chinese thinking about the natural world. The Vatican had adopted the Gregorian calendar in 1582, and several of the Jesuits were well versed in the new astronomy and mathematics that had led to the improved calculation of time. With the change of Chinese dynasties in 1644, the new Manchu rulers were eager to monopolize their control over the core intellectual apparatus of rule, including celestial auguries and the astronomical expertise they required. Jesuits found themselves as astronomers to the court, and they actively debated with Chinese elites of the old regime who attempted to retain earlier Chinese notions of the calendar. They were almost as influential in other areas of study where their mathematics gave them an advantage – from perspective painting to studies of musical pitch.

The Jesuits were not natural scientists in the modern sense. Nature was not simply an objective mechanism for them to dissect. Those ideas were just beginning to develop, mostly in Protestant northern Europe. Instead, nature was a way of seeing God at work, and the underlying mathematical beauty was part of that vision. This meshed in many ways with a Neo-Confucian view that had developed over the previous five hundred years in China, which looked to understand the transcendent principles (*tianli*) behind experience. Confucian understandings of inquiring into and extending concrete knowledge (*gezhi*) also revealed deep underlying principles that would guide a proper life. The Qing court funded research on musical intervals, for instance, because music both grew out of those transcendent principles and inculcated them in people. "Music," as the Neo-Confucian scholar Zhou Dunyi said, "is based on government."[7]

As Benjamin Elman (whose work I have been following here) argues, this helped Chinese scholars accept the new Jesuit views and integrate them into their existing views of the world. Furthermore, China by the eighteenth century had begun its own movement for evidential research (*kaozheng*). This important movement questioned the basis of much earlier knowledge, especially through close philological study of texts. Evidential research was an indigenous development, but its scholars often drew on Jesuit knowledge as part of their general skepticism toward earlier knowledge. The Jesuits for them became part of a reconstruction and revalidation of indigenous forms of knowledge.[8]

The Jesuit impact thus lasted far longer than their own presence in China. It did not cause the enormous upheaval in thought that China would see beginning in the late nineteenth century, and it rested more easily with earlier views than the new ideas of science and nature that I will discuss next. Nevertheless we can still see signs of their mathematical innovations and the glimpses of transcendence that they provided. I have a large *fengshui* compass, the outermost ring of which is neatly divided into 360 tiny boxes (see Figure 2.2). These compasses combine an enormous range of earlier Chinese thought about the ordering of the universe through yin and yang, the five elements, the ten stems and twelve branches, the eight and sixty-four trigrams, the twenty-eight asterisms, and much more. They offer a messy stratigraphy of a huge array of divination systems, each promising its own insight into the hidden transcendent order of the universe. That division of the circle into 360 degrees – a Jesuit contribution to Chinese geometry – became the most recent layer in that complex geology.

Nature as object

That Jesuit view of a divinely inspired order was already running up against Copernicus and Galileo, however. In a short, influential, and still controversial article published in 1967, Lynn White argued for a very different Christian understanding of the environment, which saw nature as tool for human exploitation. He wrote that:

> No item in the physical creation had any purpose save to serve man's purposes. And, although man's body is made of clay, he is not simply part of nature; he is made in God's image. Especially in its Western form, Christianity is the most anthropocentric religion the world has seen . . . By destroying pagan animism, Christianity made it possible to exploit nature in a mood of indifference to the feelings of natural objects.[9]

For White the removal of God from nature opened the door both to rapid technological progress and to ecological exploitation. The relevant attitudes come from Judaism, but, he argued, it was Christianity that spread them so widely.

White recognizes, of course, that Christianity is a complex faith with many strands. Certainly the Bible offers us other passages with other interpretations. White argues that Eastern forms of Christianity did not go so far in this direction, and that even Roman Christianity had alternatives – he offers us St. Francis of Assisi as a potential patron saint for ecologists. The Jesuits in China had still another view. White's article (it is only five pages long) also elides two millennia of change; more, if we include Judaism. It underplays in particular the significance of some medieval ideas like the doctrine of signatures (which saw God's messages in natural things) or the Great Chain of Being (which placed everything into a single divine hierarchy).

While we can find potential roots of this objectified version of nature in the Bible, it did not become the dominant view of nature until roughly the time of the Enlightenment. The opposition between nature and culture became a crucial backdrop for arguments about political philosophy in the eighteenth century. For some authors, Rousseau above all, these arguments brought the beginnings of a newly positive attitude toward nature, although the Hobbesian "nasty, brutish, and short" version of the natural life remained just as influential. The opposition between nature and human society was beginning to take its modern forms, with some favoring the nature side of the split and others favoring the culture side, but all accepting the split as given.

It is worth recalling for a moment just how widespread and influential the split between nature and culture was. Colonists in New England also argued about the quality and worth of a "natural" life as represented by the native peoples of the region. The Puritan hierarchy in Massachusetts, however, came down clearly on the side of industry and exploitation of nature. They silenced people like Thomas Morton, who had argued, in a way reminiscent of Rousseau, that the native peoples lived a life of abundance, superior in some ways to European society.[10] The Massachusetts Court refused to recognize native rights to any land except the small parcels that they farmed. They justified this with the claim that other native land uses – even including necessary fallow periods for shifting cultivation – did not meet the biblical injunction to be fruitful and multiply.[11]

European folk tales did not grow out of this Puritan tradition, but they also tend to see the wilderness as wicked. In so many of the tales of our childhoods, peril and destruction lurk just outside the walls of civilization – Peter and the Wolf, Little Red Riding Hood and her wolf, Hansel and Gretel and their witch, Beauty and her beast, and the list could easily be extended. The first written versions we have for all of these tales come from the late seventeenth and eighteenth centuries. Children's stories that glorify nature, from Bambi through more recent Disney inventions, tend to be several centuries newer.

The Scientific Revolution took place at roughly the same time as the philosophical revolution of the Enlightenment. It further separated free humanity as subject from rule-bound nature as object.[12] Abandoning the organic metaphors of the Renaissance and earlier (whose remnants we saw with the Jesuits in China), this view saw nature as a mechanism open to human examination and manipulation. While God was the ultimate designer of the machine in its early formulations, this newly dominant view of the world would eventually find little need for any religious underpinnings. It was Lynn White's view of nature, but with its soul removed, another weapon in the armory of human gain.

This image of nature as a mechanism to be understood through science and manipulated through engineering reached a peak during the late nineteenth and early twentieth centuries. Railroads razored their lines straight through mountains, dams plugged the most powerful rivers, steamships and telegraphs crushed the old obstacles to communication. The Panama Canal separated the Americas, undoing, in a sense, the slow drift of the continents themselves. Nature had been fully disenchanted, dispirited, and laid open for exploitation.

The technological dream of a final mastery over nature reached China during this late nineteenth-century acme of confidence in progress. The Qianlong Emperor's amusement with clever European clockworks in the eighteenth century become a wrenching realization that China was technically far behind Europe in the nineteenth. British military superiority had been clear since the first Opium War in 1842, and China (lagging behind Japan) began serious attempts to modernize its technology toward the end of the century. I will leave aside the complex internal arguments about how to achieve this, and about what role earlier Chinese values should play in the future. The main conclusion, for purposes of this book, is that most Chinese intellectuals and political elites had enthusiastically adopted this idea of science and progress by the early decades of the twentieth century. The May Fourth Movement of 1919, seen by many as a watershed moment in intellectual consciousness, placed science on the pedestal right next to democracy. Together they would build the new China.

The underlying visions of how humanity relates to the environment really had changed in the twentieth century, even though massive environmental manipulation itself was hardly new in China by then. Rice paddies, after all, are essentially a man-made environment. For its time, the scale and hubris of the Grand Canal surely matched the Three Gorges dam of today. Yet the worldview behind these projects changed in the twentieth century, in a way that ultimately encouraged massive environmental problems across China and Taiwan. Early views of heaven-and-earth as a system of energetic resonances, or of an anthropocosmism that placed human benefit as the goal of environmental manipulation, allowed massive reshaping of the land and water. They did not, however, subjugate a de-animated nature to a ruling humanity. Such a view, coming to China from post-Enlightenment Europe, came to dominate everything that had preceded it.

China had many political regimes during the early twentieth century. The Qing Dynasty lasted until 1911, followed by the Guomindang Nationalists, local warlords of all descriptions, and Communists. These various rulers disagreed with each other in many ways – often murderously so – but all were committed modernists. The Nationalists and the Communists, whose occasional united fronts and frequent internecine battles marked most of the period, disagreed greatly on what constituted democracy (though neither one did much to institutionalize it). They were largely similar, however, in their commitment to modern science, and to massive re-engineering of the environment. Both planned and eventually built systems of railroads and canals, chemical-based agricultural regimes, and large industrial engines to match the West.

We now have several good studies of state-sponsored environmental attitudes in the People's Republic of China. Vaclav Smil has shown, in depressing detail, many aspects of China's severe environmental degradation under these ideas. These include shrinking water tables after the massive introduction of tube wells in the 1960s, shocking pollution levels, and a loss of agricultural land that has greatly increased a centuries-old trend toward less land per capita.[13] Judith Shapiro documents some of the worst excesses – gigantic dam projects gone awry, the Great Leap Forward (1958–60) policy of manhandling nature in ways that contributed to massive starvation, the Cultural Revolution (1966–76) policy of decentralized and inexpensive heavy industry that polluted the air and water of the entire country. She reminds us of the slogans that so pitted humanity and progress against nature, and that so shaped policy in the People's Republic: "Man Must Conquer Nature!" (*ren ding sheng tian*), "Battling with Nature Is Boundless Joy!" (*yu tian dou, qile wu qiong*).[14]

China was far from alone in pursuing these policies. Foreign aid and investment also promoted both these massive engineering projects and the attitudes toward the environment that lay behind them. The Soviet Union provided crucial support for railroad and bridge construction in the 1950s, as well as helping China construct its industrial infrastructure. More recently, intergovernmental organizations like the World Bank or the Asian Development Bank have funded and promoted massive dams for power generation, highway construction, and other continuations of the projects of nineteenth-century modernity.

Smil and Shapiro tend to blame socialism for China's environmental ills, and there are undoubtedly some direct connections. The Cultural Revolution decentralization of heavy industry caused enormous environmental and social problems that will haunt China for a long time to come. Rapid deforestation after the decollectivization of agriculture in the early 1980s is another consequence of the specific political system in China. The substitution of short-term use rights for communal land-holding encouraged people to profit as quickly as possible from forested land, since they had no long-term interest in it. China eventually developed more effective land use rights, but much damage had already been done. It would not be difficult to multiply the examples. These specific problems are probably unique to the People's Republic, and would not have occurred under a different kind of regime.

The issues, however, run far deeper than socialism, as the Guomindang experience makes clear. A comparison with Taiwan shows that Mao's war against nature, as Shapiro dubs it, is just a variant on a much larger modernist war against nature. That war began in earnest in the nineteenth-century West, although its moral roots are much older. Both the People's Republic and Taiwan, in this context, appear to be variations on a single theme.[15]

If the Republic of China did not rival the People's Republic's later reworking of the environment while they ruled the mainland before 1949, it was only for lack of resources, not lack of ambition. We can see this clearly after the Nationalists arrived in Taiwan. With far more powerful political control and a much stronger financial base than they had on the mainland, the government embarked on a course of rapid industrialization. While people often refer to the results as an economic miracle, they were also an environmental disaster.

Taiwan's environmental history after the Guomindang's takeover in 1945 took a different course from the People's Republic, but it is every bit as grim. Taiwan trumpeted some of the exact anti-environmental slogans that Shapiro highlights for China. One section of a Taiwanese elementary school textbook from the 1970s, for example, offers a familiar title to a section on the environment: "Man Must Conquer Nature!"[16] "Nature" here is *tian* – the old term that could as easily be rendered as heaven. Conquering heaven perhaps even better captures the spirit of the slogan, and makes clear how unthinkable the idea would have been a century earlier.

The consequences of this attitude have been severe. Taiwan's water supply, for example, was seriously polluted by the mid-1980s – more or less the time everyone recognized its economy as a great success. Less than 1 percent of human excrement received even primary sewage treatment at the time. Together with massive agricultural runoff, this made many rivers unable to support fish. Every major river is seriously polluted. Air quality in Taipei has been poor, especially since motorized transport became widespread. As a basin surrounded by mountains, it traps haze and pollution in much the same way as Los Angeles. Solid waste per capita had increased by 50 percent over the previous decade, causing a crisis at the many unkempt and overflowing garbage dumps. Much the same story applies to every aspect of the island's environment.[17]

Tracing how the ideas behind these policies became so dominant will require a deeper history than I am qualified to write. It is possible, however, to sketch a few of the more important carriers that brought these ideas to a broader public. A series of 1970s Taiwanese elementary school textbooks, for example, gives a good idea of the ways children learned to think about their environment in the decade before the island saw the birth of a new consciousness in environmental protest and nature tourism.[18]

A first-grade text rhetorically asks how our daily life relates to local mountains and rivers. The answer, shown in pictures, is that we mine coal in the mountains, take fish from the rivers, and grow crops on the land. Nature is there for us to use. Social studies texts for older students emphasize the importance of "environmental improvement," by building dams for instance. Natural science texts, predictably, sound much like Western texts on the same topics. The section on forests, to give just one example, classifies them, discusses scientific management of planting and cutting to keep them profitable, and explains the many uses of timber. It also mentions forest protection, but it means primarily protection from economic loss through fire or unauthorized cutting. Other sets of texts, written for classes on ethics and morality, make no mention of the environment.

Even after the government began to promote environmental protection as a goal, the scientific view of nature continued to dominate the organismic one. The Environmental Protection Agency, for example, released an educational cartoon video in 1991.[19] The plot is vaguely modeled on Dickens' *Christmas Carol*, with a space traveler and his cute robot friend playing the part of Marley's ghost by leading a group of Taiwanese children on visits to its present pollution problems, idyllic past, and potentially horrific future of disfigured people and unbreathable air. As in the Dickens tale, the children also learn that another future is possible, but only if they change their behavior. This alternative is not a return to older ways of living with nature, but a scientific wonderland of parks built around the purified waste water from nuclear power plants. All this will be possible, they learn, but only if they stop littering.

Gazetteers (*difang zhi*), written over the centuries to compile local natural, social, and cultural histories, show a similar evolution. Before the twentieth century, most gazetteers began with a section called "territory" (*jiangyu*). This included subsections that correlated earthly territory and celestial space (*xingye*, literally "star-wilderness"), and that discussed geographic features, political boundaries, and famous sites (*xingshi*, literally shape and positional potential). Political and natural history intertwined here, as usual with a view that saw humans and the environment as parts of a single process. Modern gazetteers instead feature a *dili* (geography) section, which gives the kinds of physical information more familiar in Western geography references. Political boundaries and historical sites have been moved to other sections, and "nature" stands isolated and separated from humanity. *Dili* once meant the heavenly principles underlying the earth, and still refers to *fengshui* in some dialects (e.g., H: *teli*); now it is just geography.

Farmers' almanacs show a similar evolution. In the Qing Dynasty, such calendars typically gave times of sunrise and sunset, detailed the timing of the twenty-four solar periods that divided the year and were critical for timing agricultural activity, and gave a daily lunar calendar that clarified actions that were either beneficial or dangerous to undertake on that day. As I mentioned in the previous chapter, these recommendations grew out of the kinds of correlational theories (yin and yang, stems and branches, etc.) that allowed experts to recognize the specific potentials for good or evil of every moment in time. Village experts would use these calendars to set auspicious times for weddings and funerals; travelers would use them to schedule their trips, and businessmen to find the best days to open new shops.

By 1939, however, a Nationalist government version of the almanac had entirely removed the "superstitious" section of recommendations, and had substituted sections explaining proper political behavior and the Constitution of the Republic of China. A 1952 calendar, after they were already in Taiwan, was essentially similar. Popularly published almanacs, however, continue as updated versions of the traditional form – updated by adding Western forms of divination to the Chinese ones. They often include astrological predictions based on the Western system, as well as sections on buying and selling stocks – a new practical use for divination skills. Hong Kong almanacs also retained the earlier style, often greatly elaborated.

Almanacs in the People's Republic followed a similar path, except that the unofficial ones that eventually dominated the market in Taiwan could not be published on the mainland. A 1952 almanac maintained a streamlined version of the section on things to do or avoid each day, but also added sections on the history of the Communist Party, and regulations for punishing counter-revolutionaries, composing letters, and other useful knowledge. A traditional divination system involving flipping coins had been turned into a game, where each possible result led to a political poem instead of a divinatory verse. Later almanacs in the 1950s got rid of the divinatory information completely, revising the section into a set of recommended activities for each day (pave a road, hold a meeting . . .). By the time of the Cultural Revolution, all remnants of the earlier cosmological correlations were gone, and had been replaced with denunciations of superstition in all its forms.

Earlier Chinese ways of thinking about nature have been excised in all these media. Elementary school textbooks, local histories, and farmers' almanacs came to present nature, each in their separate ways, as something independent of human life, but available for human use. Most of these texts are also either direct products of the government or products of local elites with some kind of government backing. The only exceptions in this set of materials are some of the almanacs outside the People's Republic, which were published by commercial concerns. Significantly, these are also the only ones that show significant continuity with their late imperial equivalents in how they construe relations to the environment.

Nature for its own sake

Early histories of Western environmental ethics often focused on the growth and ultimate triumph of the idea of the cultural and technological dominance of humanity over nature. More recent work, however, shows this to be a great oversimplification. The science of ecology itself grew in part out of the concern of scientists about the rapid environmental degradation they could document around the world as a result of the economic changes of colonialism.[20] Younger than most other sciences, ecology also differs in its stress on interactive systems over simple cause and effect.

The variations are even greater, of course, outside of science. One very important critique of the optimistic view of inevitable progress through increasing control over nature came from the Romantics. The Romantics and other thinkers and writers beginning in the late eighteenth century offered alternative ways of thinking about nature. They did not much question the split between nature and culture that had been so important since the Enlightenment, but in some ways they reversed the value judgments they placed on the concepts. On the culture side they questioned the rightness of progress and rationality, and championed a kind of heroic, emotional, and intuitive self very different from the Enlightenment ideal. On the nature side, they became deeply interested in wilderness for its own sake, for the ways in which it embodied strength and will beyond any rationality.

The Romantics thus pioneered nature tourism into the wild, as part of their general questioning of social convention. The Alps – the internal edge of European civilization – became a favored destination. Mary Shelley's *Frankenstein* speaks to many of these themes, including its dystopic view of a science that creates monstrosities, the mix of terrifying power and naive nobility in the asocial monster, and the dramatic chase through the Alps themselves. Nature had been reevaluated, partly in reaction to that narrative of the triumph of human science over nature, but it was not the saccharine wilderness of *Bambi*. This nature was both terrifying and ennobling, a fit ground for heroes. It was no longer the Puritan wilderness, whose only proper use was to be fenced and farmed.

Rather tamer versions of these ideas spread widely in nineteenth-century Europe and North America. The Grand Tour, which included important legs in the wilds of the Alps, eventually became a crucial rite of passage for English gentlemen. In the United States, Emerson and especially Thoreau began writing about new ways of thinking about nature. Thoreau's experiment in the Massachusetts woods was a broad critique of urban life and social convention, although it hardly qualifies as a wilderness experience. Thoreau could easily walk to see his friends in Concord; he tallied up various supplies that he bought at the market; he even described with interest the workers who came to harvest the ice from Walden Pond and cart it off to the nearby railroad. Rather than idolizing wilderness, Thoreau offered us a way of life based on simplicity and purity of the individual self without need for the artificiality of city life and social convention. *Walden* is thus consistent with his other writings on civil disobedience, which also urged people to act according to the individual conscience without regard to social pressure.[21] There is an echo here of the Romantic heroic self in the wilderness, although it is a rather tamer image, better suited to New England than the Alps. While Thoreau did not embrace wilderness simply for its own sake, he helped to forge a very different way of thinking about nature.

By the end of the nineteenth century, though, we can see extended American arguments valorizing untouched nature for its own sake. The greatest spokesman for this view was John Muir, who wrote in secular language about experience that reads like religion: the visceral rapture of sitting alone surrounded by mountains, with no sign that there has ever been another human being on the planet. "None of Nature's landscapes are ugly so long as they are wild."[22] His work eventually helped lead to the creation of the American national park system, and shaped its underlying philosophy of preserving an untouched nature.

This goal was a fantasy in some ways, of course. The untouched wilderness in most cases could only be achieved by removing the people who had been living on the land already – often Native Americans. It ignores the ways that even environments in which no one lives still experience anthropogenic effects (like acid rain, climate change, human-carried invasive species). And it ignores the way that protecting land as a park itself influences the environment, for instance through the tourist traffic or through fire management policy. Yet this view has deep roots that have been developing over several centuries. Like the nature-as-object view, it assumes a clear separation between culture and nature. Like the Romantics and their descendants, it places a stronger inherent value on nature itself. It also implies a critique of urban life, at least in the sense that it insists on preserving a very different world for the edification and pleasure of urban users.

These various interrelated but different affirmations of the desirability of nature share the Western tradition of a nature/culture split, but reverse the more common valence that saw only evil in wilderness and nature as a tool for human comfort. We see echoes of exactly this split today when anthropocentric pro-development arguments meet anti-growth biocentrism. Both sides presume a fundamental difference between nature and culture (quite unlike Chinese anthropocosmic views). One extreme sees value only in the culture side, with nature as an object to exploit – preservation is a goal only to insure future exploitation. The other extreme values nature, sometimes to the point of suggesting drastic reduction in human population as the only way of regaining a proper balance.

Understandings of nature for its own sake did not enter China as early or as spectacularly as did scientific understandings of nature. The lever that helped split nature from culture, at least for some Chinese, was science alone, even though the other ideas were already available in European and North American thought. China had, by the early twentieth century, produced an impressive number of true cosmopolitans who were quite at home in both European and Chinese traditions. While Muir or Thoreau did not loom very large in the European and Japanese thinking that most influenced these young Chinese, the Romantics certainly were part of the material that they brought back home.

Leo Lee has documented the enormous influence that the Romantics held over Chinese literature in the 1920s. Their work, he argues, developed two main Romantic themes. The first was a concern with sentiment and depth of emotion, often a helpless sense of impending doom. The second, in some tension with the first, was the idea of the heroic individualist.[23] Far less evident, however, is the symbolic role that nature took for the development of these themes among European Romantics. The heroes and the writers of the Chinese stories lived modern urban lives and struggled with love and social convention. They did not take Grand Tours of the wilderness or brood on monsters and mountains.

They did not go live alone in the woods like Thoreau, or rhapsodize on untouched wilderness like Muir. The city remained at the core of their ideals for modernity.

Future work may shed more light, but current evidence suggests that the idea of nature (the European nature opposed to culture) as a desirable end in itself became important in China and Taiwan only toward the end of the twentieth century. Its main carrier was not so much the Western writing of the nineteenth century that I have been discussing, but more contemporary incarnations of those ideas in global environmental groups and the spread of the idea of national parks as wilderness preserves.

The earliest evidence I have found for this is from Taiwan in the 1960s. According to Hunter H. T. Eu (You Hanting), who was vice-head of the Tourism Bureau when I interviewed him in 1993, Taiwanese elites first began thinking in this way only in the mid-1960s. The first step was a report commissioned from George Ruhle in 1965, called "National Parks and Equivalent Reserves for Taiwan." Ruhle had been Chief Park Naturalist for the US National Park Service, and prepared similar reports for a number of countries. He recommended the creation of several national parks in Taiwan. All of them were in fact created, but only twenty years later. Hunter Eu himself, recommended by yet another Park Service employee who was spending time in Taiwan, underwent Park Ranger training at Grand Canyon and went on to get a graduate degree in natural resource management. Here we can see the direct globalizing influence of the American wilderness ideal carried to Taiwan through the Park Service.

The story in the People's Republic is not as clearly visible, but these alternate views of the environment began to influence people significantly later than in Taiwan. The moment when these ideas began to affect elite thinking in Taiwan was the middle of the Cultural Revolution in China. Nature for its own sake was unwelcome because it did not fit with Cultural Revolution themes of reworking nature, and even more because of its foreign origins. Only in the 1980s and especially the 1990s do we start to see organizations dedicated, for example, to the maintenance of biodiversity or to endangered species protection as an end in itself. The first formally registered environmental NGO was Friends of Nature (*Ziran zhi You*), which was founded in 1994 as the Academy for Green Culture. They have, among many other things, actively promoted protection for some endangered species (like the Tibetan antelope) and have a program to educate China's youth to "revere all life and understand the laws of ecology."[24] The aspects of Western thinking that valorized nature thus eventually grew influential in both Taiwan and China, but the story in both cases is so recent that I will take it up again in the chapters that follow.

Pastoral natures

Nature and culture do not always play out in clear opposition, even in Europe and America. Pastoralism has long offered a kind of compromise solution, where people and nature live in happy equilibrium. Historically, this bucolic view of peasant life is an urban phenomenon – peasants themselves hardly shared the same starry-eyed view of their life chances. Like the wilderness ideal, depictions of rural life served as an escape from and critique of cities with their corruptions and affectations. Unlike the wilderness or Romantic views of nature, though, pastoralism gave us a tamed landscape of human contentment. Thunder and lightning might interrupt the idyll, as in Beethoven's Sixth (Pastoral) Symphony, but the sun would always shine again.

The roots of pastoralism as a literary and artistic genre go back to Rome, but the modern heyday of its conventions ran from the Renaissance through the nineteenth century. While we use the term primarily for the arts, the ideas behind it also had important political equivalents in the expectation that a just and civil nation could be built on the sturdy foundation stones of independent yeoman farmers. In the late eighteenth century this was Thomas Jefferson's image of how the new American democracy would work.[25] By the late nineteenth century, many areas of the world experienced land reforms, promoted by liberal thinkers in the West, designed to break the hold of various communal forms of tenure (from village-level control by indigenous peoples to church lands). They had hoped and assumed that a nation of small farmers would be both more productive and more democratic. The actual results of these reforms, mostly in Africa and Latin America, were much less rosy, but that is another story.[26]

Pastoralism as a literary convention faded in the twentieth century, and Jeffersonian hopes for a society of small farmers had grown utterly implausible for the United States or Western Europe by then. Yet pastoralism took on a new life thanks to various nationalist movements that looked back to the imagined purity and simplicity of a peasant past. Beginning in the late nineteenth century, nationalist urban intellectuals had found a new interest in their rapidly disappearing rural past. This is the period when folk tales and dances were collected, and when classical composers adapted peasant songs. The Nazis ultimately led the way in this reanimation of an early rural past. Imaginary rural ancestors epitomized values of purity, discipline, and valor, all of which had been undercut by the corruptions of modern life for which fascism was the panacea. They did this with firm roots in the soil of their own homeland (*Heimat*). These ideas had environmental consequences as well, leading some to dub them as the first green party. Germany under the Nazis was the first European country to form nature reserves; it also passed laws for forest and wildlife protection.[27] Physical and mental well-being meant at least temporary escape from the city to the hinterland, and there was a fad for walking in the woods, swimming, and other outdoor recreation. Parallel with the American wilderness movement, this pastoral vision offered quite another route toward nature tourism.

While the Nazi connection throws a harsh light on the pastoral ideal, a similar vision also encouraged more benign consequences, reminding us that the late nineteenth-century German version did not have to end in fascism. The idea of a pastoral landscape – rural but tamed, a sort of garden writ large – became an important part of ameliorist schemes around the world. Landscape architects like Frederick Law Olmsted in the United States offered a pastoral landscape as a counterbalance to urban decay. This took the form, for example, of pastoral new urban areas, like Central Park and others that Olmsted created. As light rail lowered transportation costs, these ideas also did a great deal to shape the new streetcar suburbs that were beginning to sprout up. Olmsted was a great champion of the anti-urban and pastoral aesthetic that still describes most American suburbs – curving streets and gentle slopes, green yards and overhanging trees.

Many of these ideas also entered China early in the twentieth century, although none would rival "science." Land reform would prove to be the most important. Sun Yat-sen's Land to the Tiller program hoped in part for that Jeffersonian ideal of independent and hard-working smallholders, although it was not successfully carried out until the 1950s in Taiwan. The People's Republic had its own spectacular land reform, but pastoral ideals – especially the specific Jeffersonian ideals that influenced Sun Yat-sen – were not so clear. While the initial land reform did create massive numbers of independent small farmers, China would move very quickly to more communalized forms of land tenure, and this was almost surely the intention from the beginning. In addition, the Chinese Communists had a long and intimate experience of real peasant life by the time they took power in 1949. They were not urban idealists romanticizing the countryside; they were mostly peasants themselves. Pastoralist thought influenced them far less than their own revolutionary experience and Stalinist economic and social policy.

In other forms, however, some of these ideas already had a visible impact earlier in the twentieth century. Shanghai, with its dominating foreign influence, had built the first "modern" city parks – not wilderness but a taste of rural life in the city – during the late Qing Dynasty. Other cities began to emulate the idea in the first decades of the twentieth century. Hangzhou, for example, began with five small parks along the newly developed shore of West Lake. The landscape architects had been trained in Japan, and were also deeply familiar with Shanghai. Their influences, typically, did not come directly from Olmsted and other pioneers of this aesthetic, but had instead already been reworked in these other nodes of the global culture of modernity.[28]

Later in the twentieth century China would adopt more of the anti-urbanism inherent in some of the pastoral and Romantic aesthetics. During the early decades after the Republican Revolution in 1911, cities – and Shanghai above all – had appeared as the height of all that was best about modernity. They had industry, intellectual ferment, and an utterly new style. The reaction to the city tended to set in later, most clearly beginning in the 1950s. Although China's economic policies initially subsidized rapidly growing cities at the expense of rural income, based in part on Soviet theories of the price scissors, the late 1950s brought a critique of urban privilege. The Great Leap Forward was the beginning of a push to move industry out of major eastern industrial centers, and to improve educational and economic infrastructure in the countryside.

Most tellingly for the issue I am addressing, the policy of sending urban youth down to the countryside to learn from peasants also began during that period. This policy reversed the standard flow of talent into the cities, and reversed the cultural assumptions of most urban youth. The implication was that the pastoral life of the peasant was better for the soul than urban decadence and privilege. The urban young people would help the peasants advance, to be sure, but the more important goal was to improve city folk and their life of artifice with the hard work and common sense of the pastoral life. There is no reason to think that this policy was a globalized outgrowth of pastoralist critiques in the West. Instead, both Chinese and European versions grew out of the real experience of the modern city by setting up comparable rural ideals. China would continue this policy for two decades, until the end of the Cultural Revolution. Even today, though, it echoes in the "Go West" campaign that urges eastern city-dwellers to pioneer the western "frontier." The echoes of Horace Greeley and the American West of the nineteenth century are probably conscious.

Taiwan, of course, never adopted such a policy of forcing urban people to the countryside. Nevertheless, the Nationalist government there created its own version of a rural counterweight to the city. The main form was the China Anti-Communist Youth League for the Salvation of the Nation (*Zhongguo Qingnian Fangong Jiuguo Tuan*), which they usually tone down to "China Youth Corps" in English. The China Youth Corps began in 1952 under the auspices of the Ministry of Defense and under the leadership of Chiang Ching-kuo, who was Defense Minister at the time. It followed Chiang when he later became head of the Executive Yuan.[29]

The political purposes of the group are obvious from its name. Like China's Communist Youth League or the Soviet Union's Young Pioneers, they had branches at every political level, and ultimately organized activities in schools, especially high schools. In this case, the similarity is not a coincidence; Chiang Ching-kuo had spent many years in the Soviet Union during periods of ostensible united fronts between the Communists and Nationalists. We can also see echoes of prewar Germany, though, especially in the positive role that rural areas took on as models for urban youth. While military propaganda and training dominated the group in the 1950s, the China Youth Corps began bringing large groups of students to Taiwan's least settled areas from the 1960s on. They lived in hostels, exercised and hiked together, and learned to be proper nationalists through direct experience of the land. Their lives would be simple, frugal, and hard-working – an imaginary rural corrective to an imagined urban environment of corruption. This fit the generally Spartan image that Generalissimo Chiang Kai-shek himself (President and father to the head of the Youth Corps) affected, with his daily cold showers.

Although the China Youth Corps is now legally independent of the government – it became the very first group to organize under the social organizations law in 1989, after Taiwan democratized – it maintains close ties with the government. It also continues to control land and hostels in what have become Taiwan's most popular nature tourism destinations, including prime sites in what are now national parks. When I asked people in Taiwan what their first experience of nature tourism was, the great majority of people pointed to the China Youth Corps.

Conclusion

Unequal globalization from the middle of the nineteenth century offered China a new palette of options for thinking about how people relate to environments. In contrast to simple theories of globalization that see the flow of one set of ideas from a single center (e.g., hamburgers from McDonald's headquarters in Oak Brook, Illinois to the world), this flow contained multiple and interacting streams that changed character at various nodes along the way (especially in Japan) and inside China (with Shanghai playing a critical role in the twentieth century, along with the political centers of Beijing, Nanjing, and later Taipei).

At least three major streams of European and American thinking about the environment influenced China and Taiwan over the course of the twentieth century: one that saw nature primarily as an object for human use, a second that saw a non-human nature as an important end in itself, and a third that idealized a particular pastoral image of the relationship as a corrective to the ills of modern urban life. The first of these, in the guise of "Mr. Science," who was so idealized in the May Fourth era, established nearly hegemonic power over the others, and over more organismic Chinese views during the 1920s. New city parks offered hints of other views, but this remained a relatively minor theme. Scientific views completely took over the education system and the policy establishment. Only after World War II did the other views take on a stronger position. Initially, we could see this in the anti-urban aspects of political education that began in both China and Taiwan in the 1950s. To a limited extent, China's embrace of traditional Chinese medicine during this period also placed limits on the power of science. More recently still, some people in both places – including some artists, university faculty, and government officials – have begun to promote ideas of nature for its own sake.

Even these three main globalizing currents, however, had important variants that carried people in different directions. An objectified nature that exists for human benefit can be simply exploited, for example, in the hope that future science will resolve the resulting problems. The same basic stance could also support the idea of sustainable development, however. The various nature-centered views I have discussed also have different implications: Romantic nature, John Muir's sublime American wilderness, or modern biocentrism all differ significantly. Pastoralism too takes many different forms, from urban meliorism to a kind of proto-fascist nationalism. The chapters that follow explore these various streams as they met the equally varied indigenous possibilities that I discussed in the previous chapter.

NOTES

1. Benjamin Schwartz, *In Search of Wealth and Power: Yen Fu and the West* (Cambridge, MA: Harvard University Press, 1964), 45–6. Parenthetical additions are Schwartz's. Darwin himself was not fully translated until 1919.
2. Dai Nihon Pyakka Jisho Benshoshu, ed., *Tetsugaku Daijisho* (*Dictionary of Philosophy*), fifth edition (Tokyo: Dobunkan, 1924), 1147.
3. Simon Schama, *Landscape and Memory* (New York: A. A. Knopf, 1995), 15.
4. Maurice Bloch and Jean H. Bloch, "Women and the Dialectics of Nature in Eighteenth-Century French Thought," in *Nature, Culture and Gender*, ed. Carol MacCormack and Marilyn Strathern (Cambridge: Cambridge University Press, 1980), 25–41.

5. Keith Thomas, *Man and the Natural World: A History of the Modern Sensibility* (New York: Pantheon, 1983), 301–2.
6. The information in this section relies heavily on Benjamin A. Elman, "Jesuit *Scientia* and Natural Studies in Late Imperial China, 1600–1800," *Early Modern History* 6, no. 3 (2002): 209–32.
7. Translated in Wing-tsit Chan, compiler, *A Source Book in Chinese Philosophy* (Princeton: Princeton University Press, 1963), 473.
8. Elman, "Jesuit *Scientia* and Natural Studies in Late Imperial China."
9. Lynn White, "The Historical Roots of Our Ecological Crisis," *Science* 155 (10 March 1967): 1205.
10. William Cronon, *Changes in the Land: Indians, Colonists and the Ecology of New England* (New York: Hill and Wang, 1983), 55.
11. Cronon, *Changes in the Land*, 63.
12. See, for example, Bruno Latour, *We Have Never Been Modern* (Cambridge, MA: Harvard University Press, 1993).
13. Vaclav Smil, *China's Environmental Crisis: An Inquiry into the Limits of National Development* (Armonk, NY: M. E. Sharpe, 1993).
14. Judith Shapiro, *Mao's War against Nature: Politics and the Environment in Revolutionary China* (New York: Cambridge University Press, 2001).
15. For another critique of the "Mao's war against nature" idea, based on evidence of internal Chinese policy discussions, see Peter Ho, "Mao's War against Nature? The Environmental Impact of the Grain-First Campaign in China," *China Journal* 50 (July 2003): 37–59.
16. Guoli Bianyiguan, ed., *Guomin Xiaoxue Changshi Keben* (*Textbook of Common Knowledge for Elementary Schools*) (Taipei: Guoli Bianyiguan, 1974), vol. 4.
17. For details, see Steering Committee, Taiwan 2000 Study, *Taiwan 2000: Balancing Economic Growth and Environmental Protection* (Taipei, 1989).
18. Guoli Bianyiguan, ed., *Guomin Xiaoxue Changshi Keben*. I have not been able to see comparable texts from the People's Republic, but there is little reason to think they would differ significantly on these topics.
19. Xingzheng Yuan Huanjing Baohu Ju, producer, *Huanbao Xiao Yingxiong* (*Little Heroes of Environmental Protection*), Videotape (Taipei, 1991).
20. Richard H. Grove, *Green Imperialism: Colonial Expansion, Tropical Island Edens and the Origins of Environmentalism, 1600–1860* (Cambridge: Cambridge University Press, 1995).
21. Henry David Thoreau, *Walden and Civil Disobedience* (New York: Penguin, 1986).
22. John Muir, *Our National Parks* (Boston: Houghton Mifflin, 1901), 4.
23. Leo Ou-fan Lee, *The Romantic Generation of Modern Chinese Writers* (Cambridge, MA: Harvard University Press, 1973), 279–83.
24. Friends of Nature, *Environment Education*. 21 June 2002 http://www.fon.org.cn/english/1.htm.
25. Here and elsewhere in this section, I have been broadly influenced by the ideas in Leo Marx, *The Machine in the Garden: Technology and the Pastoral Ideal in America* (Oxford: Oxford University Press, 2000).
26. Joel S. Migdal, "Capitalist Penetration in the Nineteenth Century: Creating Conditions for New Patterns of Social Control," in *Power and Protest in the*

Countryside: Rural Unrest in Asia, Europe and Latin America, ed. Robert P. Weller and Scott E. Guggenheim (Durham, NC: Duke University Press, 1982), 60–3.

27. Anna Bramwell, *Ecology in the Twentieth Century: A History* (New Haven: Yale University Press, 1989), 199.
28. I am grateful to Wang Liping for her help on this.
29. I am grateful to Dr. David Pan (Pan Zhiwei) for granting me an interview on 2 August 1996, while he was Director of Overseas Services for the group.

4 Stories of stone

China has a long tradition of literati going out to areas of scenic beauty and leaving us poetic or artistic records of their experiences, from lonely contemplation to drunken poetry contests with their friends. In some ways this tradition is still with us today. It survives in the lists of important sights (the sun rising over Yellow Mountain in Anhui, for instance, but not particularly the sunset) which tourists want to see, and which grow in part out of the commemorated experiences of famous literati. It lives also in the memories of the famous paintings and poems that shape people's travels to these places – doubling direct experience with the vicarious experience of the artist.

The huge increase in nature tourism sites in both China and Taiwan over the last two decades, however, is not a direct continuation of that tradition. Governments have led much of its growth because only they control sufficient land resources. Both the Communist and the Nationalist governments have depended almost entirely on imported models of nature tourism for these developments. Neither one opposes the evocation of those old literati traditions, but neither one has made much significant effort to build on them either. Instead, at least on the surface, we have a direct globalization of American, Japanese, and United Nations models, which influences everything from the legal frameworks for the creation of the parks to the training of tour guides and rangers.

Various theories about how globalization works, as I began to discuss in the first chapter, lead us toward different expectations of how nature tourism might play out in China or Taiwan. An "avalanche" theory of globalization appears most widespread in popular literature and among anti-globalization protestors. This is the idea that globalization flows inexorably down from its heights, usually imagined to be somewhere on one of the coasts of the United States. It crushes anything in its path, and starts to prepare the next onslaught as soon as the last one is finished. Such a view would lead us to expect a world of better or worse clones of Yosemite National Park, set up to preserve a wilderness untouched by human interference. Presented like this, of course, such a view is obviously too simple, but in fact it does illustrate the way that much of the planning for state-sponsored nature tourism in China and Taiwan has taken place.

Anthropologists have never been fond of theories like this, which imply that the people we study are utterly helpless, lacking any agency in a world that simply overpowers them. We often try instead to stand our local Davids against the Goliath of globalization, as we placed them against the state in an earlier literature on resistance. People are of course not completely helpless, but subvert, rework, avoid, accommodate, and sometimes openly oppose even very powerful outside forces. These processes shape the form of power itself. For nature tourism, this view might lead us to expect a reworking of parks and reserves to accord more with local understandings of the environment, or perhaps simply a failure of global models to take root and attract visitors. My own expectations and hopes at the beginning of this research were to find something like this – an indigenous Chinese understanding of nature that might counterbalance the dominant global views. As I will discuss, this turned out to be naive, although it does describe some elements of what is happening.

Finally, a recent trend in anthropology has emphasized how, at least under some conditions, we see a creative interaction of various cultural streams, leading to something new – mélange modernities, or a global ecumene, or transnational cosmopolitanism, depending on the author.[1] Ulf Hannerz uses the term "creole cultures," which nicely evokes the sense of an innovative creation out of multiple earlier influences. This view also clarifies some of the processes involved in the development of nature tourism in China and Taiwan.

All three of these major approaches to globalization shed some light on the cases I will be discussing here, but none quite captures all of the dynamics. I will start from the most obviously Western-influenced cases of state-run national parks and nature preserves in China and Taiwan, but then successively complicate them with multiple global sources of inspiration and multiple indigenous responses that suggest many nodes of global reworking tied together in uneven flows of power, both global and national. As a way of bringing some focus to the many strands of this argument, I will keep a loose focus throughout on alternate understandings of stone. As a first step, let me tell the stories of walks through two nature tourism sites, one in China and the other in Taiwan, which first got me thinking about rocks.

Two walks

The first of these walks took place in April 1985, well before I had developed any academic interest in these topics. I had traveled to Guiping

County in rural Guangxi to do research on the Taiping Rebellion, a major nineteenth-century conflagration that had begun nearby. I was only the second foreigner in the county since 1949 – I had to get special permission from the public security office to go – and my hosts wanted to show me their town's one tourist spot, a scenic hill called West Mountain (Xishan). As we traveled the two kilometers out of town, the local officials with me described it as a site of great natural beauty. The tour began as I expected, with a broad path leading up the forested hill. I was astonished, however, to see scattered groups of people lighting sticks of incense in front of some of the larger rocks and trees as we climbed. As I looked more closely, I realized that a great many trees and stones had signs of recent incense in the ground in front of them.

Like many scenic mountains in China, this one has long hosted a set of temples. Some of these still survive on West Mountain, and house a small number of aged Buddhist monks and nuns. To the shock and dismay of my hosts – mostly officials in the county cultural office and museum – it turned out to be the birthday of the bodhisattva Guanyin, who has an important presence on the mountain. They were good Communists and educated men, as they kept reassuring me, and seemed genuinely dismayed at this blatant display of "feudal superstition." Worst, for them, was a spirit possession (locally called *tiaoshen*) session in a cave dedicated to Guanyin, which seemed to be the center of popular worship.

I asked why people offered incense at all the rocks and trees, not just the temples. I had previously worked on religion in Taiwan, and never seen anything quite like this mountain alive with hidden power. The head of the museum claimed that no one could remember the "right" places to burn incense after the Cultural Revolution had thoroughly repressed ritual for a decade. People had thus decided, he said, to treat the whole mountain as if it had divine potency (*shenling*). My unhappy hosts had been planning a quiet walk on a beautiful hill, untroubled by divine rocks and trees or a cave hazy with incense smoke and loud with supplicants to a spirit medium. Nature tourism and religion had combined in a way that neither I nor my hosts expected, but that seemed quite natural to everyone else involved. What was going on here?

The second walk was in May 1991. I had gone to Taiwan's Taroko National Park to interview its director and to see how things had changed since my first visit a dozen years earlier, before there was any sign of a National Park. I will return to some of these events in more detail below, but here I will just give four quick snapshots that show the park from different angles. The first was on the road approaching the entrance. Taroko is famous for its stunning marble gorges, but the first cliffs I saw at the edges of the park were huge scars of exposed rock – the remnants of many years of gravel mining that was just winding down within the park boundaries. I will not have much more to say about this one, except to point out the obvious: decades of incessant industrialization and pollution are the unfortunate backdrop behind any discussion of nature tourism in China or Taiwan.

The second image is of Xu Guoshi, the Park Superintendent at the time. Dr. Xu is an American-trained botanist and expert in remote sensing of tropical and subtropical forests. He showed most clearly the global – and specifically American – influences on Taiwanese nature tourism. Like most of his American equivalents, he believes in the importance of wilderness and natural preservation for its own sake, and he sees a vital education role for national parks.

The third image is of the Taiwanese artist and critic Chiang Hsun, who happened to visit while I was there. He often paints in Taroko, and as soon as he showed up, Dr. Xu cajoled him into giving a quick talk in the park headquarters lecture hall. Chiang's talk about Taroko expressed an utterly different view of the park from what the Superintendent had said to me. Chiang gave a loosely Daoist speech about water and stone. Water is soft and stone is hard, he said, water is yin to stone's yang. In the end, though, the water will conquer the stone. Every stone in the park shows its watery history, and that is what he hopes to capture in his painting.

Finally, as I was about to leave, I asked Xu about a dozen or so people splashing through a small stream looking for, and apparently pocketing, interesting rocks. When I asked if this was allowed, he told me that it was in fact illegal, but that he did not intend to enforce that law – if stealing rocks kept people coming, he was willing to allow it. He did not know, or much seem to care, what they did with the rocks. I found out much later, when a friend showed me the odd rock he had collected from Taroko: it sat on his ancestral altar. Let me leave these various images unresolved for the moment. Each suggests a different view of what nature tourism might mean at the end of the twentieth century, and the rest of this chapter will try to tease them out and show their interactions.

The influence of global models

Behind the growth of nature tourism in China and Taiwan over the last two decades hangs the backdrop of the terrible environmental cost of headlong industrial development in both places. I suggested in chapter 3 that Western images of nature versus culture, especially those with roots in natural sciences, took root in China earlier in the twentieth century than other views of nature, like Romanticism, that were also available. This was a view of nature without *qi*, stripped of its transcendent energies. Nature became simply an object of analysis, and ultimately one to be controlled for human benefit. Such a view fit with the progressivist optimism that both the Communists and the Nationalists shared – a world where big dams, big factories, and big engines were keys to human welfare, and where smokestacks evoked images of progress and not pollution.

These changes directly affected views of the natural environment. Coggins' work on tigers in southeast China, for instance, describes how the beginning of the twentieth century brought "a transformation in local perceptions of wild animals from supernatural beings to natural objects for scientific investigation, and from a source of sacred medicine that was sold in local and regional markets, to commercial commodities to be sold in a growing international market."[2] Western missionaries actively encouraged this movement, sometimes killing wildlife just to make the point that it had no spiritual power and could be shot with impunity.

The greatest symbol of this ideology at the moment is the People's Republic's construction of the massive Three Gorges Dam, but it is worth recalling that the idea for the dam first came from Sun Yat-sen, in the early years of the Republican period. Both China and Taiwan since the Second World War have pursued policies of rapid industrial growth, and both have seen serious deforestation with its attendant problems of erosion and flooding, greatly increased water and air pollution with serious health and economic consequences, major water shortages, and on through the whole list of environmental ails.

The rise of state-sponsored conservation areas and nature parks in both places, of course, shows at least a partial change of attitudes. Nevertheless, it is not hard to see the tension between these different views of nature even within the newly protected areas. The first view of Taroko along the highway from Hualian, the nearest city, as I mentioned briefly above, reveals the scars of gravel mining that continued into the 1990s. The Superintendent confirmed the problem for me when I asked what his biggest problems were with the park. On the basis of the literature from other parts of the world, I was expecting responses that might include conflicts with indigenous people, littering, or illegal taking of animals or timber. His answer, though, was that Taroko National Park's biggest problem was the other branches of government. He complained in particular about the Forestry and Mining Bureaus, both of which continued to maintain their rights to extract Park resources for commercial use. As of my interview in 1991, they were not actually exercising those rights, but they would not cede them either. Kending National Park has similar problems, with the park administration in control of only about 10 percent of the land. The rest is privately owned (about 30 percent) or under the control of other government units (about 60 percent, controlled mostly by the Forestry Bureau and the county government). In Yushan National Park, high in the mountains, the park administration controlled so little land in the early 1990s that they were having trouble finding a place to build their headquarters.

Chinese conservation areas have their own versions of these problems. In many cases, the issues turn on competing claims between lower and higher levels of government. Environmental organizations in China have brought the best-known cases to light. Beijing's Friends of Nature, for example, helped publicize how illegal logging in protected areas, sponsored by local governments in parts of Sichuan Province, was destroying habitat of the endangered Tibetan antelope.

It should be no surprise that the logic of industrialization, and simply of profit, sometimes compromises sincere efforts at the creation of nature parks for purposes of conservation, wilderness preservation, or education. Nevertheless, these efforts at park creation promote a new view of nature – reacting against or at least trying to ameliorate the problems of industrial development in China and Taiwan. They are quite different from the direct issues of pollution and waste disposal that I will take up in the following chapters on environmental protest and new government policies. I bring up these problems here just as a reminder that before globalizing ideas about national parks and conservation areas influenced Asian policy, another set of globalizing ideas about the role of nature in science and economic development had already exerted a deep influence. These ideas shaped national parks by providing a context against which they reacted, not so different from the dynamics that led to the beginnings of the American national park movement in the late nineteenth century. Parks in China and Taiwan reflect their own reactions to industrialization, but strongly influenced by numerous globalizing models.

A United States model

The rise of a wilderness aesthetic in the nineteenth-century United States helped create the world's first national parks, as well as an increase in other new forms of nature tourism. Bird watching, for example, swept rapidly through the United States with the founding of Audubon Societies in many states after the first one was founded in Massachusetts in 1897. It had grown in part out of a tradition of local natural history that began in the seventeenth century, as the Enlightenment reworking of the nature/culture distinction was becoming dominant.[3] Its other primary precursor was in movements to protect species that were being decimated by the feather trade. The Royal Society for the Protection of

Birds, for instance, began from a desire to protect the great crested grebe, whose head crest had grown so popular in hat styles of the 1850s that the bird was nearly extinct in Britain and Ireland.[4] Modern bird watching as an end in itself, however, stems from somewhat different concerns. Bird watchers document and enjoy the diversity of nature for its own sake. Its primary goal is a form of wilderness appreciation, although bird watchers often also promote conservation for the sake of maintaining diversity.

I bring this up because bird watching was one of the first signs of a changing popular conception of nature in both China and Taiwan. In China, bird watching began to be popular in the 1990s. The first bird watching organization was probably a wing of the environmental NGO Friends of Nature, founded in 1996.[5] As they describe their goals: "Through bird watching, you may get close to nature, be familiar with nature, learn scientific method and cultivate environment protection awareness."[6] Quite a few other bird watching organizations, based in cities or provinces, have sprouted up in the years since then. In some cases the connection to American or other foreign traditions is not clear, but birding tours of China have shown Chinese the extent of foreign interest. Some multinational NGOs have helped promote this, like WWF, which runs a major bird watching bulletin board.

The origins of bird watching in Taiwan go back a bit further, but also involve a combination of foreign influence and local people looking to "get close to nature." According to Hunter H. T. Eu (Yu Hanting), he and several American scientists had founded the Taipei Bird Watching Society in 1975.[7] The initial membership was almost entirely American, mostly members of the military who were still stationed in Taiwan then. Eu also used his position in the Tourism Bureau to help get government approval for Taiwan's first bird sanctuary, well in advance of any of the national parks. In spite of some important differences, both Taiwan and China show a pattern where bird watching was the leading edge of something that would evolve into a new pattern of nature tourism. Both places also showed the immediate role that foreign – especially American – influence played, both through the examples of foreign bird watchers and through direct support for new indigenous organizations.

Hunter Eu, with the American training I described in chapter 3, takes credit for getting the first budget dedicated to conservation in any government agency – NT$ 250,000 (only about US$ 6,250) to the Tourism Bureau. He also helped promote the National Park Law. It passed in 1973, although there was no serious attempt to implement it until about 1980. Given these early influences, it should be no surprise at all that Taiwan's laws and administrative models for national parks stick so closely to American models. Yosemite National Park in particular loomed large for Taiwanese planners in the 1970s and 1980s, as their park system began to take shape. George Ruhle's original report had recommended three potential sites as national parks: Taroko, Yushan, and Xueba Shan. These were the wildest sites in Taiwan, reflecting his choice of an American model of "pure" nature tourism, with roots in the nineteenth-century meeting of Romanticism and the American wilderness. Ruhle had earlier been involved in a similar effort in Thailand, which also adopted an almost purely American model for its national parks, even though Ruhle himself had expressed some doubts about the cultural appropriateness of the wilderness ideal there.[8] Two of Ruhle's recommended sites were included in Taiwan's first four national parks; the other two of those earliest national parks (Kending and Yangmingshan) both have far larger human settlements.[9]

The pure wilderness model usually attempts to resettle anyone living inside the park boundaries – this is meant to be a nature unsullied by human use. This was clearly impossible for Kending and Yangmingshan, but appeared to be the goal at the other two, at least during my research period in the 1990s. Such areas are usually home to small populations of Taiwan's aboriginal peoples, and sometimes also to retired veterans who came over after 1949 and were settled in these remote areas. The veterans are old men now, and so do not pose a long-term problem. One aboriginal village in Taroko had been resettled (with some unhappiness over compensation levels) when I interviewed there in 1991, and another was in negotiation. Yushan may allow people to stay, but, at least at a 1993 meeting of the National Park Service that I attended, they had no idea how to incorporate the aborigines into these parks, since they wanted to prevent human uses like hunting.

The same attitude that true nature has no place for humans showed up in the exhibits. These tended to be purely ecological or geographic. The only exceptions I saw involved aborigines either as subjects of slide shows or as exhibits themselves (posing for photographs for a fee or demonstrating crafts). These exhibits never showed aborigines as parts of ecosystems, even though they had interacted with these environments for millennia. Instead, viewers could learn exotica about their clothing and their tattoos. Most of the aborigine women posing for photographs at Taroko wore the costumes of quite different groups, explaining that the sexier outfits increased their chances of being photographed. Real, historical human uses of this land, either in exhibits or in living humans, had been banned (as was generally the case in US parks) in favor of this kind of spectacle of exotica.[10] Other Taiwanese uses of the land are also banned, of course. Herding, for instance, was illegal, as I learned from a guide while we waited patiently for someone's herd of about fifty cows to stroll past our car in Kending National Park.

As in the United States, the rules and regulations discouraged any direct tourist interaction with nature. Private snack and drink vendors were illegal, although this law was not very thoroughly enforced either, especially at the parks with large populations inside them. Barbecuing was illegal (and this is usually enforced), although it is one of the most desirable activities in the minds of most tourists. "Playing in the water" (*wanshui*) is just as popular in Taiwan's hot climate, and just as forbidden. And of course pulling small rocks from the stream bed to take home was illegal too. Nature, following the American model, is there for us to gaze at, but we are not part of it.

The predominantly American model also shows up in staffing and in the kinds of interpretation that the parks prepare for visitors. Many have been trained in the United States, from top managers like Dr. Xu to the rangers, who follow Hunter Eu's early example and study directly with the United States National Park Service. When I asked the head of the interpretation section at Yangmingshan National Park if there was anything uniquely Chinese or Taiwanese about the parks, he was unable to think of a single example.[11] His explanation for the rapid rise of nature tourism was simply foreign influence, a direct globalization. His counterpart at Kending National Park also explained that guides were instructed to give an interpretation based solely on "nature," and not to focus on history or on human interactions with the land.[12]

Most of the many brochures that Taiwan's Park Service produces give a similar impression. The primary bilingual introduction to the national park system features a beautiful photograph of steep and craggy mountain peaks, crusted over with ice, high in the island's interior. Its opening essay, appropriately called "The ROC [Republic of China] Bows to Mother Nature," explicitly traces the history of national parks back to Yosemite and Yellowstone.[13] The pamphlet contains seventy-four photographs, the vast majority of which (sixty-four photos) show a purified nature with no direct sign that humans had ever been there. This is not so easy, given the large populations living within two of the parks, and the large numbers of annual visitors. Most of the exceptions show small groups of serious hikers (four photographs) or small man-made objects in the distance (a boat, a weather station, a concrete pill box). The only foregrounded signs of human use are a road, a temple, and a shot of cattle on an experimental farm. A similar brochure on the full range of Taiwan's conservation areas has only a single lone hiker among all its photographs.[14]

The specific brochures for the two parks with large populations living in them – Kending and Yangmingshan – do go farther in showing human use. A Kending brochure has a photograph of sisal agriculture

Figure 4.1 Cover of an English language brochure, collected at Kending National Park.

and another of cattle grazing; both used to be important economic activities in the area.[15] It also shows some local archaeological sites. None of these past human activities on the land are highlighted in the park itself, however. When I went to see the archaeological site in 1993, for instance, I found only a boarded over hole in the ground. The vast majority of the photographs in this brochure again show an untrammeled nature, although it is very difficult to experience anything but large crowds there. The brochure's cover is a good example (Figure 4.1): it shows a beautiful, clear beach, shining in the dawn sunlight. It does not show the tourists packed cheek by jowl, or the raw sewage that ran into the water from the park just off to the left, or the nuclear power plant just off to the right. A few people told me that the effluent from the power plant made the water pleasantly warm for swimming, but I decided not to check for myself. The image the park management wanted to convey, even at a place like this, was of a nature untouched by human hands.

So far, this sounds like a straightforward story of globalization from Yosemite on down to the rest of the world. From top park management to the information given to casual tourists, the park system appeared dedicated to the preservation of unsullied wilderness, with only the slightest recognition of past and continuing human interactions with the landscape. As we shall see, though, there are also other views of parks available, even within the small world of state-run parks in Taiwan, and even more if we look beyond.

A Japanese role

Now that there is a freeway, my original field site of Sanxia Township is only about twenty minutes away from Taipei by car, instead of an hour and a half. Sanxia lies at the edge of the massive mountain range that dominates Taiwan's central axis. This makes it one of the closest places to the capital city for people who want to enjoy any kind of nature tourism. The result has been a boom in parks of various sorts, one of which the government runs: Full Moon Forest Recreation Area (*Manyue Yuan Senlin Youlequ*). Unlike the national parks I have been discussing, Full Moon was run by the Forestry Bureau of Taiwan's provincial government, not by the national government.[16] It began as an experimental forestry station under the Japanese occupation, but is now purely a tourist site, focused on two spectacular waterfalls within about a kilometer of the headquarters.

In some ways, the management sounded very much like the national park management, with their view of a nature that had no place for humans except as observers. As my informant from the Provincial Forestry Bureau explained, most of the visitors had no interest in wild nature. They just wanted to play in the water and then barbecue a meal. Yet, she explained, the Forestry Bureau was dedicated to preservation, and had no intention of changing just to meet market demands. She thought that perhaps people would slowly learn to appreciate nature properly.

As with the national parks, both water play and barbecuing were forbidden. Unlike the national parks, though, people seemed to ignore these rules completely. Nearly everyone seemed to be splashing around or cooking. "We don't want to get yelled at," the manager told me. "We only have a staff of four, and so we can't enforce anything." While the national parks also compromised their ideals to an extent – as when people take strange rocks from the stream bed at Taroko – Full Moon appeared to have given in completely to more human uses of the park, in spite of the manager's statement of ideals.

Some management policies encouraged these alternate ways of thinking about how people should enjoy nature. For example, this park included a course of rounded stones, laid out in a straight path about 20 meters long and 1 meter wide. Visitors were supposed to walk the path in their bare feet, hoping to gain health benefits from the massaging effects of the stones. This harks back to very different notions of human relations to the environment, with roots in Chinese medicine, where a proper interaction with the environment improves the quality of life. I have never seen anything like this at a national park in Taiwan, although I know of some others at non-nature tourism sites, like the Sun Yat-sen mausoleum in Taipei.

This park also featured a "forest shower" (*senlin yu*) – an exercise course that stretched through a large stand of planted pine trees. This is the sort of thing where a visitor does a few sit-ups at one station, walks a few dozen meters to the next station to do a chin-up, and so on. I had seen such exercise courses occasionally in the United States, but never heard the term "forest shower." Doing these exercises in the woods, people explained, had particular health benefits that doing them in a gym would not – a kind of energy showered down from the trees themselves. Again we see humans and their environment sharing a kind of energy that can be directed for human benefit, and that looks very different from official ideas about preserving nature for its own sake.

I was curious about why a provincial park would construct these kinds of activities when the national parks did not. The answer was Japan, which was the main inspiration for adding these features to nature parks.[17] Just as national park leaders often trained in the United States, the provincial park leaders in the forestry administration typically trained in Japan. Officials in the provincial government had almost entirely Taiwanese roots, of course, while mainlanders still dominated the central government. Having gone through half a century of colonialism, Taiwanese very often spoke fluent Japanese – a skill far more rare in the central government. They were also much more willing to look to Japan for models. Many Taiwanese have a kind of nostalgia for the Japanese period, and recognize the benefits they gained along with the detriments of colonialism. For mainlanders, on the other hand, memories of the Japanese focused instead on the shorter but much more horrific Japanese invasion and occupation of China. Finally, the provincial forest service itself, along with many parks like Full Moon, were direct outgrowths of the Japanese period in ways that the national parks were not.

These ideas thus reveal a very different globalizing mechanism than the one that shaped the national park system. The specific borrowing from Japan did not always take root in Taiwan any better than the American borrowing in the national parks. The "forest shower" at Full Moon was being allowed to rot, and had never been very popular. Other direct emulations of Japanese park activities, like "boot camp" programs for corporate executives, had also proved unpopular. Both the Japanese and the American models have had their clearest influence on park managers alone, and I will take up more popularly based versions of nature tourism later in the chapter.

The flows, counterflows, and interchanges of globalization are already complex here. The United States model of nature and nature tourism had been important for Japan (as for every country) as it developed its own nature park system, but both took their own routes once they got to Japan. The topic of the evolution of Japanese thinking about nature takes me too far afield from this book, but perhaps it is enough simply to note the changing political significance of "nature" in Japan as it first picked up social Darwinian ideas of progress and competition, and then further developed them into a nationalist justification of Japan as a nation uniquely in harmony with nature.[18] Japan's national park law is far older than Taiwan's, dating back to 1931. By the time Taiwanese provincial parks were in a position to emulate global models, Japan had spent decades developing its own mixed-use models of parks in which wilderness tourism played only a secondary role.[19]

A United Nations globalization

The People's Republic of China founded its first nature reserve in 1956, with the emphasis placed almost completely on scientific research rather than conservation, education, or tourism. Consistent with their broader environmental values at the time, the main goal was a better understanding of ecosystems in order to improve production. Only a few reserves were set up, though, in part because of the social upheavals and subsequent starvation that resulted from the Great Leap Forward. When things had calmed down in the early 1960s, as the leadership pursued a less radical course, the State Council revised the regulations on nature reserves. In 1962 they called for reserves to be set up in every province, and now emphasized conservation over science. Limits on hunting played a major role, and they completely prohibited hunting of some species, like the giant panda. The leaders' new push for wildlife conservation reacted to the starvation of the previous years; nature continued to be important primarily as a support for the development of the human population.[20]

While the new policies resulted in a total of nineteen reserves, many of them became dysfunctional during the Cultural Revolution decade (1966–76), and no new ones were created. The opening up that began soon afterwards again saw the central government encouraging nature reserves, and the 1980s brought a huge surge in new ones. The result was well over a thousand reserves by the year 2000. County governments manage most of these, which means that many of them are poorly funded, and some have no formal administrative structures at all.[21]

These problems led to further regulatory adjustment in the mid-1990s. In making these changes, China has increasingly looked to international models. Unlike Taiwan, however, they have drawn less on American or Japanese models, and much more on relatively recent models out of the United Nations and the World Conservation Union (IUCN). The IUCN, as its name implies, focuses primarily on maintenance of biodiversity, and on protecting natural and "associated cultural" resources. Within this, they recognize a wide variety of functions from pure protection to tourism, education, sustainable resource use, and maintenance of what they call "cultural and traditional attributes."[22] Of their six categories of nature reserves, only the first three involve total protection (and China had only four such reserves by 2000). The others make way for increasing human use. The most recently introduced category (stemming from 1992) involves areas dedicated to preserving sustainable use, that is, primarily to protect people who rely on the reserves for their basic welfare. This change follows a broad trend among intergovernmental organizations through the 1980s and 1990s to recognize human demands on the environment, and not to follow the US model of setting aside huge swaths of land to protect as wilderness. China, like the United Nations and many other countries, uses this scheme to classify its reserves.

UNESCO's biosphere reserve program goes even farther in building human needs into the project. This program began in 1970 with primarily scientific and conservation aims of protecting genetic diversity in a full range of the world's ecosystems. After the United Nations Conference on Environment and Development in 1992, however, they became dedicated to fostering working examples of sustainable development. Even more than the IUCN, this program now places development directly alongside conservation in an attempt to reconcile biodiversity with sustainable use. It tries to achieve this by demarking three biosphere zones: a core where preservation is the overarching goal and there is no human activity beyond scientific monitoring and research (or possibly "traditional extractive uses by local communities"), a buffer zone that protects the core area but can also be used for tourism, experiments in ecological rehabilitation, or research on economic productivity consistent with conservation, and an outer transition area where local inhabitants, governments, and all others work together for sustainable development.[23] China had designated twenty-four Biosphere Reserves by 2004, giving it the fourth most in the world.

Both of these schemes share with the American model the idea that nature must be protected from humans, rather than seeing humanity and nature as part of a single anthropocosmic system, for instance. We can see this in the IUCN fully protected categories and in the UNESCO idea of a core zone. Nevertheless, both evolved away from the US national park model in the 1990s to allow for much more economic use of protected land by embracing the ideal of sustainable development.[24] The increasing dominance of this new model in world discourse came at just the moment China was rethinking its nature reserve system. These new global ideals have shaped China's system far more than we saw in Taiwan.

Wolong, in the western mountains of Sichuan province, offers an early Chinese example. This reserve dates back to 1963, when protection of endangered species first became a goal. Because it is the largest and most developed of the giant panda reserves, and home to the panda breeding station, Wolong became a centerpiece of Chinese conservation. It was one of China's first entries into the Biosphere Reserve program, and continues to be a flagship.

Thanks to the pandas, Wolong is more thoroughly dedicated to conservation goals than most Chinese reserves. It also attracts strong global support from environmental nongovernmental organizations – especially WWF (formerly World Wildlife Fund), which takes the panda as its logo. WWF, whose founders had also been involved in the early conservation efforts of both UNESCO and the IUCN, has been less interested in new ideals of sustainable development than those groups.

In spite of these pressures toward a pure conservation model, Wolong still includes a resident population of about 4,000 people, who rely on the panda habitat for firewood, pasture and other needs.[25] They live primarily in the valley that cuts through the heart of the reserve. The result is that what appears to be a large and contiguous panda habitat on the map is in fact several smaller and largely unconnected habitats. Conservationists have been unhappy about the human population, but China is not actively resettling people. In part, this is because such resettlement, involving mostly minorities, would be expensive and very much under the eye of the world. Yet such problems are exactly the kind of issue that has encouraged global conservation discussions to take human development issues more seriously. More recently, Wolong has actively tried to attract tourist income by building an up-scale hotel and other amenities. Even in this most conservation oriented of reserves, China has built in a human population more than the US national park model suggests.

The differences between the Chinese and Taiwanese cases illustrate several important points about the processes through which ideas about nature have globalized. First, as I have been arguing, globalizing forces are not unitary, and we have seen related but significantly different influences emanating from the United States, Japan, and the United Nations and other global groups. Each of these acts as a kind of node that reworks ideas and sends them out again. Second, the timing of entry into this complex global flow of ideas is important. There is only about a decade between Taiwan's development of national parks and China's reworking of its nature reserve system, but those were precisely the years when global conservation discourse embraced sustainable development. These ideas thus had a far greater impact in China than in Taiwan.[26] Finally, globalizing ideas also flow through channels worn by history. Taiwan was thus far more likely to look to the United States for models than China, and Taiwan's provincial government was more likely to look to Japan than its national government.

Chinese natures

These various global models have powerfully shaped legal frameworks and administrative structures. Nevertheless, neither they nor the governments who adopt them determine how people will actually use and interpret these resources. Turning toward problems of interpretation immediately forefronts various locally born traditions of nature appreciation that appear to have had very little effect on official state policies, but that importantly affect consumption. Let me begin to explore this by returning to the case of Chiang Hsun, the Taiwanese artist and writer.

He has written on his fascination with the interactions of water and stone:

> It isn't enough that Taroko's great mountains show the vigor and force thrust up when the mountains were created. Because the Liwu River has wound round them, stroking, slapping, grinding and eroding, their bulk has, for eons, been inscribed with the water's tattoos. The waters of the Liwu each stamp themselves on the marble cliffs before they flow into the great sea without a glance back. You can see the flying spray of the rapids, you can see the cycling of the waves, you can see the gyrations of the frothing crests, you can see the line of the ripples piercing their way toward the great sea; these are the corpses of water that died

on the rocks, etched memories of a past love that they have left for millions and millions of years – this is a kind of tender affection carved into the bones, never to be removed.[27]

Chiang had been painting at Taroko for a while, and one of the park's early publications featured his work along with a selection of several other artists.[28] Unlike some of the others in that collection, Chiang paints in a style that evokes earlier traditions of Chinese landscape painting – from the techniques of brush on paper to the use of calligraphy and the application of a chop. Figure 4.2 shows his painting of Yanzikou (Swallow Caves) in Taroko, where swirling rapids ages ago have eroded holes in the sheer cliffs. This spot particularly emphasizes the interaction of water and rock that Chiang finds compelling. He accentuates the effect further through his depiction of the stream meandering at the bottom of the cliffs; it seems to dissolve into the rock itself as we follow it up the painting.

Chiang's paintings and writings about Taroko evoke more than just a general Chinese landscape tradition; they draw in particular on China's long history of rock aesthetics. The most desired stones were the ones where the flow of *qi* was clear. Sometimes this took the form of an exposed rock face whose marbling itself resembled a landscape painting. The most valued, though, were the large "strange" rocks (*qishi*, see chapter 2) pierced through with eroded holes, especially the ones from the bed of Lake Taihu. A whole aesthetic vocabulary had developed around these stones by late imperial times, and collectors would pay a fortune for particularly fine examples that they might place in a garden. The ideal rock should be lean (*shou*), meaning that its shape should reveal its internal structuring of *qi*. It should also be textured (*zhou*), with a complex surface whose microstructures manifested the fractal flow of *qi*. Finally, it should be pierced (*tou*), penetrated with holes that evoke the motion of the *qi*.[29] All of these features make tangible the living flow of *qi* that is normally invisible. All also result from that yin and yang interaction of water and stone that Chiang celebrated.

In painting "nature" at an American-inspired national park, Chiang was thus not simply adopting an imported wilderness aesthetic. His use of a self-consciously Chinese style recalls for us that painting, like the landscape itself, is a creative manipulation of *qi* that unites humans and the environment in a single web of energy. The traditional use of calligraphy and application of a chop (itself carved from special stones) further place the painter himself into the environment, and the evocation of traditional rock aesthetics – accentuated by the naturally "pierced" cliff walls he painted at Yanzikou – adds to the feeling. Chiang may have been

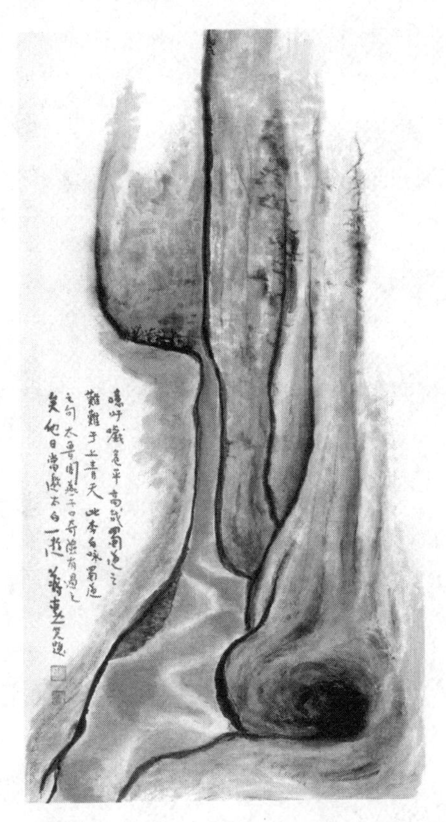

Figure 4.2 The artist and critic Chiang Hsun's painting of Yanzikou in Taroko National Park. The original hangs in the park's museum.

sitting in a globalized construction, but he chose to show the experience in a distinctly local idiom for thinking about the environment. Faced with the same effects of modernity that had led to Western responses like Romanticism or the wilderness movement, Chiang has offered us a uniquely Chinese response with roots in the anthropocosmic world and in the power of marginal places that I discussed in chapter 2.

Chiang, of course, is hardly alone in doing this. Many, many painters in both China and Taiwan continue to develop earlier idioms of Chinese landscape painting, although not all in exactly the same way as Chiang. I have been emphasizing the diversity of globalizing understandings of the environment, and the continued development of indigenous understandings is equally diverse. Even within this narrow range stemming from a late traditional elite art form we can see many lines of development. Chiang departs from the tradition, for example, in generally having no

Figure 4.3 Chu Ko's landscape of Taroko National Park, showing a famous tunnel. The original hangs in the park's museum.

sign of human presence in his paintings. He avoids the tiny peasants or the distant hut that typify nearly all late imperial landscapes. Here perhaps Chiang is borrowing from a Western landscape tradition, or from the wilderness goals of the national park movement, even though his primary interest lies in the interplay of yin and yang, water and stone.

Other artists, even others painting the same park and drawing loosely on the same Chinese artistic traditions, work things out differently. Figure 4.3 shows another painting of Taroko, this time by an artist named Chu Ko. Like Chiang Hsun, Chu is extending an obviously Chinese landscape painting tradition. Both artists seem fascinated with the line and flow of the stone, with its tangible and visible *qi*. Both further humanize the painting by adding their own calligraphy and chops, though Chu typically does this with a greater sense of humor – his line of calligraphy is falling down the edge of the cliff. Both also evoke those weird rocks by featuring big holes. Chu's hole, however, is obviously man-made. He is also happy to show the railings and the tiny tourists enjoying both the view of the marble canyon and the wonder of this neat round tunnel blasted straight through the rock. More than Chiang, Chu seems comfortable with a human presence, and most of his paintings have small people or pagodas in ways quite reminiscent of the earlier landscape tradition.

It is too much of a simplification to classify Chiang and Chu as nativist reactions to modernity or globalization, even though both draw primarily on older Chinese artistic idioms. Both men feel the pull of this American-style national park for reasons that would be familiar to Americans: they live in a noisy, crowded, polluted city from which they want a moment's respite, they want an escape from the competition and commodities of daily life, and they appreciate Taroko for the chance it offers to think about and experience their world in a different way. These are, in brief, modern men dealing with their modern world. Unlike some other painters of Taroko, though, and quite unlike the park's designers, they choose to deal with that world in self-conscious reference to Chinese tradition.

The result – this fascination with flowing *qi*, with the play of yin and yang – is of course quite different from what happened in the West. The results from the two artists are also quite different from each other, with Chiang much closer to a wilderness ethic translated into a Chinese understanding of the environment, and Chu less interested in wilderness than in an anthropocosmic world that does not reject human intervention. As I discussed in chapter 2, they already had a wide range of older Chinese landscape appreciation on which to base different ideas. Each artist comes to his own creative reworking of the problems of modernity and tradition, environment and humanity, oil paints and inkstones.

It would not be difficult to expand greatly the enumeration of artists rethinking these issues by pushing the Chinese landscape tradition ahead. There are many in both Taiwan and the People's Republic. Nor would it be hard to document further how their solutions differ from each other. I am no art historian, though, and I doubt it would change the conclusion that many artists – like many people in general – are facing the problems of nature in modern life by embracing both globalizing ideas like national parks and indigenous traditions with a broad popular resonance like landscape paintings, in ways that are leading to creative new forms.

Looking at Chinese landscape traditions, or at poetry or any other elite genre we might examine, barely scratches the surface of the entire Chinese repertoire of possibilities for thinking about the environment, or even just for thinking about rocks. As a way of beginning to consider some of those other resources, let me return to the small stones people poached out of the stream bed at Taroko and brought home to place on their ancestral altars. Ancestral altars hold tablets to commemorate the ancestors, an incense pot and other paraphernalia of worship, and often a god image or two. In rural Taiwan, like much of south China (at least when not interrupted by the Communist suppression of ancestor worship), altar tables are often among the most elaborate pieces of furniture in the house, and sit in the main room, where guests are entertained. They very typically hold souvenirs of trips, decorative knick-knacks, amulets picked up while visiting temples, or important family photographs – and occasionally strange rocks from Taroko.

It hardly makes sense, in the Chinese religious context, to ask if this placement implies sacralizing the stones and treating them as a kind of deity, or instead juxtaposes sacred and profane. For most Taiwanese and Chinese, most of the time, these ideas are not so clearly divided as Durkheim might imply. The term we usually translate as worship in Chinese (*bai*) more literally means to offer respect. This respect can be to a god (*bai shen*) or ancestor (*bai zuxian*), but can also be to one's in-laws (*bai qin*) or to some important person (*baifang*).[30] Gods and ancestors are as much part of the world of *qi* as living humans, or rocks for that matter. There is certainly no incense pot dedicated to anybody's souvenir Taroko stone, and I very much doubt that anyone offers prayers. The souvenirs are there because it is a public place of honor, a shrine to the family's images and memories of itself. In that sense, these stones are very much like the ancestors and gods with whom they share the table, and whose incense smoke they also enjoy.

Yet people sometimes do dedicate incense pots, offer prayers, and make vows to stones. Taiwan and some parts of China are dotted with little shrines to rocks, and occasionally with larger temples for them. Little has been written on these shrines to "stone gods" (*shitou gong*; H: *chiou-thau kong*), but they are widespread.[31] Stones that people worship are usually prodigies of some sort. Some have an unusual appearance – often resembling a human face or an animal form, but usually not the kind of lean, textured, and pierced appearance of the elite aesthetic. Others behave oddly, for instance by turning up in a farmer's field even though she moves it repeatedly. Ultimately, such stones must withstand the test of practice that all deities undergo. People will worship if their wishes are granted, and not if they are ignored. Exactly the same process happens for sacred trees in some parts of China, and this is surely part of what was involved in the generalized tree worship I described from West Mountain in Guangxi.[32]

The Stone Immortal temple (*Shixian Gong Miao*) in the mountains of Sanxia provides another example. This temple had a wide local following, and many people told me variants of its origin story. A woman, they said, was not getting along with her daughter-in-law (or her neighbor, according to some). One day, she found a large stone in her path, and moved it aside. The next day it was back, and she moved it again. After it had reappeared several times, she thought maybe there was something unusual about the stone, and tried worshiping it. She soon gained the upper hand in her dealings with her daughter-in-law (or neighbor), and others started coming to worship the stone after word got out. Eventually they constructed a small temple around it, and people from all around the township would occasionally make the long, sweaty climb to offer incense there. As the site expanded, two other large stones began to receive worship along with a tree (see Figure 4.4).

The Patriarch of the Eight Trigrams (*Bagua Zushi*) temple in the town of Yingge had a slightly different story. In this case, it was the uncanny resemblance of the stone to a turtle that initially attracted attention – according to legend, the eight trigrams had been discovered inscribed on a turtle's shell in ancient times; this deity's name is thus an indirect reference to turtles. More centrally located than the Stone Immortal temple, this one gradually grew in wealth until it fully resembled a god temple. This process included anthropomorphizing the deity, so that the original stone itself is no longer visible, but instead sits in a small shrine in the back.

It is tempting to call this offering of incense and prayers to rocks and trees a kind of nature worship. It would also be misleading, however, in the same way as it is misleading to translate *tian* as nature. People worship rock deities because they are somehow extraordinary, and above all because they are efficacious (*ling*) – they have the ability, as Sangren puts it, to mediate between order and disorder.[33] In this however, they are exactly like every other Chinese deity. People honor them and ask for their help; in return the deities can expect repayment in the form of donations, embroidered robes and gold medals, or occasional puppet shows.

As we have seen with *qi*, there is no particular separation between the human and natural world from this point of view. The Patriarch of the Eight Trigrams could evolve into a human image because nature was never really an independent category from humanity. In this context, perhaps it is worth noting that the male protagonist in *The Story of Stone*

Figure 4.4 Stone god on the altar of its small temple in the mountains of Sanxia, Taiwan. It wears robes and gold medals presented by grateful worshipers.

(*Shitou Ji*, also called *The Dream of the Red Chamber*), one of the most important works of fiction in late imperial China, was a piece of extraordinary jade born on earth as a human.

A stone taken from the stream bed at Taroko evokes all of these images: family souvenirs sharing the incense smoke and honor of the ancestral altar, the aesthetics of the bizarre stones that graced elite gardens, minor temples to efficacious rocks, and the powers that emanate from inaccessible places at the geographic margins of civilization. It is not, however, a very strong evoker of the globalizing wilderness ethic that created the park itself, which requires leaving the rock in place. People do talk about the glories of the scenery at Taroko, and the delights of escaping from the city; in this they sound no different from their American counterparts. The very act of picking up those stones and taking them home, however, already shows another sensibility at play. This is not an active resistance to globalizing ideas. It is, in its own way, a bricolage of indigenous resources, new ways of life, and globalizing culture that is every bit as creative as the paintings of Chiang Hsun or Chu Ko.

The ties between nature tourism and religion run deep in China. Most of China's primary pilgrimage sites had been in relatively inaccessible places. The various sacred mountains that attracted the most pilgrims mostly lie at some distance from major cities, and the famous temples they shelter may be several days' hike up the mountain. The temples – dedicated to various Buddhist or Daoist deities, depending on the site – were always the centers of worship, but pilgrimage itself could be referred to as *chaoshan*, paying respect to the mountain. Late imperial descriptions of trips up these mountains often seem to combine experiences we might otherwise separate as religious and natural pilgrimage. A Ming Dynasty censor, for instance, climbed Mount Tai to ask for help from the divinity, but most of his description is of the view of the sunrise and other famous sites.[34] Others reported on the strange natural phenomena they witnessed, bizarre clouds and inexplicable lights. As one Northern Song traveler wrote:

> Shang-ying [the author] donned pilgrim's garments, burned incense, and bowed repeatedly. Before he had risen from even the first prostration, however, he saw the "golden bridge" and an aureole, gold-edged and deep violet-blue within. But he harbored doubts about these visions, thinking they might be just the effects of the sort of color that is produced when clouds catch the rays of the setting sun. Later, however, when it had grown quite dark, three columns of rosy light arose directly in front of the mountain, and his doubts abruptly vanished.[35]

During my own trip up Yellow Mountain in Anhui, I could see an odd circular rainbow as I looked down from the high peak to the clouds below me. People standing there told me how fortunate this was, because I was granted a rare sight of the *foguang*, Buddha's aura.

I have only traveled on one Chinese pilgrimage. This was in 1978, when friends and neighbors in Sanxia organized a trip down the island's west coast to all the most famous Mazu temples. Taiwan has no sacred mountains, and its pilgrimage sites (none of which had ever been very important by broader Chinese standards) are all urban. We sat in a rented bus, watching smuggled mainland martial arts movies and singing songs to each other. We sat for hours and hours – there were still no major highways in Taiwan – stopping only at roadside restaurants with which the travel agency arranging the trip clearly had cut a deal. We would finally be released when we got to one of these temples, but only long enough to burn some incense, collect an amulet, and use the bathroom. We got a full hour in the most famous spots, but usually half that and then back on the bus. Nights were spent in such nasty hotels that we all thought the travel agent must be getting a kickback.

On the last day of the southward journey, though, having burnt our incense at the final temple, we kept going farther south. We went all the way down to the southern tip of the island, to what is now Kending National Park. At that time it was just a famous botanical garden and a beautiful beach, both of which we visited. Our pilgrimage had culminated in nature.

When I interviewed travel agents about nature tourism, fifteen years later, the ties to pilgrimage remained clear. Many of the older agents I talked to had primarily arranged pilgrimages before, and had more recently added nature tourism trips for school groups and companies. They pointed out that these two sides of their business were not really separate. Groups going to a national park, for instance, would often stop at a famous temple or two to burn some incense, and pilgrimages continue to take in natural scenery. In addition, the infrastructure for the two forms of tourism turns out to be the same: the same travel agencies, the same singing on the bus, the same roadside restaurants and dodgy hotels, and (I assume) the same kickbacks.

All of this draws, to some extent, on the idea of the power of the margins that I developed in chapter 2. Inaccessible places have accessible, but sometimes difficult and dangerous powers. Temples both draw on and add to those powers, which can be seen as clearly in wishes granted as in strange lights, clouds, or rocks. Cultural tourism to temples is thus not so very different from natural tourism to mountains and beaches. From this point of view, my experience on West Mountain in Guangxi, where people had lit incense in front of every big tree and rock, is not so strange. My initial impression of a jarring juxtaposition of scenery viewing and religious worship forced a distinction that was not very salient to most of the people involved. Secular and sacred tourism in China and Taiwan both draw on a single experience of power.

In contrast, the United States National Park Service draws a clear line between natural and cultural landscapes. Similar ideas underlie all attempts to preserve a wilderness with no human contact, even the UNESCO biosphere reserve idea with its core of untouched nature. Built on these various global models, government sponsored reserves in Taiwan or China leave very little room for the kinds of interpretations I have been discussing. Visitors to these places, on the other hand, have a lot of freedom of interpretation, as we have seen in the paintings of Chiang and Chu, the people collecting rocks from Taroko, or those lighting incense on West Mountain. Visitors appear to draw on a palette that includes a wide range of both local and global resources for thinking about their environment.

Nature tourism markets

Some of this becomes even clearer if we examine market-based nature tourism. The government can, if it chooses, largely ignore market pressures to set up its own models of nature tourism. Nature entrepreneurs, however, have to respond to the desires of their market. Taiwan by the late 1980s already had several hundred sites run as profit-making businesses, at least part of whose market appeal rested on nature enjoyment through gardens, scenery, hiking, water-play, or any of the many other possibilities. Restrictions on private land ownership in China mean that the government is almost always more closely involved there, but many of the dynamics are similar because profit motives drive many of the new parks in China as much as in Taiwan.

I explored this first and more thoroughly in Taiwan. Its smaller size makes it far more tractable for research trying to cover the full range of nature tourism. Taiwan also has better and more broadly available resources on the topic, from guidebooks that attempt to cover every single site to published surveys of park users.[36] I will thus begin in Taiwan, but more piecemeal research in China suggests that many of the same processes are at work.

Comprehensive tourist guidebooks offer one useful starting point in Taiwan. I analyzed in some detail a six-volume set published in 1990, called *Taiwan's Most Beautiful Places*.[37] Of the 1,140 places this set of books describes, about 40 percent offered scenery or wilderness as their main feature. Private entrepreneurs ran very few of these sites, which tended to be significantly larger and more remote than the others. Of the rest, about 15 percent were temples, 30 percent were historical landmarks, and the remaining 15 percent represented various new forms of tourism that began to thrive in the 1970s and 1980s – amusement parks, camping sites, tourist farms, sports venues, formal gardens, and others. Even places like temples and amusement parks, though, often had at least an aspect of nature tourism, like a garden or a waterfall. Most of the private entrepreneurs were concentrated in the category of new, mixed forms of tourism, accounting for well over half the sites in this category.[38] The entrepreneurial sites tended to be the smallest (except for temples), at least in part because land is expensive and difficult to consolidate. They also involved the shortest travel times for visitors, clearly for market reasons.[39]

The most recently created places were these new kinds of tourist sites (average founding date of 1976) and the remote wilderness sites (average of 1973), followed by the scenic sites (1967); the historical landmarks and temples were decades older.[40] The dates in the guidebooks imply that Taiwanese became interested in several new forms of tourism sometime in the 1970s. One of these new forms was wilderness tourism, with the government as the primary promoter. The other consisted of a set of humanized activities in nature – everything from water parks to green showers. Many of them combined several different types of activities. Private entrepreneurs were the main investors in these.

As a way of going farther into this, I interviewed an opportunity sample of 270 informants at twenty-four sites chosen to represent the range of variation in the guidebooks.[41] Many people confirmed that their tourism habits had changed over the course of the previous decade or so, and that rural places now appealed much more to them than urban activities. Many attributed this to better transportation (most people had arrived by private car) and to the relatively new concepts of vacations and leisure time. Many also spoke of the desire to escape urban life, with its work pressures, artificial environment, and security worries.

The interviews often raised environmental issues. Some took a human-centered view that nature tourism was just another way of using the environment to relax. Many others, however, complained about sites that artificially sculpted nature to satisfy a perceived market. One man complained, for instance, about all the people going to sing karaoke at a scenic site; he saw it as an urban corruption of the rural beauty. The majority at every site said that their favorite tourism spot would be distant mountains and wilderness.

On the other hand, we also found a large gap between what people say and what they do. One sign of this was in comments from various official nature guides I interviewed at some of the national parks. Li Yuanguang, the chief of the interpretation section at Kending National Park, for instance, complained that none of the visitors are really interested in nature for its own sake, but instead come just for the excitement (*re'nao*). One of the guides there, working for just his second day after two weeks of training, explained unhappily that people showed little interest in the natural history he had been trained to explain. "Can you eat it?" they asked. "Can you use it for medicine?" A more experienced guide told me he had developed various interpretations to fit the desires of his audience. For older people, he embroidered legends and stories. The younger ones would listen to more natural history, but only if he concentrated on the human uses and dangers of the wild plants and animals. All the guides I talked to agreed that most people's interest in nature focused only on its benefits and risks for humans.

Many of the visitors who extolled the virtues of wilderness in my interviews were in fact at amusement parks, contrived gardens, or other sites with no trace of wilderness. Even those at more remote sites often liked the concept better than the reality. At one moderately remote site, for instance, six of ten people claimed to prefer wilderness sites, but three of them complained that the path to a very nearby waterfall was too "exotic and bumpy." Even the man who complained about the karaoke was happily singing away a few hours after the interview. Of the 270 interviews, only one person had ever been to a truly remote area. In practice, people prefer their nature tamed – a waterfall with a nice shelter nearby, to play mahjongg if it rains.

People gave two reasons for this. First, their leisure time was limited, and actual wilderness was just too far away. Second, most traveled with their families (about 55 percent), and said that the desires of their children drove their decisions.[42] Children, they said, want fun, exciting, and different places. Families thus searched for the new and fresh (*xinxian*), and often did not return to the same place twice. Interviews with owners of some of these sites confirm the impression. These are profit-seeking businesses, much more interested in supply and demand than changing views of nature. When capital and capacity allowed, owners mostly wanted to create a mixed-use product that would attract and retain the most customers. They would have some natural forest and a garden for the parents and old people, an amusement park for the smaller children, water slides and riskier rides to excite the older ones, a hotel with a conference room, karaoke for tour groups, and a temple just for good measure. They consistently strove to bring in new and different entertainments to respond to the market demand for novelty, everything from a visiting Russian circus to the largest statues of important religious figures. Monster truck shows were a favorite during the interview period. These are locally called *Jipu Anuo* – Jeep Arnolds – in honor of Arnold Schwarzenegger.[43]

The result of all this has been a burgeoning of a new form of mélange tourism, attempting to offer something for everybody. While I do not have comparable interview data from China, the shape of many of the actual parks created there since the 1990s implies that very similar mechanisms are at work. Full or partial state ownership is more common there than in Taiwan, but market demand has also promoted new forms of mixed-use tourism. Let me show this with some examples, first from Taiwan and then from China.

Sanxia turned out to be well placed for the new tourism opportunities. It lies at the edge of the mountains that dominate Taiwan, close enough to Taipei to offer relatively easy transportation by car or motorbike, but far enough away to offer a range of rural opportunities, from rice paddies to strenuous mountain hiking. In 1993 I knew of six nature tourism sites that had opened just in the upper hills of one of Sanxia's small river valleys – an area called Big Leopard Creek (*Da Bao Xi*). One of these was Full Moon, the provincial park I discussed above. One was an unowned and unsupervised spot where people gathered to play in the water of the creek, and the other four were run by entrepreneurs. I will pick out just some of these spots to show the range of variation.

Plankroot (*Dabangen*, lit. Banyan Root) was the most impressive operation. The land had been held by a Japanese company during the colonial period. The Taiwanese government took it over in 1945. The government landholding company had tried to run it as a tourist site (called Haishan Amusement Park) in the 1980s, but it was not successful. They leased the land to private investors in 1987. The new company invested a lot, but also lost money until the current group took over in 1991.[44] The manager estimated that the various owners had invested about NT$ 120 million (roughly US$ 3.5 million), and new construction continued. The manager, who had four years of experience in similar enterprises in Japan, hoped to build a place where people could come for a quiet, calm, and natural vacation. If he had enough capital, he would build a luxurious resort.

He kept coming back to "leisure" (*xiuxian*) as the key term in his thinking about the market, and he felt that taking more advantage of the pristine forest environment (including some spectacular banyans after which the place is named) would work better than previous attempts at amusement parks. On the other hand, he thought he could do better than government parks because he was not limited to the idea of pristine nature. Indeed, much of his money was going into water engineering. Taiwanese tourists, he told me, want to see and play in water when they come to a place like this. Plankroot had a swimming pool, but that was not enough. Lacking a proper stream, he was building one from the ground up.

A bit farther upstream, Bee World (*Mifeng Shijie*) is a different kind of place altogether. This began as the farm of four brothers and their aged mother, who had moved up from southern Taiwan. Remarkably, they were still living together as a joint family. They raised bees, because the tangerine groves in the area made for good honey. At some point in the 1980s they opened a roadside stand to sell honey and royal jelly to people driving by. People seemed interested, and they soon expanded by giving educational tours of the hives and by selling bottles of a special drink made by steeping fierce tiger-head hornets (*hutou feng*) in strong liquor. The expensive result has medicinal uses, and the hornets sitting in the bottom of the bottles seem attractive to people.

By the early 1990s business was booming, and they built a camping area, a water play area, and finally a seventy-bed hotel. When I was there in 1993 they were putting the finishing touches on a new Chinese style garden. The old woman, with whom I spent most of my time, clearly still could not believe the luck of a mountain farming family bringing in this kind of money. "Do you know what that thing cost?" she asked me, pointing to a large "strange rock" in the traditional style. "A million NT (just under US$ 30,000)!" And she laughed. They still sold their various bee products, but the educational tours of the hives seemed to have evaporated. Partly, the decline of the tangerine industry had forced them to move the hives higher into the mountains. Mostly, though, she told me the bees frightened the customers, so they moved them away. People want barbecues and water play, she said, not natural history.

As the last stop in Sanxia, there was a nameless place that gave easy access to the creek itself. People crowded there to climb on the rocks and splash in the fast-running mountain water. No one took responsibility for the site, but the township government had put up numerous warning signs – several dozen people drown there every year, usually when sudden torrents higher in the mountains cause flash flooding. It was crowded anyway. The rubbish was as striking as the crowd – massive amounts of litter floated in the quieter pools and piled up on the banks, smelling fetid in Taiwan's subtropical heat. Both public and private park managers go to great trouble and expense to remove litter that people toss everywhere. The entrepreneurs resigned themselves to this as part of the cost of doing business; the national park administrators complained about low educational levels. No one, however, would go to that trouble over this unclaimed spot. There were not even any trash receptacles.

Figure 4.5 The Eight Immortals Water Park, showing a swimming pool, a happy whale, and several of the immortals – the strange rocks in the background.

I will not describe any other Taiwanese sites in detail, except to note briefly some other typical examples of mélange tourism. Jidong Gardens, near the town of Caodun, for example, had a typical combination of nature and other attractions. There were bumper cars and other amusement park rides, oversized images of Confucius, Jesus, Guanyin and others, and some demarcated nature views. Dragon Creek Gardens (near Shimen Reservoir) featured a new Chinese-style garden, complete with strange rocks and a nine-bend bridge. The manager explained that Taiwan already had a lot of European gardens, and that the market seemed better now for a Chinese one – they had to be new and different. Perhaps just to be safe, though, the Chinese garden suddenly blended into an Italian formal garden, all straight lines and formal geometry, broken up occasionally with an ornate classical sculpture. To be even more safe, they also had a pool, some kiddy rides, an archery area, barbecuing facilities, and a water buffalo. The Eight Immortals Water Park offered another sort of variant: it was a standard water park with slides and rides, but with the added attraction of the Eight Immortals in the form of eight gigantic strange rocks (see Figure 4.5).

The last site I will mention is Dongshan River Park, which is part of a large water control and urban improvement project of the Ilan city government. Only one part of this project was done when I visited in 1993, but it was already crowded with local people. The heart of it was a large, shallow pool of water, with stone paths that ran at or just underneath the surface of the water. The paths turned back and forth at right angles, reminiscent both of the straight geometries of European formal gardens and of the traditional Chinese nine-bend bridge. The park made extensive use of stone, but not the strange rocks of Chinese tradition, or even the less strange stone of Japanese or Western rock gardens. Instead, large rocks had been heaped into enormous pyramids (see Figure 4.6). It was a park of straight lines, squares, and triangles – a high modern geometry softened by the lapping of the water on the toes of visitors. For some, perhaps, the stone brings other, more natural evocations. The huge pyramids resemble the symmetries of Mount Fuji, a shape well known in Taiwan, and the landscape architects were in fact Japanese. This park has a singleness of vision that the commercial parks avoid, but it does very little to foster the image of a pure nature that the national park system promotes. It is thus significantly different from the other places I have discussed, and I bring it up largely to show that there are even more ways of thinking about relationships to the environment, and even just stone, than the many Chinese and Western possibilities I have discussed.

The People's Republic of China does not have the large numbers of private, entrepreneurial nature sites that Taiwan developed. Limitations

Figure 4.6 Dongshan River Park, Ilan. The simple geometries of the rocks and the gently flooded paths have attracted crowds.

on private landholding make them largely impossible. On the other hand, governments from Beijing down to local counties see great potential in developing tourism, including nature tourism. While globalizing standards of nature preservation have shaped some of the most important sites, like the Wolong Panda Reserve I discussed earlier, profit motives drive many of these newer sites. While ownership is often different from Taiwan's situation, market pressures appear to be pushing these sites into mélange forms very similar to what developed in Taiwan in the 1980s.

In some cases this involves knitting nature tourism and religion together again, although in somewhat different ways from earlier Chinese pilgrimage patterns. The Guangxi West Mountain site that I have discussed involved a grassroots reintroduction of religion to a place the government saw as nature tourism, which local cadres found uncomfortable and unfortunate. At some larger and more important sites, however, the government has actively promoted the combination. Mount Emei in Sichuan, for instance, is one of China's four "sacred" Buddhist mountains, and has long attracted pilgrims. Typically, it was as famous for its natural phenomena as its temples – tourists/pilgrims took in the "sea of clouds" at dawn, and hoped to see Buddha's auras and other strange optical effects. Many of the important religious objects were destroyed during the Cultural Revolution, and China invested a lot in the early 1990s to rebuild the area for tourism. Together with the nearby giant Buddha in Leshan, it was listed as a UNESCO World Heritage Site in 1996.

When I went in 1997, most people drove or took a cable car to the peak, instead of making the long, hard hike of bygone pilgrims. The main temple complexes at the peak have been renovated, and destroyed religious objects have been replaced with similar ones from other temples or, more often, with modern substitutes. Tourists still try to see the same natural sites, but the temples are the main attraction for most of the Chinese. Speaking as someone who has spent a lot of time in Chinese temples, though, the reconstruction struck me as more the appearance of religion than the practice. There are monks and worshipers, but the broad impression is much more of a place designed by Communist bureaucrats to look like a temple than of a continuation of a millennium of Buddhist worship. At worst, it deteriorates into a sort of religion theme park – one pavilion features an enormous, obese plaster Maitreya, at whom tourists are encouraged to toss coins. Hitting him in the right spot makes the deity give off huge peals of deep laughter, mildly distorted by the speaker system.

Foreigners often come instead primarily for birding. As one American reporter rather breezily dismissed the entire human aspect of the landscape: "Sidestepping the manmade attractions is easy enough. Nothing added in the last couple thousand years can detract from a mountain that took millions of years to craft."[45] Other foreign tours concentrate on the mountain's martial arts tradition, although it is not as famous as the Shaolin Monastery. The result of all this is a mountain designed to meet several markets at once. These include the physical world in its appeal as pure nature (endemic bird species and craggy mountains scenes), as the spiritual power of the margins (strange lights and Buddha's auras), and as a recollection of old elite tourism recorded in their writings (famous sights like the clouds at dawn). They also include religion both in practice and as an odd curiosity.

A very different sort of example of religious and natural tourism combined comes from northern Shaanxi, as described in a recent ethnography by Adam Yuet Chau.[46] A local man, a kind of religious entrepreneur, had led an ambitious reconstruction effort for a local dragon king temple in the 1980s. Under his leadership, the temple gradually resumed its local position and again began to attract very large crowds, especially for the famous opera performances at its annual temple fair. Given China's discomfort with local religion (or "feudal superstition" as the government calls it), the temple had to take great pains to achieve some kind of political legitimacy. The most innovative and successful of these attempts involved the creation in 1988 of a hilly land arboretum, in collaboration with an official in the prefectural Forestry Bureau. Within a few years, the project began to attract foreign attention from Japan and elsewhere. The leader ended up involved with national and international NGOs, and the arboretum was featured as a kind of green development. Groups came from Japan and Beijing to plant trees and to admire the little oasis of green in the parched landscape of northwest China. At the same time, the temple's and its leaders' positions were enhanced because income from their "superstitious" activities subsidized the arboretum. To my knowledge, this particular arrangement is unique in China, but the result – another combination of religious and nature tourism – is a regular pattern.[47]

Hainan Island, in China's far south, has developed still another permutation on the combination of religion and environment. The island began to pursue tourism as a major economic goal in the late 1990s, with almost 8 million visits by the end of the decade.[48] The vast majority of the visitors are domestic (including Hong Kong) or overseas Chinese. One of the centerpieces they have been developing (with a planned budget of over US$ 800 million) is the Nanshan Buddhist Culture Park. Unlike Mount Emei, or even the dragon king temple, this was never an important religious center. Instead, it offers religion primarily as theme park and as museum piece: an American firm designed the park. One of the main attractions is what claims to be the largest statue of the Bodhisattva Guanyin – bigger than the Statue of Liberty – standing in the water just offshore. The park is also an "ecological environment restoration and protection" zone, and complements other more strictly environmental attractions in the area. They still plan to add a golf course, resort hotel, and mythology sculpture park.

Each of these cases suggests that when nature tourism reacts to the market, rather than directly reflecting state environmental policies, we see an immediate interaction of global and indigenous cultures of nature. We have an American firm designing a theme park based on Chinese religion and environmental restoration in Hainan, and a Chinese temple recruiting international environmental groups to help it build an arboretum in Shaanxi. Chinese rock gardens blend into European formal gardens at Dragon Creek, and protected stones from an American-style national park show up on people's ancestor altars in Taiwan.

Conclusion

Given the wide political and economic gulf between Taiwan and China, even after several decades of China's market-based reforms, I had not expected nature tourism to evolve so much in parallel. One reason for the similarity is the shared cultural heritage of Taiwan and the People's Republic of China, of course. Another reason is that policy-makers in both places reflect globalizing discourses about nature.

By the late twentieth century, both China and Taiwan increasingly pursued alternate strands of Western environmental thinking aimed at resource and wildlife conservation and at a new wilderness aesthetic. China preferred the United Nations model and Taiwan preferred the United States. This is partly because of their different historical relations to the US, and partly because China began to do this more recently, when the United Nations model was more elaborated and widespread. Both models, though, put a dehumanized idea of nature at the center of their policy goals. Both grew from a post-Enlightenment understanding of nature as opposed to culture, reworked in the nineteenth century by various streams of Romanticism and nature appreciation, and further developed by the environmental consciousness of the twentieth century. By the last decades of the twentieth century, neither China nor Taiwan could ignore these discourses. They dominate international discussions of nature conservation, shaping the language of international treaties, academic meetings, and nongovernmental pressure groups.

The resemblance between nature tourism patterns across the Taiwan Strait also stems from similarities between the two governments. The two political systems have differed enormously for over a century, of course, but nature has provided one realm where they overlap. First, elites in both places emulated and admired modernity throughout the twentieth century and beyond. They were anxious to adopt new ideas instead of adapting older Chinese ideas, and this has included several strands of Western thinking about nature. In addition, much nature tourism in both places reflects the realities of domestic market demand. Taiwan's national parks and some of China's nature reserves are partially insulated from this because they are heavily subsidized. Private nature tourism in Taiwan and many profit-seeking government tourist sites in China, however, must adapt to the desires of their visitors. That is why we so often see a combination of religion and nature tourism that recalls earlier Chinese pilgrimage practices, along with other creative forms of mélange tourism. Shared domestic demand for tourism that reflects both global and older Chinese traditions overcomes most of the differences in ownership patterns in the two places.

The kinds of syncretic places that have blossomed seem to support the sorts of globalization theory that focus on creole cultures or cosmopolitanism rather than an unstoppable force out of Hollywood (or Yosemite, in this case) or a straightforward local resistance to it. The simple models of a monolithic globalization or of a localizing resistance cannot account as well for the multiple lines of both global and indigenous nature discourse that I have been discussing. The many influences on Taiwanese and Chinese nature tourism include the *qi*-based power of certain objects (like some stones or trees), old patterns of pilgrimage, imperial Chinese traditions of landscape painting and poetry, the post-Enlightenment opposition of nature and culture, the American wilderness movement, anti-urban pastoralisms (variously realized through the Chinese practice of sending youth down to the countryside and the Taiwanese China Youth Corps), and so on. All of this combines into a complex and creative array of different nature tourism patterns, from the paintings of Chiang Hsun or Chu Ko to the hornet liquor of Bee World.

Yet, it is misleading to be too optimistic about these creole cultures and mélange modernities. While those images do leave room for intricate variation in the "local" and the "global," and do allow for genuinely innovative responses by people, they also tend to underplay the enormous differences in the organizational power of various discourses. At the highest levels of power, just a few lines of global thinking about nature completely dominate, and there is little trace of anything indigenously Chinese. This includes the government bureaucrats who create the legal frameworks for nature tourism, the school curricula that promote certain understandings of the relationship between humanity and environment, and the administrative structures that shape nature tourism sites directly. It also includes the intellectuals and professionals who sometimes consult for and sometimes critique their governments' policies.

Mélange nature turns up instead at the limits of the political and professional elite's ability to exercise control. This happens, for example, when people go to government parks and reserves to take strange stones home or barbecue. These activities are illegal, but lie beyond the managers' will or power to control. It also happens when nature tourism sites have to respond to market demands by promoting religion or amusement park rides. These are the venues where the most creative combinations take place. The ideas they are playing with, however, seem unlikely to shape policy very directly, or even to become knit together into some newly organized way of thinking about the environment. Grounded in both local and global experience, these mélanges are likely to remain scattered, disorganized, and unsystematized. Much the same pattern holds in the following two chapters, which turn to environmental protest and to policy implementation.

NOTES

1. Arjun Appadurai, *Modernity at Large: Cultural Dimensions of Globalization* (Minneapolis: University of Minnesota Press, 1996); Ulf Hannerz, *Transnational Connections: Culture, People, Places* (London: Routledge, 1996).
2. Chris Coggins, *The Tiger and the Pangolin: Nature, Culture, and Conservation in China* (Honolulu: University of Hawai'i Press, 2003), 72–4.
3. Felton Gibbons and Deborah Strom, *Neighbors to the Birds: A History of Birdwatching in America* (New York: W. W. Norton, 1988).
4. Royal Society for the Protection of Birds, *History of the RSPB*. 2004, 18 March 2004, http://www.rspb.org.uk/about/history/index.asp.
5. Hong Kong is a rather different situation, with the first groups founded in the 1950s.
6. Friends of Nature, *FON's Bird Watching Group*. 18 March 2004 http://www.fon.org.cn/index.php?id=255.
7. I interviewed Hunter Eu on 4 August 1993. At the time, he was Deputy Director-General of the National Tourism Bureau, where he had spent most of his career.
8. Pinkaew Laungaramsri, "On the Politics of Nature Conservation in Thailand," *Kyoto Review of Southeast Asia*, 2 October 2002, 18 March 2004, http://kyotoreview.cseas.kyoto-u.ac.jp/issue/issue1/.
9. Two further national parks were added later, for a current total of six.
10. This situation may be changing at Taroko under a new Superintendant who seems more intent on building aboriginal life in than any of his predecessors or colleagues at other parks in Taiwan. My description concerns the situation as it stood in the 1990s.
11. This took place at the park headquarters on 29 May 1991.
12. Interviewed at Kending, 25 July 1993.
13. Construction and Planning Administration, Ministry of the Interior, *A Journey through the National Parks of the Republic of China* (*Zhonghua Minguo Taiwan Diqu Guojia Gongyuan Jianjie*) (1985).
14. *Island of Diversity: Nature Conservation in Taiwan* (Taipei: Council of Agriculture and Department of National Parks, 1992).

15. *Kenting National Park, Republic of China* (Taiwan: Kenting National Park Headquarters, n.d.).
16. The national and provincial governments control almost identical territories, of course. The separate status of the provincial government was a result of the Republic of China's claim to govern all of China from its temporary base in Taiwan. Later in the 1990s the provincial government was dissolved, reflecting both the need to cut the budget and the changed political situation. Full Moon is thus now under national administration. When I interviewed park managers in 1993, however, provincial control was not yet in question.
17. The research proving the benefits of forest showers, I was told, came from Germany. I was not able to confirm this, but the manager told me she knew about the German research through Japan.
18. Julia Adeney Thomas, "'To Become as One Dead': Nature and the Political Subject in Modern Japan," in *The Moral Authority of Nature*, ed. Lorraine Daston and Fernando Vidal (Chicago: University of Chicago Press, 2004), 308–30. See also Conrad Totman, *The Green Archipelago* (Berkeley: University of California Press, 1989).
19. Hisayoshi Mitsuda and Charles Geisler, "Imperiled Parks and Imperiled People: Lessons from Japan's Shiretoko National Park," *Environmental History Review* 16 (1992): 26.
20. See E. Elena Songster, "Reserving Nature for Communist Conservation," paper presented at the Annual Meeting of the Association for Asian Studies, 27–30 March, New York, 2003.
21. Coggins, *The Tiger and the Pangolin*, 15.
22. World Conservation Union (IUCN), *Guidelines for Protected Area Management Categories*. 29 October 2001, 31 March 2004, www.wcmc.org.uk/protected_areas/categories/eng/c2.htm.
23. See UNESCO, *Biosphere Reserves in a Nutshell*. 19 March 2004, 1 April 2004, http://www.unesco.org/mab/nutshell.htm.
24. The United States has also felt the influence of these changes, and has been designating places as biosphere reserves. Nearly all the US reserves were registered as soon as the program began, however, well before the emphasis on sustainable development.
25. Jianguo Liu *et al.*, "A Framework for Evaluating the Effects of Human Factors on Wildlife Habitat: The Case of Giant Pandas," *Conservation Biology* 13, no. 6 (December 1999): 1360–70.
26. Some sites in China do lean toward the Yosemite model, partly to appeal to the international ecotourism market for such places, and partly with influence and funding from international (often US-based) organizations promoting that model.
27. *Xi Shan Qing* (*Feelings on Streams and Mountains*), ed. by Wenqing Huang and Guiyu Zhuang (Taroko: Taroko National Park Administration, 1987), 49.
28. *Xi Shan Qing* (*Feelings on Streams and Mountains*).
29. This discussion relies on John Hay, *Kernels of Energy, Bones of Earth: The Rock in Chinese Art* (New York: China Institute in America, 1985), 99–125.

30. I develop this idea at greater length in Robert P. Weller, "Worship, Teachings, and State Power in China and Taiwan," in *Realms of Freedom in Modern China*, ed. William C. Kirby (Stanford: Stanford University Press, 2004), 285–314.
31. For a recent exception, see Chien Yu, "Three Types of Chinese Deities – Stone, Tree, and Land" (PhD diss., Lancaster University, 1997).
32. Hui-t'ien Feng and Wolfram Eberhard, "On the Folklore of Chekiang: The Tree Temples of Chin-Hua (Chekiang)," in *Studies in Chinese Folklore and Related Essays*, ed. Wolfram Eberhard, vol. 23, Indiana University Folklore Institute Monograph Series (The Hague: Mouton, 1970), 19–24; Yu, "Three Types of Chinese Deities."
33. P. Steven Sangren, *History and Magical Power in a Chinese Community* (Stanford: Stanford University Press, 1987), 141.
34. Pei-yi Wu, "An Ambivalent Pilgrim to T'ai Shan in the Seventeenth Century," in *Pilgrims and Sacred Sites in China*, ed. Susan Naquin and Chün Fang Yü (Berkeley: University of California Press, 1992), 70–1.
35. Translated in Robert M. Gimello, "Chang Shang-Ying on Wu-T'ai Shan," in *Pilgrims and Sacred Sites in China*, ed. Susan Naquin and Yü Chün Fang (Berkeley: University of California Press, 1992), 104.
36. Taiwan is also more open to survey research led by foreign scholars, on which some of these findings are based.
37. Life Away from Home Magazine, ed., *Taiwan Zui Jia Quchu* (*Taiwan's Most Beautiful Places*), 6 vols. (Taipei: Huwai Shenghou Zazhi, 1990). I am grateful to Chien-yu Julia Huang, who served as research assistant for this part of the research. We classified the sites into five types, based on the distributions of the types of categories reported for each: historical landmarks (primarily archaeology, education, history, gardens, and scenery), scenic sites (ocean and river views, waterfalls, camping, walking, scenery), remote wilderness sites (mountain and river views, waterfalls, climbing), temples, and sites with new forms of tourism (amusement parks, camping, tourist farms, gardens, sports facilities, etc.).
38. Overall, private businesses owned about 15 percent of all the sites documented in these guidebooks, and were involved in mixed ownership arrangements for another 15 percent.
39. These sites averaged 302 hectares, less than half the size of the historical sites (averaging 697 hectares) and far smaller than the purely scenic or remote sites (typically several thousand hectares). Travel times to both temples and these new tourism sites averaged 1.2 hours, compared to 2.2 hours for scenic sites and 2.7 hours for remote ones.
40. The averages were 1915 for temples, and 1950 for historical landmarks.
41. I am grateful to my two field assistants for this portion of the project, Chien-yu Julia Huang and Liu Yicheng. The interviews took place in July 1993.
42. Of the rest, about half were groups of friends, typically about ten people, and the other half split between school groups and groups of co-workers (often 100 or more people).
43. One side effect of this search for novelty is that the smaller parks tend to come and go fairly quickly. Once the novelty wears off, there is little left to draw customers. Some appeared to be little more than attempts to keep land

tax rates low by running a business on land that was really just being held for speculation. Taiwan's land tax system, with roots in Sun Yat-sen's interest in Henry George, is intended to discourage speculation by putting prohibitive taxes on unused land.

44. For a description of this earlier incarnation of the place, then called Xiaoyao You, see Stevan Harrell, "Playing in the Valley: A Metonym of Modernization in Taiwan," in *Cultural Change in Postwar Taiwan*, ed. Stevan Harrell and Chün-chieh Huang (Boulder, CO: Westview, 1994), 161–83.
45. Ron Gluckman, *Getting to the Top*. 24 February 2003, 3 May 2004, http://www.gluckman.com/Emei.html.
46. Adam Yuet Chau, *Miraculous Response: Doing Popular Religion in Contemporary China* (Stanford: Stanford University Press, in press).
47. I have ignored the relations between ethnic and nature tourism here, even though they are quite important in both China and Taiwan. The topic is too large to take on here, and deserves its own book.
48. Most of the information on Hainan tourism comes from Chris Cockel, "Tourism as a Development Solution or a Development Disaster: The Case Study of Hainan Island, South China" (PhD diss., School of Oriental and African Studies, 1999).

5 Garbage wars and spiritual environments

On the night of 5 May 1990, about a hundred local residents gathered in a community temple in the Houjing neighborhood of Gaoxiong, Taiwan's second-largest city. It was the eve before a referendum on the construction of a new naphtha cracker – a kind of light oil refinery – and people had come to ask the advice of Shen Nong, an agricultural god. They offered incense to the god, and then performed the simplest form of divination by throwing a pair of crescent-shaped "moonblocks" (H: *poe*) to answer their question: should they vote to oppose construction no matter what kind of compensation the government offered? "Yes," came the reply. To make sure, they threw the moonblocks again, with the same result. Against all odds, in fact, people performed this divination eleven times in a row, and each time the answer was "yes."

Word spread about this remarkable set of divinations, and the crowd quickly grew. Every newcomer added more sticks of incense to the temple's incense pot, to show respect for the god. The smoke and smell grew with the crowd, until the incense in the pot suddenly erupted into a roaring fire. People take this to indicate a powerful manifestation of the deity, and it brought even more residents to the temple. From within the crowd, an old woman began to shake and speak wildly. She had been possessed by Guanyin, a bodhisattva associated with mercy and nurturance. Pulling the crowd's attention, the deity-woman chanted that Houjing would be doomed if the naphtha cracker were built.

The next day the community voted to oppose construction and not to compromise. Observers were astonished – recent national polls had shown over 80 percent of people in favor of construction, and local sentiment held that the government would not have agreed to the referendum unless they were sure of victory. Many people credited the religious events of the night before with swaying opinions against construction.[1] The government decided to build the naphtha cracker anyway, but these events and many other protest activities helped get guarantees of improved pollution controls and the promise of NT$ 1.5 billion (about US$ 60 million) for a foundation to benefit the neighborhood.

There had been earlier religious interventions as well, along with many other mobilizations of local social and cultural ties. The temple scene on the eve of the referendum was simply the final act in a drama that played out for well over three years, centering around a long blockade of one of the gates to the industrial compound where the new factory would be sited. Religion is not always important in Taiwanese environmental protest, but as one of the few kinds of ties that could unite a community, it has a powerful organizing potential.

Typically, however, temples organize only on a very local scale. Taiwanese (and Chinese) worship mostly takes place in homes and in local community temples. Sometimes these temples honor deities who are only known locally; others worship famous deities with titles granted by past emperors. Either way, though, the temples themselves are largely independent from each other. At most they form small networks of daughter temples that branched off from an older temple. Even then, senior temples have no direct control over junior ones. Local committees run the temples, hiring priests as needed. Temples become successful not so much because they house a god enfeoffed by the emperor, but because of stories about their local miracles. When the god where I lived saved soldiers from exploding bombs during the Second World War, for instance, he only warned the locals.

When temples become involved in the environmental movement, they retain this sort of localism. When Guanyin appeared before the referendum, she did not speak against pollution in general. She spoke instead about the defense of the neighborhood, and this typifies most godly interventions – they are interested in the environment only to benefit the human population within their territory. There are echoes here of the anthropocosmic ideas I have discussed earlier, and of the localism inherent in *fengshui* or the worship of extraordinary stones and trees.

After I had interviewed various participants in these Houjing events, I learned that an academic friend, himself active in national-level environmentalism, had suggested to the organizers that their use of religion was inappropriate. To some extent, modern urban intellectuals may be uncomfortable with the village religion of their childhoods. More importantly, however, local temple worship does not mesh with their more biocentric environmentalism. People like my friend value the environment for its own sake. This leads them to a universalism at loggerheads with the purely local interests of the temples and their deities, and to a biocentrism at odds with this very human-centered religion.

I will return below in more detail to specific case studies of local and national environmental action, but I began with this anecdote because it raises two very general questions. First, in what ways do people's understandings of nature influence when and how they take environmental action? What are the cultural and social resources that shape their behavior? Second, as the story implies, the broad rubric of "environmental action" can lump together some very different understandings of the relationship between humanity and nature. In particular, the cases I will present here suggest that the main ideas powering grassroots demonstrations are localist and human-centered, while national and international organizations tend toward a much more thoroughly global and universalist environmental discourse. This is true in both Taiwan and China, in spite of the deep political differences that shape the possibilities for protest in each place.

Garbage wars and dead crabs: local protest

I will start with the most local levels of protest, first in Taiwan and then in China. Unlike the larger forms of environmental organization (which I take up later in the chapter), local protest organizations tend to be ephemeral and ad hoc. They address a particular issue, and usually dissolve once the issue passes.

Taiwan

Taiwan began to develop an environmental movement even before the state of emergency was lifted in 1987. Both local environmental protest and a few environmental nongovernmental organizations (NGOs) date back to about the late 1970s. Any kind of protest carried a certain political risk at that time, but people would still sometimes try it because of a combination of circumstances. First, Taiwan's pollution problems became increasingly severe. When people demonstrated, they usually claimed major forms of damage like noxious smoke that forced school evacuation or poisoned water that wiped out rice crops. Some people in Houjing claimed that existing refineries leaked so much oil that their tap water would ignite at the touch of a match. Second, the government legitimized environmental concerns through activities like the upgrading of the Environmental Protection Agency to Cabinet status and founding the national parks during the 1980s. Protest against environmental abuse thus became safer than protest aimed more directly at political or economic issues. Finally, Taiwan's politics had relaxed slightly even before the major changes of 1987.

A trickle of local demonstrations grew through the 1980s, and developed rapidly after a local movement successfully prevented Dupont from building a titanium dioxide plant in 1986.[2] This successful resistance to a multinational giant became a model to other movements. When the state of emergency was finally lifted, and when it became much easier for national groups to organize, Taiwan saw a rapid boom in numbers of both protests and environmental NGOs. Companies and the government paid over NT$ 12 billion (about US$ 500 million) in environmental compensation just from 1988 to 1990.[3]

Among the thousands of local protests that occurred over the last two decades of the twentieth century, roughly a third involved battles over garbage dumps.[4] Very little research has been reported on what Taiwanese newspapers dubbed the "garbage wars," even though this was by far the most common reason for protest. Field research among piles of garbage in a subtropical climate is not very appealing, but I was drawn to the topic by a particularly spectacular garbage war in Sanxia during the early summer of 1991.[5]

Sanxia's garbage made headlines in May, when the newspapers reported that the current dump had been shut down by local villagers. This dump had been created as a short-term solution to the town's solid waste problem while a better site was found. Thirteen years had gone by, though, with no new site. The county government had proposed placing a regional sanitary landfill high in Sanxia's mountains, but the elected county assembly had just voted it down. The blockade of the old dump began the same day, and garbage began to pile up in the hot and humid streets.

The township head desperately tried to get neighboring towns to take the garbage. The Tucheng government and later the Yingge government, Sanxia's closest neighbors, agreed. In both cases, though, local people refused to take in other people's trash, and they blockaded their own dumps until the deal fell through. Some angry residents of Sanxia began dumping their garbage in front of the township head's house, sometimes setting it on fire first.[6]

Expecting to find an organized village community protesting ill-treatment by the government, I headed out to Sanxia and found something quite different. Unable to get any response from the township government – they were ignoring their phones – I went out to the village of Tianfu to see the old dump. I had assumed this would be the center of some excitement, but instead I found almost nobody. The dump itself was just mountains of garbage, directly abutting a stream that flowed into the water supply for the main town of Sanxia and ultimately for Taipei's western suburbs. It was hot, and smelled, and flies buzzed all around. I did not stay long.

The "blockade" itself was unmanned. It consisted of a banner saying they refused to accept any more garbage, and two wrecked cars they had managed to pile on top of each other, blocking the dirt access road to the dump. This was my first clue that I had misunderstood the dynamics. After all, the township government could have cleared the old cars away in moments, using the tractor already working in the dump. Instead, this undefended blockade was respected, even as it caused chaos on the streets of the town.

Eventually, a friend managed to get the secret personal phone number of the township head, Liu Wenxiu, who agreed to see me. There were about a dozen people gathered in his office when I got there, and garbage was the only item on the agenda. To my surprise, this inner circle included Tianfu's village head, the man apparently behind the blockade. As they explained the history for me, I began to understand why he seemed so friendly with Liu Wenxiu. Liu supported the idea of a regional dump, but Sanxia's two representatives in the county assembly (Lin Muzong and Wang Mingli) had led the fight to kill it. Sanxia has a long history of two warring political factions; Liu was in one faction and the two representatives were in the other.

This particular battle dated back a year earlier, when the county assembly first considered the regional landfill. The two representatives had got the motion tabled at that point, and also organized a protest meeting in Sanxia.[7] At the protest – attended mostly by local political leaders and reporters – people complained about the numbers of outside garbage trucks that would roar through town. They said Sanxia would account for less than 10 percent of the garbage, but have to accept all the pollution, in exchange for inadequate compensation. Most of their bile, though, concerned a boondoggle trip to visit European sanitary landfills, paid for by the county but for the benefit of the township. They had allowed Liu Wenxiu to organize the trip, and he had taken only his own faction friends. This was the sort of patronage on which Taiwanese factions are based, and through which township heads stay in power.[8]

The next phase of the battle took place as I sat there. Liu Wenxiu took a phone call, and suddenly took off, with his entourage in tow, and me in his wake. It turned out that the garbage trucks had been making their rounds through the town even as we were speaking. Unable to use a landfill, they dumped their huge loads by the major river bed – hundreds of tons of garbage. At the time this was a construction site for a new highway. Liu claimed it was legal to dump there because the government had taken the land by eminent domain. He also seemed pleased at the fury of the man whose land abutted the site – a cousin of one of the county assembly representatives who bore the brunt of his anger.

A few days later the old dump caught fire. Some people suspected arson, while others pointed out that gigantic heaps of festering garbage often burst into spontaneous flames in Taiwan's heat. The fire department never came, either because they can do little against such fires, or because the township head told them not to, depending on which faction was telling the story. In the end they compromised. A new sanitary landfill was built in the mountains, but only for use by the township itself.

This was thus not a village protesting against state-sponsored pollution of its land, air, and water. It was one local faction (with the two assembly representatives) at war with another faction (with the township head and the Tianfu village head), using garbage dumps as the weapon. That is why the villagers of Tianfu seemed so unconcerned, and why there was no need to defend the blockade. The villagers disliked the dump, I was told when I finally found some, but this was never really their fight.

This local political dynamic turned out to typify every "garbage war" I examined in detail, although it rarely played a decisive role in other forms of environmental protest. The southern town of Caodun, for example, had played out a similar drama in 1990, but involving two township governments instead of two factions within one township. Caodun's dump burned its garbage every night in open fires. They were just at the edge of the township, and the stench and smoke blew into the neighboring township of Wufeng. Officials in Wufeng had no authority over Caodun, and county officials did nothing. Finally, the chairman of Wufeng's township assembly and several of the representatives took a surveyor to the dump, and declared that it had encroached over the border. With this as justification, they blockaded the access road by digging a ditch with a backhoe, leaving just enough room for small farm vehicles to pass, but not garbage trucks. Caodun township officials quickly arrived, and an angry and unresolved argument followed. In this case, the blockade forced the county government that supervised both townships to take action, and they closed the Caodun dump two weeks later. They buried the remaining garbage with a thin cap of soil, although much had already risen to the surface when I visited in 1992.

Garbage protests nearly always center around the most local politics, even though other forms of environmental action rarely do. One reason for this is that solid waste disposal does not threaten national economic strategy the way protests against nuclear power plants, light oil refineries, or multinational chemical firms do. Taiwan's garbage problems were intractable by the early 1990s – population density was very high, consumption had been increasing rapidly, and the dreadful state of most existing dumps at that time encouraged strong opposition to new landfills from the local population. Higher levels of government – even just county governments, as we saw in both the Sanxia and Caodun cases – tended to dither until the crisis blew up. The political costs were high and the rewards few. On the other hand, garbage collection is an inevitable issue at the most local level. It is one of those services that can quickly put people out of office if it works badly. Just as importantly in the Taiwanese context, it is one of the flows of patronage – jobs, rents for dump sites, compensation payments, and occasional boondoggles to Europe – through which the local factions have long functioned.

For all sides in these arguments, the primary concern is for the quality of human life: removing garbage, keeping drinking water safe, finding appropriate levels of compensation. No one in these garbage wars discussed other kinds of long-term solutions, like reducing consumption or increasing recycling. In this, and in the inherent localism of everyone's goals – no one wants any part of anyone else's garbage – these actions are consistent with a view of the environment as a place in which humans are a privileged part of the whole.

When we move away from garbage wars to disputes about industrial pollution, the most local levels of politics decline in importance. Little patronage is at stake in most such disputes. In addition, nearly all factions in all towns were affiliated with the ruling GMD until after 1987, when it became legal to organize an opposition party. None of them thus had an interest in going against what they perceived to be the interests of higher levels of government. Instead of relying primarily on factions, other kinds of local ties often came into play, including religion, kinship, and sometimes even underworld organizations. Outside environmental organizations are also far more likely to add their expertise in industrial actions than in garbage wars, especially for issues of nuclear power or very large industry.

The Houjing naphtha cracker with which I began this chapter is a good example. They were protesting against China Petrochemical, a company directly owned by the central government. Local politicians mostly kept their heads down, and factions became involved only indirectly, through their ties to other kinds of organizations. The local people learned of plans to build the new naphtha cracker from the newspapers in June 1987. There had been no prior consultation. A couple of local small businessmen organized a petition to the government, but it received no response. Within a month they had given up pursuing relatively passive and legal channels, and set up a blockade of one of the gates to the existing refinery compound.

When a worker drove a truck into the demonstrators in August, hundreds of people traveled to Taipei to demonstrate against construction, and to present another petition. It was at this point that one of the community temples first became openly involved, when the temple committee offered to set up a life insurance fund of NT$ 2 million for anyone killed during the demonstrations. It made for good publicity, and they knew it was very unlikely that they would actually ever have to pay.

There was another, somewhat smaller protest trip to Taipei in October, which became famous for blocking the entrance to the Executive Yuan – the first time this had ever happened. By around this time, several developments further complicated the situation. First, workers at the existing China Petrochemical refineries (some of which dated back to the Japanese period) became increasingly unhappy about the protests. Second, national and regional environmental groups (Taiwan Greenpeace, the Taiwan Environmental Protection Union, and others) began to get involved.

The next major religious intervention came in December, when the police removed the blockade of the gate in the middle of the night. The protest organizers used a religious parade to reinstate it, because religious parade permits are granted almost automatically, while a protest parade permit seemed highly unlikely. In an event the newspaper dubbed the Battle of the Coffins, they carried coffins and funeral wreaths to be set up at the factory gate, thus recreating the blockade. The excuse was that they were commemorating a man who had recently immolated himself in Taipei, although the issue had nothing to do with this protest. Instead of writing the dead man's name on the wreaths, though, they wrote in the names of top factory managers. They also brought along the temple's performing martial arts troupe. These are standard parts of religious parades, especially in southern Taiwan, but they involve real weapons and young men trained in their use. The idea was to take advantage of the respect for funeral symbolism, upset the factory managers, and intimidate the police – a thousand of whom were waiting at the factory gate. It worked, and the blockade was back up.

By agreement with the police, they removed the coffins in January 1988, but the banner remained up. Just as with the Sanxia garbage dump, that sufficed. The blockade remained up for more than two more years. The protests became quieter, except on a few occasions where something unusual happened to upset the balance – after a refinery worker beat and robbed one of the protest leaders, or several times after unusual emissions from the existing refineries. As often happens in long actions, the protesters split into "doves" who were willing to compromise and "hawks" who were not.

With the doves looking stronger, the government agreed to the referendum in May 1990. This was the occasion for the scene in the temple that I described at the beginning of this chapter. It had also led to what people dubbed the "night of the gangsters." Both newspapers and some informants said that the company had hired gangsters in the days and nights before the referendum to intimidate protest leaders and to bribe ordinary residents. There was some speculation that this offended enough people to have the reverse of its intended effect during the vote.

I asked one of the top protest organizers how he felt about the intervention of gangsters. Gangsters cost money, of course, and China Petrochemical had far more of that than the protesters. To my surprise, he brushed this off. He said that the company hired a lot of gangsters at the beginning. These were local, small gangsters, not the big organized crime bosses – the people locally called "street corner bosses" (H: *kak-thau*). They had wrecked his business office. Yet, he explained, these are local people. He had gone to school with them and served in the army with them. Thus the protesters could draw on local loyalties and personal ties to neutralize this threat. He solved the problem, he told me, just by going to talk to them.[9] Little work has been done on the Taiwanese underworld, for obvious reasons, but this is consistent with what we know of the integration of local gangster groups into society.[10] This is quite a different form of social capital from temples or lineages, but important all the same.

The hawk position won the referendum, but the government ignored the results. The protesters finally lifted the blockade in November 1990, after 1,202 days. In addition to getting the promise of a very large compensation package, the long protest also led to a permanent local branch of the Taiwan Environmental Protection Union, and became a model for later demonstrations.

Just as in the garbage wars, this protest relied on fundamentally local forms of social organization – temples, township-based factions, even neighborhood gangsters. These forms receive support from the cultural emphasis on personal connections, kinship, and localist religious practice. The Houjing case also showed an extremely common evolution, where people first try legal mechanisms like petitions, but receive little response. They follow this with extra-legal mechanisms like street marches and especially long-term blockades. In the vast majority of cases, they also ultimately settle for some form of financial compensation.

Let me give a couple of additional quick examples in support of these patterns. Dalinpu and Hongmaogang are small neighborhoods that sit together like an island in a sea of heavy industry in Gaoxiong. Protesters there were unhappy at what they considered high pollution levels, and upset that at least one of the areas would have to be resettled elsewhere to make room for industrial expansion. There were intermittent protests and petitions during 1988 and 1989. At that time they did not have support from the local community temple. Like most such temples, wealthy and powerful people controlled the committee, and they were more sympathetic to the government and factories than to the protesters.

This still did not prevent the protesters from using the temple. Any worshipers can borrow a god's image from the temple – they need the god's permission (achieved through divination), but not the temple committee's. Protest organizers borrowed one of the images and placed it in the local police station, "just to keep everybody honest," they told me. Laughing, they said the police prayed to the image for winning numbers in an illegal lottery.

The second use of the temple was in 1992, when the organizers planned to block the main gate to a Taipower compound in an angry demonstration. Again they went to the temple to borrow a god image. They threw moonblocks to ask the god if he was willing to accompany them in their protest. The answer was yes, and the incense pot burst into flame, just as in Houjing. The protest turned violent, although the god went back to the temple first. About sixty people were hurt, the organizers told me, and seven were arrested, mostly for throwing rocks at the police as they chased everyone back toward the temple. This event changed the minds of the temple committee, which agreed to bail everyone out. I asked about gangsters here, too, and was again told that it was not such a great problem: "They have their gangsters and we have our gangsters."

Let me turn to Sanxia's Jialong plastic pellet factory as the final case. This was primarily a village-level action, although it also brought in some outside support. The local people claimed that the factory had polluted the ground water, causing problems for their rice crop and a local fishing pond, and giving their well water a bad smell. They asked the county office of the Environmental Protection Agency (EPA) to investigate, and that the factory install piped water for them. The EPA investigated, but found no serious problem. More small demonstrations followed. After a few weeks, they managed to connect to the Taiwan Environmental Protection Union, which tested the water independently and found more serious problems. The factory closed temporarily, only to be met with a blockade after it tried to reopen. The blockade continued for six months, with both sides asking for government intervention, but no significant action. The factory, in a typical rhetorical move, accused the villagers of just wanting to squeeze compensation money out of them; the villagers threatened to shut the factory down one way or another. The blockade was finally removed by force, but the factory had not reopened by the time of my fieldwork. In this case very few villagers were employed by the factory, and it was not difficult to mobilize village neighborhood ties for the protests. There was also the typical progression from petition to blockade, although they never got to compensation. The alternative in some cases, especially for factories based on cheap labor like this one, was to move the operation to the mainland. Finally, this case also shows the recalcitrant and indecisive role of the environmental protection bureaucracy, which was caught between conflicting claims and different levels of government.

These cases share some fundamental features, most of which turn out to be important in China, too. First, there is a repeated pattern of movement from petitions to blockades to compensation. Cross-culturally, the move from legal, peaceful means of protest to extra-legal ones is no surprise. The specific technique of blockading is more unusual, however, because it tends to be granted a kind of cultural legitimacy by both sides in Taiwan and China. That is why some blockades remain up for months, or even years, with no need for much more than a banner and a guard or two.

Second, different levels of government act in different ways according to the case. This has been most clear with the involvement of township-level government in Taiwan only in garbage wars. The plastic pellet factory case also suggests the complex role that the environmental protection bureaucracy plays, often with conflicting pressures from the central government to protect the environment without challenging economic interests. We will see this kind of dynamic again in China.

Third, although national NGOs sometimes became involved, the predominant organizational resources were inherently local. None of the ties that form the core of these protests – temples, lineages, neighborhoods, or even local gangster groups – extend beyond the county level, and most are limited to the township or village.[11] Furthermore, the urban elites who run the NGOs tend to dislike these forms of organization. This is partly because the NGOs have no natural ties to them, but most importantly because of the differences they imply in the view of nature. In contrast to the hopes of the universalistic and biocentric NGO elites, all of these local forms of organization work to serve only their particular locality, with a primary emphasis on human welfare. Temple religion shows this most clearly. When deities intercede on behalf of the environment, it is expressly for the purposes of protecting the humans or the gods themselves. One temple, I was told, decided to join a protest against water pollution only when they realized that the god would have to be in contact with this water during an annual festival. This is not an image of humans in fundamental conflict with nature. Instead, it is consistent with earlier Chinese views of an anthropocosmic universe, where human benefit is desirable, but only as part of a larger system of order.

China

The obvious political differences between Taiwan and China mean that grassroots environmental protest takes different forms. There are many fewer tactical alliances between national NGOs and local protests in

China, because of the dangerous political consequences of organizing protest at anything above the most local level. With far less press coverage of protests, China has also not seen the development of "model" protests that inspire others, the way the anti-Dupont movement, or later Houjing's naphtha cracker protest did in Taiwan. These features also mean that it is far harder for us to document environmental protest in China, both qualitatively and quantitatively, than in Taiwan.

Nevertheless, we know that local protest over environmental conditions occurs all over China, often peacefully through letters or petitions to officials, sometimes extra-legally with street protests or blockades, and occasionally violently. The growth in environmental protest has to do with China's increasingly awful environmental conditions, of course, although that is not a sufficient condition – many areas have had serious environmental problems for decades, but protest developed only more recently. In fact, protest of all kinds has increased in China, in part because the government has created more open space for it. In some cases, these protests may indicate a decline in political control, but more generally they show a government willing to accept popular feedback in this form, as long as it remains local and not threatening to the fundamental political structure.[12] As long as protests remain easy to control, they provide a valuable source of information for a government unwilling to adopt fully democratic mechanisms, but recognizing that a top-down system needs some further ways of achieving good governance at local levels. In that sense, they are like the village-level elections that now exist everywhere in China. They stem less from any long-term commitment to procedural democracy than from a need to control corrupt officials locally.

In some ways this resembles the situation in Taiwan around 1980, when sporadic environmental demonstrations began to occur around the island, but no larger forms of protest organization were possible. Neither government would tolerate any form of protest or political organization that might challenge its control, but both made some room for environmental protest as a way of addressing local problems. On the other hand, one important difference is that the Chinese government today has a more elaborated environmental bureaucracy, with more established mechanisms for legal protest, like writing letters to environmental protection bureaus or calling environmental hotlines. In that sense it resembles the current situation in Taiwan more than the situation around 1980.

Authoritarian control in both its current Chinese and earlier Taiwanese versions has left open space for local and informal social ties. In Taiwan before 1987, that is why things like temples and lineages remained so salient – as long as they remained local and politically quiescent, the government allowed them to continue. China's Cultural Revolution period in particular brought a much stronger attempt to remove all social forms beyond the state itself. Even that never fully succeeded, however, and the period since then has seen a regrowth of local, apolitical forms of society that the state permits, including temples and lineages in some areas.

In a way reminiscent of the situation with nature parks, as I discussed in the previous chapter, local environmental protests in China and Taiwan look more like each other than one might initially expect. This is especially true in the social and cultural resources on which they draw. The research base is much thinner for China, but let me still illustrate the point with some examples.

China's garbage protests have not been nearly as widespread or pressing as Taiwan's, but they do occur. In July 1997, for instance, several hundred residents of Beijing's Haidian district blockaded the access road to a local dump with cars and bicycles. They unfurled banners demanding closure of the dump. They claimed that it was polluting their air and groundwater, and making people sick. Residents said they were never informed that a garbage dump was being built before it opened a few months earlier.[13] They had petitioned to the Beijing Environmental Protection Bureau in June, but inaction had led to this more forceful protest. I have no further information on this particular protest, which makes it impossible to compare the political dynamics with Taiwan. Nevertheless, the pattern here strongly recalls the common Taiwan evolution from petition to blockade. This one was allowed to remain up at least for several days, and a number of garbage trucks had been forced to turn around. As in Taiwan, the government seemed to respect blockade as an appropriate form of protest.

A second case shows the complex local political dynamics more clearly. This one comes from a rural county under the jurisdiction of Anqing city, in southern Anhui Province. I ran into this during a broader study of pollution, health, and environmental attitudes in the region, and it was the only legal case involving the environment that turned up in that project.[14] China had passed a series of laws and regulations concerning the environment during the 1990s, which created at least the theoretical possibility of using the law to deal with polluters directly. More generally, the government was also campaigning broadly at this time to broaden knowledge of the legal system. Like their greater lenience toward demonstrations, this probably indicated the hope of building a new mechanism for local feedback and control, rather than a dedication to rule of law. People have used lawsuits with increasing frequency all around China, although they remain a relatively unusual means of approaching environmental problems.

In this case the plaintiff was a man named Gao, who had contracted about 10,000 mu of a lake in one of Anqing's rural counties in 1998. He was raising crabs. In 1999 he claimed that the water was severely polluted by leakage from a nearby factory that processed waste oil from one of urban Anqing's refineries. He put his personal losses at RMB 600,000 (roughly US$ 75,000), in addition to the public losses from the pollution flowing down into the Yangzi River. He had the county Environmental Protection Bureau test the water in late June of that year. Their test in fact showed somewhat elevated levels of oil. Nevertheless, they concluded that no harm had been done, and they refused to act. This is hardly unusual, because the local environmental bureaucracy usually must respect the county government's need to show economic growth. Just like several of the Taiwan cases, they took no action.

Mr. Gao argued that most of the pollution had dissipated by the time of the test, and that their sample was taken from very deep water. Had they tested promptly and properly, he claimed, the pollution levels would have been much higher. Frustrated at the local level, he pushed his complaint further. First he went over the heads of the county bureaucrats to their superiors in the municipal Environmental Protection Bureau. He also petitioned other offices in the municipal government. In his letter, he blamed the negative decision at the local level on the fact that the factory pays the county RMB 800,000 (roughly US$ 100,000) in taxes each year. This was also the point when he sued the county-level Environmental Protection Bureau (EPB) in court. Probably under his leadership, the local village also submitted a petition complaining about the smell from the factory, and lamenting the way it turned their seedlings and their mountain streams black. They asked for the factory to be closed and for RMB 1,000 in compensation for each villager. There are close to one hundred signatures, probably accounting for most of the household heads in this village of about three hundred people.

None of these documents speaks about the needs of the environment in the abstract. They are couched instead in the language of human gains and losses, of economics, politics, and law. Gao himself sometimes used a very traditional language for this. His petition to the head of the municipal Environmental Protection Bureau begins:

> Amidst all your busy duties, receiving this report undoubtedly just adds to your troubles. Yet we foolish subjects (*yumin*) have no choice but presumptuously to submit this letter. From ancient times "heaven is high and the emperor is far away," but why is the nationally promulgated Environmental Protection Law never properly enforced in my home town? The point of this "wasted talk and trifling speech" is to beg the bureau chief to take seriously what your foolish subject has reported here.

Gao goes on to spell out his losses in detail, and to imply that the law has been subverted by economic interests at the county level. In spite of his language that recalls a late imperial subject addressing a magistrate, he speaks primarily as an unhappy entrepreneur, just as the village petition speaks for unhappy farmers. This is an environmentalism in a way that resonates with older Chinese anthropocosmic views and with a globalized (and nationalized) language of economic progress, but it has few ties to the broader international or elite environmental discourse.

Unfortunately, the case was not resolved when our project ended. Nevertheless, even unclosed it illustrates many of the dynamics that typify environmental policy on the ground: a local environmental protection bureaucracy closely tied to the economic interests of the county government, some difference of interest between different levels of government, and the overwhelming importance of purely political mechanisms like petitions. There is no monolithic state here: we have villagers supporting an outsider businessman, the local environmental bureaucracy supporting a factory, a rural factory tied to an urban factory, and a rural Environmental Protection Bureau opposed to the higher-level Bureau.

This is consistent with the findings of recent research in Sichuan, showing the conflictual results of a local government promoting industrial growth while the central government demands environmental cleanup.[15] It is also consistent with studies of administrative lawsuits generally in China, where plaintiffs use a full range of political options – lawsuits, appeals to higher levels, personal connections, threats of collective action – in the hopes of finding an angle into the system that will let them accomplish their goals.[16] This environmental case is fundamentally similar, including its primary focus on economic welfare, not the environment for its own sake.

One final case from China helps to reveal a social and cultural dynamic very like Taiwan's. This was a village in Gansu, studied by the anthropologist Jun Jing, which had been in a long dispute with a large province-run fertilizer factory over pollution of the Yellow River that affected drinking water for humans and animals and damaged crops.[17] Jing shows that local lineage and temple ties lay at the heart of the protest, even though the names on the documents were those of political leaders. The Kong lineage, tracing its ancestry to Confucius himself, accounted for 85 percent of the population. Like all lineages with a strong institutional base, their formal activities had been shut down during the Cultural Revolution. By 1991, however, they had reconstructed their ancestral hall, and lineage members dominated all the important local political positions.

The temples entered into the protests especially in the 1980s. This was the period when China's birth control campaign was greatly limiting births, and the local people became especially concerned over high rates of stillbirths and birth defects, which they blamed on pollution from the fertilizer factory. It is no coincidence that they rebuilt a set of four temples dedicated to fertility goddesses at just this time. The temples had been razed during the Cultural Revolution. This became the major issue in protests against the factory at the time. The village Party Secretary, who led some of the protests, did not condone "feudal superstitions" like the worship of fertility goddesses. Jing reports, though, that he had been seen taking offerings from the temple late at night, as part of a ritual attempt to enhance the health of his children.

When the villagers protested the factory during this period, they phrased the issue primarily in these terms of fertility and lineage. They demanded safe drinking water to ensure their ability to reproduce, or that factory officials and their children drink bottles of contaminated water from the river. As in every case of local protest I have examined, this is more an anti-pollution movement than an environmentalist one. Its goals concentrate on human benefit. Yet it would be misleading to stop there, without putting people's motives into a broader cultural and historical context. Lineage and temple shape people's actions just as much as pure economic interest.[18] As in Taiwan, these ties survived in part because they more successfully resisted authoritarian political control that left no room for social organizations with more contemporary origins. By surviving, though, they also shaped people's desires and understandings.

General features of local protest

In spite of their very different histories of capitalism and communism, some important economic similarities push the Chinese and Taiwanese cases to resemble each other in many ways. Chinese industry, and much of its pollution, had long been state-owned. Even since the economic reforms, with the rise of private entrepreneurs, most larger businesses must maintain very close ties to government officials. Taiwan, in contrast, had always allowed for free market business. Yet Taiwan also had significant amounts of state-owned industry, including some of the most polluting sectors, like Houjing's oil refining. Big business there too tended to retain close ties to the state, and state policy was insistently pro-industry until recently. That is one reason why Taiwan before 1987 and China today have similar patterns of protest.

There are also important differences, of course, most of which result from Taiwan's democratization. National-level NGOs in Taiwan found it politically safe to support local movements only in the late 1980s, when the media also finally became free enough to play a more important role.

In China, however, these kinds of alliances are rare, because the political consequences remain severe. The same is true of alliances among grassroots protest groups that might try to organize on any scale beyond the local. China has opened much more space for local protest, but absolutely not for anything on a larger scale.

Beyond this, however, both places show similar patterns. I will take up the role of the state more thoroughly in the following chapter, but here we can already see how different levels of the state may act on different interests, leading to varying sorts of behavior. The environmental protection bureaucracy tended to be quiet in both cases – frequently called upon but rarely taking decisive action. This happened, for instance, in the Taiwanese plastic pellet factory, where the EPA did nothing until after independent testing by an NGO. The local EPB also did nothing in Gao's crab dispute in China, until he appealed to higher levels. This is predictable as long as environmental protection bureaucracies have little independent power, and government priorities remain geared toward economic growth. Local levels of government in general, in both China and Taiwan, tend to stay out of local environmental disputes, especially where larger industries are involved. They generally have little clout, and prefer to leave these problems for higher levels. The big exceptions here are Taiwan's garbage wars – the only frequent case where the local government does have some control, and where its patronage base could be threatened.

The general absence of local political groups helps open more space for other kinds of social ties in organizing these movements. While factions dominated Sanxia's garbage war because of the local political implications of landfills, in all the other cases we can see some combination of ties through neighborhood, temple, lineage, and occasionally local gangsters. These ties are even more important given the authoritarian history of both China and Taiwan. These more traditional-looking relationships survived beneath the notice of the state, while other kinds of organization (NGOs or unions, for example) had no space to develop independently. Villagers had few other ties on which to draw.

Both China and Taiwan also seem to share a pattern where they begin with relatively peaceful and legally sanctioned means of protest – writing letters to environmental officials or submitting petitions to local government. In both cases, these actions rarely led to any concrete results.[19] People probably continue to indulge in them because they create a moral justification for the extra-legal protests that often follow. This can take many forms, from the usual street marches and rallies outside government offices to more creative events like Houjing's use of a militarized religious parade or a mock funeral.

The most striking such mechanism is the blockade, which occurs regularly in both Taiwan and China, and seems much more common than in other parts of the world. Blockades are remarkable in part because governments often allow them to continue for long periods. There seems to be a kind of moral economy, where both sides accept this as a legitimate form of protest. That is why just a banner often suffices, with the addition of a guard or two for a very large and inflammatory case like Houjing. The reasons behind this need more research, but the phenomenon suggests that there may be a greater willingness to blur distinctions of public and private property than in some other parts of the world.

Most of these demonstrations finally achieve a resolution that involves compensation payments. Compensation inevitably brings up moral issues. Companies regularly accuse demonstrators of protesting simply out of greed. For that reason, protesting groups almost never begin by raising issues of compensation. Instead, they argue about the welfare of their children and the quality of their lives and livelihoods. This also helps us understand why temples and lineages so often play important roles. Both provide moral justifications in addition to their significant organizational (and sometimes financial) resources. Neither temple nor lineage deals directly with the environment, but both imply certain relationships between humans and nature. Lineages embody values of filial piety and proper intergenerational relationships, but these also require creation and preservation of an ancestral estate that would ideally last as long as the lineage – forever, or so people hope.

This is not an ideal of nature for its own sake, but it does require a long-term view of nature that can easily oppose pollution. Local temple religion similarly puts human interests and morality at its core, but also easily reads polluting factories as an enemy of those things. These are hardly environmentalist philosophies, and they have not served well for issues like endangered species protection, where China has long had a poor record. Yet they also will not justify a rapacious approach to the environment, and place a focus on the long-term viability of the local ecosystem – seen as a unit focused on its human population.

Institutionalizing environmentalism

Environmental activism extends far beyond grassroots protest. Its other main wing consists of standing institutions dedicated to environmental issues – groups usually discussed as a subset of the broader set of nongovernmental or nonprofit organizations. These groups may became involved in protests, but most also have other kinds of activities and some never protest at all. They might organize recycling drives, sponsor flea markets to promote reuse of old goods (a new idea in China and Taiwan), or encourage people to bring their own chopsticks and cups to restaurants to reduce the use of disposable ones. Some create nature walks for children, sponsor lectures and debates, or lobby the government. Unlike the grassroots groups, which tend to be temporary, ad hoc, and focused around a specific goal, these groups attempt to create a permanent structure to promote long-term goals.

NGOs in general have increased rapidly around the world since the 1980s, and both Taiwan and China have been part of this growth. Before Taiwan's democratization, the legal framework for NGOs was essentially corporatist: each social sector was allowed one organization, which received a monopoly as representative of that sector in return for political loyalty. Such groups could still lobby and bargain for the benefit of their members, but they could act only within strictly controlled political parameters. All of this changed there after 1987, when Taiwan opened up much more space for NGOs. They allowed organizations to exist legally without registering, and no longer put limits on numbers of organizations. Most of the registration procedures were to allow donors to receive tax benefits, and they now concern fiscal control far more than political subservience. The number of these organizations has skyrocketed as a result of these changes.[20]

In China, independent social organizations had been dissolved into socialist mass organizations over the course of the 1950s, and even those had little presence during the radical years of the Cultural Revolution. The ideal during that period was to merge state and society into one unit. This changed, however, with the economic reforms, when China abandoned its totalitarian model. Part of the transformation was an enormous increase in private and social space, at least as long as there was no political challenge involved. China also made legal space for NGOs during this period, but its model was very much corporatist, roughly along the lines of Taiwan before 1987. Even this, however, has allowed a massive growth in NGOs of all kinds, including environmental ones.

Under corporatist arrangements, NGOs either accommodate to the state or find themselves dismantled. Those that survive tend to have the centralized structures that authoritarian states prefer to deal with. They also look modern in the sense that they are strongly institutionalized, with clear bureaucratic mechanisms, dealing with issues that these self-consciously modernizing states find appropriate. Neither local community temples nor lineages, for example, have these features. The result in many authoritarian regimes with roughly corporatist relations to society is a bifurcation between local, informal associations that survive beyond the gaze of the state, and these centralized, formally organized NGOs that survive by working closely with the state.[21]

This continues to be the case in China today, where autonomy is not an important goal for most NGOs, who can better pursue their agendas by cooperating with the state. Lineages cannot legally organize (although they may remake themselves as history museums, for instance) and village temples are still branded as "feudal superstition." Even in Taiwan, where democratization has fundamentally altered this relationship, most NGOs prefer cooperative means of pursuing their goals. On the other hand, local social arrangements like temples have become increasingly prominent there, as politicians must now use all possible means to mobilize local support.

Both Chinese and Taiwanese NGOs at the national level have actively pursued global connections, although for somewhat different reasons. In China, they are driven primarily by the same concerns that NGOs everywhere share – the need for expertise and, above all, the need for cash. In the environmental field as in most others, the best-known NGOs receive significant funding and advice from abroad, making for a strong global influence. The dynamic in Taiwan is more unusual, however, because of Taiwan's difficult diplomatic position. Recognized by only a few small countries, Taiwan's government has encouraged NGOs to serve as a kind of informal diplomatic channel. Taiwanese NGOs thus undertake activities abroad far more than similar organizations in most non-Western countries. Either way, these processes encourage NGOs in China and Taiwan to speak a global discourse, rather than to develop more indigenously rooted ideas.

Taiwan

Taiwan's environmental NGOs predate democratization by almost a decade. One early pioneer was Huang Shunxing, who had been elected to the national legislature in 1979, running as a non-party (i.e., anti-KMT) candidate. He was a very early opponent of nuclear power, and founder of the magazine *Life and Environment* (*Shenghuo yu Huanjing*). The magazine folded for financial reasons after a few issues, but it is widely seen as the first national-level environmental effort.[22]

The other crucial early leader was Lin Junyi, who founded Taiwan Greenpeace in 1982. In retrospect, it might be best to consider Taiwan Greenpeace as a kind of proxy NGO. For people who wanted to pressure the authoritarian regime without taking the radical steps that would land them in prison, NGOs in certain sectors offered some possibilities. The trick was to find areas where the NGO could show that it acted completely in accordance with avowed government policies, while in fact criticizing specific government actions. Environment was a particularly fruitful field for this, because the government officially embraced environmental protection, but had an industrial policy that often threatened the environment. Similar kinds of proxy NGOs developed in Taiwan around women's rights and consumer protection, and the same issues seem to offer opportunities for proxy NGOs in many authoritarian regimes.

The main evidence that Taiwan Greenpeace was a proxy is hindsight. After democratization, Lin was elected to national office, and Taiwan Greenpeace gradually faded into unimportance. Lin was not simply being utilitarian – he continued to pursue environmental politics from within the government – but the NGO was his organization of choice only under the unusual circumstances of Taiwan's gentle authoritarian opening in the early 1980s. His group was an important voice that helped nudge Taiwan to democratize by criticizing policy and increasing the space for acceptable dissent. Other groups, however, would take over the actual work of lobbying for environmental protection.

Environmental groups, like NGOs in every other sector, boomed after corporatist controls were lifted in 1987. Taiwan Greenpeace may have faded out, but many new organizations took its place. The most important of these during the time of my research was the Taiwan Environmental Protection Union (TEPU, *Taiwan Huanjing Baohu Lianmeng*), which was founded just a few months after the "state of emergency" and effective martial law ended. Unlike most of the other national-level groups (including Taiwan Greenpeace), TEPU attempted to be a union of grassroots groups. It had nine branches around the island, almost all of which had begun as large local demonstrations where a few leaders had become radicalized enough to start a branch. Their Gaoxiong branch, for instance, had its roots in the Houjing demonstration against the naphtha cracker.

When I interviewed their chairman, Liu Zhicheng, in 1992, the group had about 1,200 members. Their executive committee included the leaders of the nine branches, seven more people elected by the general membership, and another seven taken from their academic advisory committee. This gave academics a very large voice in the group. Academics dominated other groups (including Taiwan Greenpeace) even more thoroughly. Many of these academics have foreign graduate degrees, usually from the United States, and this is often the direct root for their environmentalism. Liu himself has an American PhD in environmental engineering, and had been interested in environmental issues ever since taking an undergraduate sociology course on environmental protest (from another professor with an American degree).

I was thus not especially surprised to find Liu's responses to my questions sounding very much like certain kinds of global environmental discourse. There was nothing identifiably Taiwanese or Chinese about his positions. Talking about the relation between environmental protection and economic development, for instance, he argued that perhaps some kind of sustainable development might eventually be possible, but that for now development should be scaled back while we concentrate on the environment. By prioritizing an environment seen as endangered by humans pursuing their interests, he echoed a common international position, but one with very few roots in Chinese traditions. When I asked about the role of religion in Taiwan's protests, he agreed that temples were sometimes very important, but he did not advocate using them either organizationally or ideologically. This kind of attitude typified most of the other major groups at the time, like New Environment, which consisted mostly of urban academics.

The only partial exceptions to this pattern were women's groups and Buddhist groups. The most important women's environmental group during my research period had actually branched off from New Environment in 1989. It was called the Housewives' Union Foundation for Environmental Protection (*Zhufu Lianmeng Huanjing Baohu Jijinhui*), and many of the founders were the wives of New Environment leaders.[23] They split in part because they found New Environment too academic – too many seminars, talks and workshops, and not enough actual changing the environment. They also felt that housewives were an important group with little representation. On the other hand, their secretary-general (Lin Yupei) told me that TEPU's activities, which often included organizing street demonstrations, were too radical for most of their contributors.

Many of their activities at the time aimed to change consumer behavior. They encouraged people to separate garbage for recycling, and to carry their own cups and shopping bags. They tried to train "environmental mamas" who would go back to their apartment blocks and organize other women to promote these activities. They have also published various materials aimed at children or families, like a set of environmentally oriented walking tours, or comic books promoting recycling, proper disposal of trash, and good personal hygiene.

Their other main form of activity concerned child-raising, and ranged from reading groups to summer camps for teenagers. They stretched the idea of environment to cover this kind of thing under the rubric of protecting the "spiritual environment" (*xinling huanjing*). This already implies a significantly different understanding of the environment from TEPU's leaders. Humans remain at the core here. Lin maintained this idea even when talking about economic issues. She saw close ties between humanity and nature: "The world needs people." This also fit some globalizing discourse, both on environment and on family life, and the group actively translated foreign works ranging from John Muir to child-rearing guides. Yet it was a significantly different attitude from most of the other environmental NGOs, and one that fit more easily with older Chinese views of how people relate to their environment.

The final important variant has come from several of the modernizing Buddhist groups that have become so popular in Taiwan over the last two decades. Several of these groups claim over a million lay followers, although most of the leadership is monastic. All of them share a concern with what they call "humanistic Buddhism" (*renjian fojiao*), and for some this includes environmental concerns. Their activities tend to be similar to the Housewives' Union, but with no involvement at all in street demonstrations. They recycle, promote simpler lifestyles and more limited consumption, and also discuss the "spiritual environment" of children. The leader of the largest group, for instance, says she uses every piece of paper three times – first writing with pencil, then with pen, and finally with a calligraphy brush. In this and many other ways she promotes a simple lifestyle for her millions of followers, minimizing demands on the environment.[24]

Positions like hers form the beginnings of a specifically Buddhist environmentalism. Living a simple life in part creates more resources to share with the poor – a concrete realization of the bodhisattva ideal. Reducing consumption also brings lay followers closer to a monastic abandonment of the false desires of this world, even though they remain at home. Buddhist vegetarianism, which has important environmental consequences, grows out of the idea that the Buddha-nature is in all things.

The most influential groups within Taiwan's environmental movement have been the ones dominated by urban academics, like TEPU or New Environment. These are also the groups that most closely match the important strand of global environmental discourse that sees human activity, especially economic activity, as a threat to an environment that they imagine primarily in non-human terms. This view has strong roots in Western thought, as I have discussed especially in chapter 3, and makes little use of any indigenous Chinese tradition. The women's groups also attend closely to global trends, but feel a much stronger influence from those that center on human welfare. That is why they often grasp onto a broad extension of the concept of environment to include something like the "spiritual environment," whose concerns are almost entirely within the human world. This meshes more easily with some older Chinese ideas about humans and nature. The Buddhists' concrete activities differ little from the women's associations, but they are rooted much more explicitly in indigenous traditions of knowledge, especially in the Buddhist traditions that I discussed in chapter 2. It is surely no coincidence that the women's and Buddhist groups tend to have much wider followings than the more intellectual groups, even though the latter have been far more successful at garnering media attention and ultimately affecting policy.

China

China began to allow limited space for independent social organizations in the early 1980s. The first real regulatory framework for "social organizations" (*shehui tuanti*) – the closest equivalent to NGOs – came in 1984. These regulations forced organizations to jump difficult political hurdles to gain official registration. National-level groups had to establish a need for the association, acquiesce to strict controls, and gain explicit permission from the State Council and the Central Committee of the Communist Party. Even with these strictures, though, the numbers of organizations grew rapidly, especially at local levels.[25]

The 1989 demonstrations in Tiananmen caused China to rein in NGOs over the next few years, and much the same happened again after the crackdown against Falungong in 1999. Both events led to temporary declines in the numbers of organizations, but the generally increasing trend resumed again after a few years in both cases. The regulations had been revised in the 1990s, though, to make the basic corporatist structure of just one organization per social sector more explicit. The result in some ways is similar to Taiwan's situation before 1987, with large organizations closely tied to the state, and localized groups with little or no legal support but largely ignored if they remain small and apolitical.

The Chinese situation is a bit more complex, however, because a large number of organizations that seem like NGOs have "registrations of convenience" that disguise their nature. Just as private entrepreneurs sometimes used to register as collective enterprises by making a deal with a collective, some NGOs register as for-profit companies or as branches of other administrative units. This is one of the reasons that China has so many more NGOs than the basic corporatist approach would seem to allow. Levels of autonomy, of course, are very low for any of the recognized groups.[26]

The result has been a significant number of environmentalist groups. Most of these initially concentrated in Beijing, but campus-based student groups have recently increased rapidly as well. Friends of Nature is one of the oldest and best-known groups. It was founded in 1994 by Liang Congjie, a historian from one of modern China's preeminent intellectual families. When Friends of Nature registered as an official "social organization," the corporatist slot for an environmental group had already been taken. Liang solved the problem by claiming an interest in traditional ideas about nature, which let him register under the Academy of Chinese Culture in the state-sponsored Chinese Academy of Social Sciences.

His group undertakes various educational programs, as well as the bird watching group that I mentioned in the previous chapter. It is most famous, though, for its efforts at protecting endangered species. The group tends to identify issues where local economic interests (often with ties to the local government) conflict with national environmental policy. They will send field investigators and mobilize people to write letters and petitions to the central government. One of their most famous victories led to a logging ban in an area of Yunnan that was home to an endangered species of monkey. This kind of action can be bold or even dangerous in the local context. At the national level, however, it always meshes with the announced aims of the central government. Neither this group nor any of the other influential NGOs attempts serious challenges of basic policy, like the reliance on nuclear power or the construction of the Three Gorges dam.

Without the benefits of hindsight, it is difficult to classify these groups as proxy NGOs, similar to Taiwan Greenpeace. Liang's history would be consistent with this – he was involved with a gently dissident journal before starting the environmental group. All of the leaders have a genuine commitment to the environment, and all seem interested in carefully pushing the boundaries of the space allowed for social organization. They are very careful, though, and recognize that they will not be able to pursue their agendas at all if their organizations are crushed. The array of activities of all the important national environmental organizations thus meshes with official policy, even if it sometimes clashes with real interests on the ground – they plant trees, protest illegal logging and poaching, recycle garbage, and run educational programs. Liang pushes the envelope more than some, but manages this because he is so very well connected at high political levels.

These groups depend significantly more than the Taiwanese ones on foreign financing. In this, they resemble NGOs in all fields in most of the developing world. The need for foreign support means that these groups must speak within the conceptual space of their donors as well as of the Chinese government. None of them thus seems to draw anything obvious from any indigenous Chinese traditions. When I asked Liang about this, thinking that his affiliation with the Academy of Chinese Culture would mean he had an interest in indigenous views of nature, he soon clarified my mistake. China's biggest problem, he told me, was the environmental ignorance of the peasantry, and thus it was crucial to offer educational programs. He had no interest at all in what those peasants may actually have believed about nature, or how they had managed to create relatively stable and very long-lasting ecosystems like rice paddies. Instead, his flagship issues of endangered species protection fit better with a view of nature threatened by an external humanity – a view with few Chinese roots.

Northwest Yunnan provides a revealing and complex example.[27] With tight restrictions now on its timber industry, this region has turned to tourism as a major source of income. At the same time, it has also seen significant investment from international environmental NGOs, and particularly from the Nature Conservancy, which is based in the United States. One of their goals is to establish a national park, modeled after Yellowstone, that would highlight the spectacular mountains of the area and help to protect several endangered species. The centerpiece would be the 6,740 meter glaciated peak known as Meili Snow Mountain (from the Mandarin) or Mount Khabadkarpo (from the Tibetan).

Khabadkarpo is a sacred mountain to the Tibetans who constitute much of the local population, and indeed to Tibetans everywhere. Tibetan pilgrims come from all over China to circumambulate the peak – a trek of about two weeks. More recently it has attracted numerous mountaineering and adventure travelers from China and abroad. This is a significant source of income for the region, but also a significant source of tension for the local people who resent these attacks on their mountain. Litzinger tells how during one attempt to scale the peak in 1991 the local women began to curse the mountain god for allowing itself to be humiliated like this. They even raised their skirts toward it as an insult. The team was in fact wiped out by an avalanche, and the villagers prayed for forgiveness the next day, but also praised the mountain.[28]

This issue became central in discussions with the Nature Conservancy and the local government about their long-term plans. At least three images of nature seem to be at stake here. The first is the Tibetan idea of sacred mountains, which we see in a range of behaviors from pilgrimage to women shouting insults. This is different from anything I have discussed, and serves as a useful reminder of how wide the full range of indigenous Chinese ideas about the environment really is if we include all the ethnicities beyond just the majority Han Chinese I have been concerned with here. For my purposes, it is enough just to note that this Tibetan understanding of the mountain was an important shaper of local responses to the possibilities of tourism. The second idea of nature comes from the mountaineers, who "conquer" peaks through "assaults" from "base camps." The combat imagery immediately calls to mind a view of man against nature, where the human goal is to dominate. Finally, we have the international environmentalists, who also separate humanity from nature, but want to preserve rather than conquer – this is the Yellowstone model that was so important to Taiwan's national parks as well.

The result of the discussions was an alliance in which the people promoting the indigenous sacred mountain idea and the conservationists united against the mountaineers. When they wrote their petition, they necessarily couched it in the language of national and international biodiversity and ethnic rights protection. This was true even in the most literal sense – it was written in Chinese and English, but not Tibetan.[29] There was significant internal disagreement, for instance, about whether to refer to the mountain by its Chinese or Tibetan name, but they eventually chose the Chinese version. Much the same kind of thing happened at the broad level of arguing about why mountaineering should be banned. Local Tibetan understandings of the mountain were mentioned, but only as an instance of Tibetan culture that was protected by national law. It was never taken seriously as a way of understanding the environment. Other arguments about biodiversity protection had no particular local roots at all. The petition was to be delivered by none other than Liang Congjie of Friends of Nature, owing to his powerful connections. This case shows a complex interaction of local, national, and global actors, but the final language of their decision drew far more on national and global understandings of nature than on local ones.

We can see another kind of resolution from Herrold's study of Caohai Nature Reserve in Guizhou.[30] As part of an attempt to preserve rare black-necked cranes, the provincial government restored part of a lake that had been drained for farmland. From an environmentalist point of view, the project was a success, and the migratory birds returned to the area. Caohai was typical of the kind of "pure nature" ideal of many of the parks and reserves I discussed in chapter 4. From the point of view of the local people, however, it was both utterly unexpected and economically problematic as many of their former activities were criminalized. There were frequent protests and some physical threats against reserve employees. Anger seemed to peak in 1992, just as the government upgraded it from a provincial to a national reserve.

At this point two American NGOs became involved, the International Crane Foundation (a conservation group) and the Trickle Up Program (a development group). In this case, the rather different agendas of the two NGOs combined. Trickle Up saw an opportunity for rural development through its association with the nature reserve, and the crane conservationists hoped for a way of easing tensions with their nature reserve by tying it to development goals. The alliance also meshed with new international thinking about the need to tie development and conservation issues together instead of opposing parks to people. The result was a microcredit program tied to the nature reserve administration rather than the local government. At least for the short run, this succeeded in significantly lowering tension. In this case, the development side of international discourse (which is somewhat beyond the scope of this book) meshed with local demands to use the environment for their economic survival instead of for the cranes, and they were able to negotiate a compromise. The microcredit program substituted a new kind of economic opportunity through the reserve for the old activities that had been lost. This allowed the international and national conservationist agenda to continue, at least as long as funding continued.

NGOs and environmental discourses

These cases begin to show the complexity of the discursive fields that come into play for any specific issue. We have various environmental ideas sometimes cooperating and sometimes conflicting, including images of humanity in control of nature, or needing to protect nature from itself, or as a core part of nature. We also find these environmentalisms sometimes allied with and sometimes opposed to other global discourses like development, and to other national discourses like the protection of national minorities.

In nearly every case, though, a fairly simple pattern emerges in the relationship between NGOs and more grassroots movements. The issues and organizations that are most important locally – like village temples, lineages, political factions, or mountains that can be insulted with a lifted skirt – tend to disappear when we turn to the national and international organizations. Those big organizations may sometimes disagree with each other, but they share a globalized language that ranges from biodiversity to human rights. This happens in part because the elites who run these groups are highly educated, steeped in the values of modernity. The universalizing values of the global discourses also appeal to them because they generalize across the many different local situations, even though things like temples and lineages may be more effective at local organizing. Finally, these elites speak a global language of environment because that opens the door to international funding (in China's case) and international substitutes for diplomacy (in Taiwan's case).

Significances

These cases of grassroots movements and national organizations show the power of globalizing visions of nature to diffuse through the centers of intellectual control, but also show how diluted the effects can become when we get down to the people actually protesting on behalf of their environment. The national organizations are good at lobbying for new laws, addressing the media, and speaking to other intellectuals and professionals. The bulk of environmental action, however, takes place elsewhere, among people whose motivations are above all local and personal. They protest on behalf of the health of their children, the value of their crops, or the quality of their lives, but they rarely embrace the abstract and universalizing ideals of the national elites, like biodiversity for its own sake or the dangers of nuclear energy. They organize using local cultural resources for local ends. National groups and local protests sometimes unite for strategic purposes, but that does not necessarily mean they fully share their ultimate goals.

This situation is common in many parts of the world. The famous Chipko "tree-hugging" movement in the mountains of northern India, for instance, began as a local peasant protest over their declining rights to use local forest land as government controls increased. Various national-level movements allied with the locals in a complex dynamic. These included ecofeminists who were drawn to the visible role of women in the protest, environmentalists who saw this as a way of protecting the forest from harvesting, Marxists who saw it as a tale of exploited peasants, and so on. The result was a distinction between what Ramachandra Guha calls the "public" and "private" faces of the movement. Privately, it was the continuation of a century-long struggle over land and forest rights, but publicly – that is, in the hands of national and global elites – it was an environmental movement that formed part of whatever broader view of nature they were promoting.[31]

The Brazilian Kayapo provided an equally famous example of local environmental protest awkwardly allied with larger organizations. According to Terence Turner, the Kayapo view themselves as an important part of the production of human, social, and natural life, without any concept of a separable "nature."[32] In 1989, Kayapo leaders managed to pull in a huge range of global environmental NGOs to support them at a large media event to oppose construction of a World Bank funded dam. The leaders had to motivate hundreds of their people to make the trek to the event, while at the same time effectively mobilizing these global forces. They chose to do this by performing a major annual ritual that would both bring Kayapo in and show their unique culture to the world. Ironically, this required them to cut down a gigantic forest tree. They managed to pull this off successfully, but the ritual already revealed a potential tension between the Kayapo happily sacrificing a tree to guarantee social reproduction and global NGOs who preferred to romanticize them as protectors of nature. The tension became real later, when it became clear that the Kayapo were not nearly so interested in stopping gold mining or especially mahogany logging on their land.[33]

The cultural differences between local movements and national or international organizations suggest that there are limits on the ability of global discourse to penetrate everywhere. For most people in Taiwan and China, as for the north Indian hill farmers or the Brazilian Kayapo, understandings of nature with long and local historical roots remain salient in guiding their environmental action. They will ally with NGOs that have different views, but in most cases they do that without adopting the NGOs' understandings of the world. Globalization – in this case primarily of views of nature that took shape in the West after the Enlightenment – acts most powerfully only on the elites. They are the ones most likely to feel the influence of a nature/culture split, either the version that wants to conquer a dehumanized nature or the one that wants to protect it.

Diverse views of nature survive best in local contexts, but they do not lend themselves to broader institutionalization, at least in China and Taiwan. This is partly because the authoritarian history of both places prevented any grassroots organization from becoming significant on a large scale. It is also because the specific ideas that are called into play, from lineage ties to village temples, do not generalize well beyond the local level in the Chinese context. It is difficult to see how any of the indigenous potentials for an alternative environmentalism might be realized on a large scale, at least without a fundamental change in elite attitudes. The only nudge in that direction so far has come from the Buddhists, but the environmental aspect of their thinking remains less developed than others, and they have had little influence on China so far.

NOTES

1. See Robert P. Weller and Hsin-Huang Michael Hsiao, "Culture, Gender and Community in Taiwan's Environmental Movement," in *Environmental Movements in Asia*, ed. Arne Kalland and Gerard Persoon (Surrey: Curzon, 1998), 83–109.
2. James Reardon-Anderson, *Pollution, Politics, and Foreign Investment in Taiwan: The Lukang Rebellion* (Armonk, NY: M. E. Sharpe, 1992).
3. Weller and Hsiao, "Culture, Gender and Community in Taiwan's Environmental Movement."
4. Ming-Sho Ho, "The Environmental Movements in the Democratic Transition in Taiwan," paper presented at the Conference on Civil Society, Social Movements, and Democratization on Both Sides of the Taiwan Strait (Boston University, 24–25 April 2001), 8.
5. I am grateful to Hsin-Huang Michael Hsiao and Julia Huang for help on this aspect of the research. I am especially in the debt of Liu Xiuyuan, without whom I would never have understood Sanxia's political intrigues.

6. This information comes from the Taipei County editions of *Minzhong Ribao* (14 May 1991) and *Taiwan Shibao* (16 May 1991).
7. See the local editions of *Ziyou Ribao* and *Minzhong Ribao* for 21 September 1990.
8. I later interviewed Lin Muzong, one of the two county representatives, who made similar arguments and placed all the blame squarely on manipulation by Liu Wenxiu.
9. According to local rumors, his sister was married to an important local street corner head, but I did not try to confirm this.
10. For a fictionalized but highly evocative description, see chapter 5 of Margery Wolf, *The House of Lim: A Study of a Chinese Farm Family* (New York: Appleton-Century-Crofts, 1968).
11. I have not given examples of the role of kinship and lineage, but they are also sometimes important, for example in Taiwan's movement against construction of a fourth nuclear power plant.
12. See Jean C. Oi, "Realms of Freedom in Post-Mao China," in *Realms of Freedom in Modern China*, ed. William C. Kirby (Stanford: Stanford University Press, 2004), 264–84.
13. Weihe Guan and Ray Zhang, "Beijing Residents Protest against Garbage Dump," *China News Digest*, no. GL97-098 11 July 1997, 11 July 1997, www.cnd.org.
14. For more information on the project, see William P. Alford *et al.*, "The Human Dimensions of Pollution Policy Implementation: Air Quality in Rural China," *Journal of Contemporary China* 11 (2002): 495–513. I am grateful to Li Jiansheng, a postdoctoral affiliate of the program, who collected much of this material in 1999. I have copies of the lawsuit, the County Environmental Protection Bureau report, and various petitions from the plaintiff and local villagers.
15. Bryan D. Tilt, "Risk, Pollution and Sustainability in Rural Sichuan, China" (PhD diss., University of Washington, 2004).
16. Kevin J. O'Brien and Lianjiang Li, "Suing the Local State: Administrative Litigation in Rural China," *China Journal* 51 (January 2004): 75–96.
17. Jun Jing, "Environmental Protests in Rural China," in *Chinese Society: Change, Conflict and Resistance*, ed. Mark Selden and Elizabeth J. Perry (New York: Routledge, 2000).
18. On the important role of lineage and temple generally in rural China today, see Lily Lee Tsai, "Cadres, Temple and Lineage Institutions, and Governance in Rural China," *The China Journal* 48 (July 2002): 1–27.
19. I have discussed elsewhere how letters to the EPA increased enormously when they did start responding more effectively for a while in Taiwan. The EPA later found its budget cut, however. See Robert P. Weller, *Alternate Civilities: Democracy and Culture in China and Taiwan* (Boulder, CO: Westview, 1999), 121–5.
20. Hsin-Huang Michael Hsiao, "NGOs, the State, and Democracy under Globalization: The Case of Taiwan," in *Civil Life, Globalization, and Political Change in Asia: Organizing between Family and State*, ed. Robert P. Weller (London: Routledge, 2005).

21. For more detail on the argument, see the introductory chapter in Robert P. Weller, ed., *Civil Life, Globalization, and Political Change in Asia: Organizing between Family and State* (London: Routledge, 2005). The essays by Hsiao, Chan, and Weller have more detail on the Chinese and Taiwanese cases.
22. Huang himself eventually left Taiwan for the People's Republic.
23. Hwei-syin Lu, "Women's Self-Growth Groups and Empowerment of the 'Uterine Family' in Taiwan," *Bulletin of the Institute of Ethnology, Academia Sinica* 71 (1991): 29–62.
24. This is based on interviews with the Ven. Zhengyan, head of this group (Ciji Gongdehui, the Compassion Merit Foundation), in 1993. Other information on Buddhist groups comes from Wu Muxin, head of the environment committee of Jinghua, a much smaller group, in 1992. For more information on the recycling activities of Zhengyan's group, see Wei'an Zhang, "Fuojiao Ciji Gongde Hui Yu Ziyuan Huishou [The Buddhist Compassion Merit Society and Recycling]," paper presented at the Workshop on Culture, Media and Society in Contemporary Taiwan (Harvard University, 12 June 1996).
25. Kin-man Chan, "Development of NGOs under a Post-Totalitarian Regime: The Case of China," in *Civil Life, Globalization, and Political Change in Asia: Organizing between Family and State*, ed. Robert P. Weller (London: Routledge, 2005); M. Pei, "Chinese Intermediate Associations: An Empirical Analysis," *Modern China* 24, no. 3 (July 1998): 285–318.
26. Robert P. Weller *et al.*, *Dangdai Huaren Chengshi Shehui de Minjian Zuzhi: Taibei, Xianggang, Guangzhou, Xiamen de Bijiao Fenxi* (*Civil Associations in Contemporary Chinese Urban Societies: A Comparative Analysis of Taibei, Hong Kong, Guangzhou, and Xiamen*), Occasional Paper 123 (Hong Kong: Chinese University of Hong Kong, Institute of Asia-Pacific Studies, 2002).
27. This case comes from Ralph Litzinger, "The Mobilization of 'Nature': Perspectives from Northwest Yunnan," *China Quarterly* 118 (June 2004): 488–505.
28. Litzinger, "The Mobilization of 'Nature.'"
29. The full text is in Litzinger, "The Mobilization of 'Nature.'"
30. Melinda Herrold, "From Adversary to Partner: The Evolving Role of a Nature Reserve in the Lives of Reserve Residents," paper presented at the Annual Meeting, Association for Asian Studies, New York, 2003.
31. Ramachandra Guha, *The Unquiet Woods: Ecological Change and Peasant Resistance in the Himalaya* (Berkeley: University of California Press, 1989), 178.
32. Terence Turner, "Indigenous Rights, Environmental Protection and the Struggle over Forest Resources in the Amazon: The Case of the Brazilian Kayapo," in *Earth, Air, Fire, and Water: The Humanities and the Environment*, ed. Jill Conway, Kenneth Keniston, and Leo Marx (Amherst: University of Massachusetts Press, 2000).
33. Brazilian Yanomami have been involved in similarly complex alliances, where appeals to global organizations leave them open to charges of not being nationalistic. See Beth A. Conklin, "Shamans versus Pirates in the Amazonian Treasure Chest," *American Anthropologist* 104, no. 4 (2002): 1050–61.

6 On "policies from above and countermeasures from below"

Both the Chinese and the Taiwanese governments have transformed their environmental policies since the 1980s, in part because their ways of thinking about nature have changed. China has replaced military images of the human conquest of nature, so popular during the Cultural Revolution and before, with closures of polluting factories, bans on leaded gas, and sales of organic food. China was the first country to produce a United Nations Agenda 21 document (outlining plans for sustainable development) under the Rio agreements of 1992. It has established an elaborate system of environmental regulations and the agencies to support them. It has staged periodic environmental campaigns, for instance promoting reforestation after the Yangzi River floods of 1998, or opposing pollution of the Huai River by paper factories. As I discussed in the previous chapter, it has also allowed foreign and indigenous environmental NGOs to play an active (if carefully delimited) role. Taiwan's actions have been roughly similar, although they are less tied to United Nations agreements because of the island's diplomatic limbo. Generally a few years in advance of China, Taiwan has also greatly increased the power and influence of its Environmental Protection Agency, passed or strengthened laws to protect endangered species and improve the quality of air and water, and cut back on extractive industries like forestry and mining.

Striking as these changes are, examining actual implementation of these policies exposes a much more complex and ambiguous situation. Farmers in poor areas of China, for instance, often illegally open up steep fields, leading to soil erosion. Others will cut down roadside trees for firewood, thus removing important windbreaks. Local governments may connive with timber companies in illegal logging, or look the other way as factories pollute water and air. Elaborate legal provisions seem to have little effect, and massive propaganda campaigns seem to reach few people. Taiwan's greater rule of law and more open political system, which allows for independent monitoring, make the situation somewhat better there. As we shall see, though, even Taiwan sometimes has serious implementation problems. Some of the most significant obstacles to carrying out policy lie in mismatches among the alternate understandings of the relationship between humans and environment that I have been discussing.

A Chinese cliché provides a useful starting point for issues of policy implementation: "there are policies from above and countermeasures from below" (*shang you zhengce, xia you duice*). Anthropologists often expound on native phrases as a way of getting at some fundamental and untranslatable cultural essence, but that is not my intention here. I focus on it instead because its two parallel contrasts – between above and below and between policies and countermeasures – resonate so strongly with some of the main social scientific approaches to state/society relations and to globalization.

The contrast between above and below in the cliché is general enough to capture political and economic hierarchy of all sorts – global and local, state and people, or higher and lower levels of government. For anthropologists of China, interest in this has greatly increased over the last several decades, when our work routinely began to transcend the boundaries of the village to include broader relations of power.[1] Like the field as a whole, we discovered the state (above), but we also usually set it up as a unified power that stood outside the village (below). For political scientists, the contrast plays out more between competing higher and lower levels of government – typically Beijing above and counties below. While political scientists rarely reach all the way down to villagers, their examination of local government helped show the dynamic complexity and internal competition that characterized the "state." They showed us how interests varied between lower and higher levels of government, across regions, and even within different agencies at the same level.

Their work suggests that taking the "state" as a whole is a misleading reification. Even more, these complexities require us to move beyond the simple hierarchy of above and below, and even beyond an image of the state as an orderly hierarchy where power ramifies down from the top to lower branches, like descent flowing down a genealogical chart. The anthropological concept of heterarchy, which recognizes that hierarchy is complicated and compromised by units whose relative power may vary, may provide a better metaphor.[2] Heterarchy does not result in the unified structure of an organizational chart, but rather in a conglomerate of multiple, competing orders of power and authority.

Taking a step beyond the state to the global, and beyond politics to economic and cultural power, leads in the same direction. As I have discussed in earlier chapters, the global is not simply a unified force standing apart from the local. In fact, it is even less uniformly hierarchical than the state, and more characterized by multiple and competing nodes of power. One of this chapter's themes will be the need to find better metaphors for understanding these dynamics than above and below, state and village, or global and local.

The other revealing contrast in the cliché is between policies and countermeasures. The Chinese terms here reveal more than the English. The second character in both terms is *ce*, plans. "Policy" in Chinese is *zhengce*. The first character, *zheng*, is short for *zhengfu* – government – but more literally means officially authorized or orthodox. "Countermeasures" are *duice*, with the character *dui* meaning opposition or duality. The contrast is thus between authorized plans and oppositional plans, monologue and dialogue, hierarchy and heterarchy. In setting up this opposition, the Chinese phrase again echoes some current lines of thought in the social sciences, especially those that emphasize the possibilities of resistance to state or global power.

Unlike totalitarian political theory, which once shaped our understanding of a purely top-down power flow in China, and unlike those Hollywood or Wall Street versions of globalization that also see an unstoppable force, this image allows for effective resistance. Something like this has characterized most of the anthropological thinking on these issues since the field entered these debates. At the more political end is the work of someone like Mayfair Yang, who places the "popular" (*minjian*) in opposition to state-controlled images of society.[3] For globalization, the best-known work in the China field has been James Watson's argument for the localization of even a multinational giant like McDonald's.[4] One of the attractions to anthropologists is that these images of power and resistance grant some autonomy and agency to the people we study, unlike the purely top-down theories.

If we complicate the ideas of above and below with some more heterarchical image of power, however, the duality of policies and countermeasures seems inadequate. The image in the cliché implies a sort of chess game, with each side matching wits against the other. There is not much room in this image for complex sets of different interests among the many players. The chess image also overemphasizes the rationality of the decision-making, and the direct translation of strategy into action. As the examples in this chapter will show, we need instead to imagine a world where rational strategizing struggles with a vast array of unintended consequences, unknown conditions, and unspoken assumptions.

Some cases of environmental policy

The data I will draw on in this chapter come primarily from three sources. The first is qualitative work in an urban neighborhood of Tianjin. The second is a survey of environmental behaviors and values among rural households in the Anqing metropolitan area (southern Anhui Province), supplemented with some more ethnographic work.[5] Finally, I will also develop one case involving Kending National Park in Taiwan. I have already discussed Kending in the context of nature tourism, but here I will expand on the political complications of arguments over land use in the park.

Tianjin is one of China's largest cities, with a population of about 10 million. While it may not compare with Shanghai or Guangzhou in the speed of its economic development, it has taken part in the general economic boom of coastal cities under the economic reforms. The late 1990s brought significant changes in the city's environmental policies and attitudes, with particular attempts to address air quality. The municipal government began to close down state-owned urban factories, moving them out to more distant suburbs. Like some of the other large eastern cities, it banned the use of leaded gasoline in cars at this time. Like most northern cities, pollution from coal provided one of the most obvious and annoying air quality problems, especially during the winter heating season. Tianjin has systematically tried to move people from coal to natural gas for domestic use – a case I will discuss in some detail below.

Tianjin's population also has a relatively strong awareness of environmental issues by China's standards. Like environmental surveys from around the world, surveys in China show a strong correlation between education and knowledge of problems like acid rain, holes in the ozone layer, or shrinking biodiversity. One study based on letters of complaint to environmental officials, for instance, concludes that "a 1% increase in the literacy rate seems to induce a 2% increase in environmental complaints."[6] A Beijing survey came to a similar conclusion in 1999, and added that over 98 percent of respondents with a college education follow daily air quality reports, while only 60 percent of those without a college education follow them.[7] Education levels are higher in all these coastal cities than in rural or inland China, and so environmental concerns are greater.

Even in Tianjin, however, informal interviews suggest that people make little connection, for instance, between fuel use and health. When they complain about the environment (which they often do), the issues usually relate to dust and ash from factories that make their houses dirty, smells and noises that annoy them, or litter left by street vendors. They are much less aware of problems that are not immediately obvious to the senses, like greenhouse gas emission or acid rain.

At the same time, mothers of young children in particular often go out of their way to decrease their families' exposure to pollution. Beginning in the very late 1990s, some in the neighborhood of our study began to frequent an organic food store and purchase other health foods for their children. Some bought air purifiers for their houses. For a while there was even a fad for "oxygen bars," where one could breathe oxygen through a mask for a few minutes. Mothers did this especially for children preparing for college entrance exams, in the hopes that it would improve their brain function. This very general glance at Tianjin shows the important changes that took place in both city policy and popular environmental consciousness during the late 1990s. It suggests at least a significant degree of government success in getting its policies implemented.

The situation in rural Anqing, however, is quite different. The late 1990s saw a number of important environmental campaigns there. In 1996 alone, according to the government, 240 Anhui provincial government offices and 2,376 officials had mounted 1,921 television and other mass media programs, held 128 training courses, and undertaken 340 other activities in environmental "propaganda and education."[8] This does not even include the standard school exposure to basic information about sanitation, and required activities like litter clean-ups and tree planting. This was also the year that saw the beginning of the widely publicized campaign to limit pollution on the Huai River, which led to the claimed closing of over 1,000 paper mills.[9] Much of this activity took place in northern Anhui, just before our survey in the southern part of the same province.

In contrast to what these impressive statistics might imply, our survey found extremely low levels of awareness about any of these campaigns. Only 12 percent of our sample said they had ever heard about or participated in any environmental campaign, and most of these were referring to the ubiquitous tree-planting drives. As another example, most families burnt rice stalks in their fields after the harvest to add to soil fertility and help eliminate pests. Only 36 percent saw this as even relatively harmful to the environment, even though the resulting smoke had forced the shutdown of the municipal airport during our interview period. Even more surprisingly, 63 percent of the respondents did not even recognize the term *huanjing baohu* (environmental protection).

Either government campaigns are not reaching people, or people are ignoring them completely. One reason for this is education – not the overnight education of propaganda campaigns, but the long-term investment in educating the public. Quite unlike Tianjin, less than half the people in our sample had gone beyond elementary school, and 39 percent had no formal schooling at all.[10] Rural Anqing also showed none of the environmental fads – oxygen bars and organic foods, for instance – that swept Tianjin at the same period quite apart from any government policies. Anqing has many policies that might lead to changed environmental behavior – new legal mechanisms to control pollution and to empower people to deal with problems, extensive propaganda campaigns, and a strengthened environmental protection bureaucracy – but little seems to have had much of an impact.[11]

The situation in Taiwan is unlike either place in China. In a recent island-wide survey, for instance, 92 percent knew that the law requires environmental impact studies for major projects, 60 percent knew that nuclear power provided most of Taiwan's electricity, and 81 percent claimed that they will definitely or probably vote for a green candidate in the next election.[12] This results partly from the much higher education levels in Taiwan even than in Tianjin.

These environmentalist answers to surveys, however, also reflect the new kinds of information flows and modes of action that democracy brought to the island. An organization like TEPU, for example, offers independent scientific assessment of the environment in a way that is impossible in China. The rapid blossoming of independent print media since democratization has also given people access both to information about environmental problems and to different opinions about what should be done. The gradual broadening of elections to the highest levels after 1987 also helped open up environmental debate. Before 1987, elections involved only one party and offices at the county level and lower. Just as in China's village-level elections today, environment was rarely an issue because these levels of government had so little control over environmental policy.[13] We saw this in the previous chapter, in the way that local governments tended to duck all environmental problems except the unavoidable landfill issues.

The situation changed, however, when electoral politics became national and when various opposition leaders coalesced into the Democratic Progressive Party (DPP). Many environmentalists tended to support the DPP. This was not so much because they favored its environmental policies – it did not have a very clear environmental platform, and waffled on major issues like nuclear power – as because they opposed the policies of the ruling GMD. This alliance only began to evolve further when the DPP was finally elected to the Presidency in 2000. This evolving political situation set the stage for the case I will discuss below, focusing on land use issues at Kending, but in the context of changing party politics.

Above and below

China

Tianjin offers a good example of the complex interactions between political levels and kinds of hierarchy. At the most local urban levels, we can see this in the actions of the lowest levels of political organization, the neighborhood committees (*jumin weiyuanhui*) and street committees (*jiedao banshi chu*).[14] In Tianjin a neighborhood committee typically takes responsibility for about 400 households. The committee itself is usually five to seven people, who are often retired cadres given a small monthly stipend to help implement policy on the ground. While there may be a façade of elections in some cases, these people have generally been chosen by higher levels of government. Street committees are the next level up, and typically include about twenty to twenty-five neighborhood committees. These units are very loosely comparable to village committees and township governments in the countryside, which are also usually staffed by local people who are not part of the national cadre system. For most people, work units in state-owned enterprises were more important instruments of local state policy, but neighborhood committees took responsibility for people not part of work units and for a few core policy arenas like monitoring compliance with the birth control campaign.

With the reforms of the 1980s and 1990s, the role of these groups has changed considerably. One of the major changes has been to make them more responsible for their own finances. This is one small part of a broad fiscal change in government, where units at all levels have to reduce expenses, in part by forcing lower levels to raise their own funding. Some government regulatory offices thus became quasi-independent "NGOs" expected to live off dues and fees, just as some schools have to offer nighttime English classes to raise enough money to teach during the day. Neighborhood and street committees now often start their own enterprises, or rent their office space out to factories.

Given their fiscal needs by the mid-1990s, these units stood to gain little from promoting environmental issues. Like township governments at the same period, they had a strong economic incentive to ignore both polluting industry and citizen complaints about the environment, as long as the polluters brought them some income. In one Tianjin district, for example, residents complained about piles of coal ash from several nearby factories in the late 1990s. The factories were storing the ash for a few days at a time on a local street. The wind tended to scatter the ash, especially in the winter, and it blew into the surrounding apartments and a local elementary school. The street committee at that time took no action, however, in spite of complaints from the residents. They were charging the factories to use the site, and using the income for salary bonuses and travel. Without local political support for the complaints, the municipal Environmental Protection Bureau also took no action. For the same reasons, neighborhood and street committees have tended to support street vendors who burn a lot of coal, because they pay licensing fees.

This general situation in the 1990s typified both rural and urban areas, where economic gain motivated local leaders far more than environmental policy implementation. Neighborhood and street committees could not function without these outside sources of income, but they had little incentive to promote environmental regulations. Nevertheless, our interviews indicate that the situation has been changing, at least in Tianjin. By the year 2000, the very same street committee had set up a twenty-four-hour environmental hotline to hear complaints from citizens. They guaranteed that someone would arrive at the polluted area within five minutes, and that they would take action within a day.

This change in attitudes has something to do with the increasing environmental concern among the general urban population. Hotlines and environmental offices were flooded with petitions and complaints around that time. Yet this change probably reflects a new emphasis in central policy more than a new public consciousness. This was just the same time when Tianjin and other cities began to enforce new laws about coal burning and the use of unleaded automobile fuel. Unlike the countryside, where such changes have not been very much in evidence, China's government had decided to clean up the most glaring urban environmental problems, beginning in the late 1990s.

Even the increase in popular complaints resulted partially from changed policy – people complained more because government offices suddenly showed themselves more willing to listen, and sometimes to take action. The central government had significantly strengthened the independent power of urban Environmental Protection Bureaus at just around this time. Their new efficacy in addressing at least some pollution concerns helps explain the rash of complaints they received in 2000.[15] The enormous expansion of the environmental protection bureaucracy is one of the largest changes over the last two decades. It now has ministerial status at its highest level and ideally extends down to every county at the lowest. In principle, this has created for the first time an arm of government that will monitor the environment and enforce policy.

In practice, however, this mission has often been compromised. At the lowest level, the career trajectories of environmental officials tend to tie primarily to how well their county or urban district meets its primary political goals. These goals are currently defined overwhelmingly in economic terms, and low levels of central financial support have forced many rural counties to look for money in any way possible.[16] Especially during the heyday of township and village enterprises in the 1990s, low-level environmental bureaucrats simply could not afford to alienate industries that were producing their incomes. They also had little incentive to promote programs like changes in household fuel use, for which there was no centrally controlled infrastructure. While they did have the power to collect fines for pollution, they often had trouble collecting these funds, and then lost control of the income as it was funneled into other local projects.[17] Significant change only occurred at the very end of the century, when central policy made the environment a political priority in urban areas.

Tianjin's neighborhoods show the inadequacy of conceiving authority in the linear terms of above and below. Over the course of just a few years, we can see the reworking of the ways that neighborhood and street committees changed their form of interaction with the people under their nominal control. They acted not simply as the conduit from above to below – the way they were initially conceived by the government – but responded to the competing pushes and pulls of the local residents, the businesses that provided them with income, and the district and city governments. Even those higher levels of government are not simply "above." They are themselves complex mixes of competing interests and agencies, as my brief discussion of the role of their Environmental Protection Bureaus suggests.

The rural research in Anqing shows a similar kind of complex configuration of power, but one that has so far had much less influence on environmental behavior. The kinds of major new political directions that led to greater power for environmental officials in large cities in just the last few years have not taken place in many rural areas. This is partly because the fiscal struggle still overwhelms other issues in such regions, but also because rural areas are not on the front lines of China's presentation of itself to the world as modern and up-to-date. Tianjin competes with other world cities for transnational industry and finance, and for important global cultural and athletic events. Cleaning up the environment is part of the image they need to project. Rural areas like Anqing do not have the same priority for issues like the environment.

Nevertheless, there have been some important attempts; they just have little success to show. One of these has been the widespread introduction of competitive elections for village committee membership – something roughly comparable to the urban neighborhood committee, but at this point far more democratically chosen. These elections appear in large part to be attempts to weed out corrupt and incompetent local leaders without the political and economic costs of direct supervision from higher authorities. In principle, they should also help foster a local leadership that is more sensitive to local priorities, potentially including the environment. All villages in our study area in Anqing held regular elections, and in some cases these were hotly contested. Some of the local people estimated that candidates for village head might spend as much as 5,000–10,000 yuan on their campaigns.

In spite of this, our survey does not provide much cause for optimism for the influence of local elections on environmental behavior. Only about a third of the sample had voted (82 of 244 people), and 54 percent told us that they were "not interested at all" in the elections. The lack of enthusiasm reflects the widespread opinion that these officials have little independent power, and that they serve primarily as conduits for higher levels of authority. More than two-thirds (168 of 244 people) felt that elections had no actual effect on village affairs. Similarly, only 10 percent had ever attended a village committee meeting, and most of those reported that they did not speak. Most felt that village-level officials are concerned primarily with birth control, taxation, and education. These are all issues promoted heavily by township and county-level cadres, whose promotion chances rely heavily on their performance in these few areas.

Village-level elections thus appear to have little effect on environmental behavior, and this is unlikely to change unless local government becomes more genuinely independent of the central state, or unless the higher authorities make the environment as important an issue as revenue generation and birth control. Unlike the much less democratic neighborhood committees in Tianjin, village committees have not responded to changing environmental policy from above or changing sensitivities from below. In spite of the elections, village committees in practice continue to fit a simple hierarchical model of above and below much more than their urban counterparts. Village committees' behavior, and the local people's quite proper assessment of their interests, shows that the message they are getting from higher political levels continues to focus on economic growth and birth control. The many environmental propaganda campaigns are not translating into policy directives that might change local behavior; even local cadres behave as if the campaigns were mere lip service.

China's attempt to develop some form of rule by law might also be expected to have an effect, although it is inherently limited by the lack of an independent judiciary. Beijing since the late 1970s has created twenty national laws on the environment, issued hundreds of national regulations, and joined thirty multilateral instruments.[18] At the time of our research, China was also in the midst of a major campaign (*pufa jiaoyu*, education to spread the law) to broaden public knowledge of the legal system and to encourage people to use the law effectively.

Nevertheless, we found very little use of legal mechanisms in either Anqing or Tianjin. Only five people from our Anqing sample had ever gone to court over any matter, and none of these involved the environment. Only three had ever consulted a lawyer. Only eighteen had heard of the widely trumpeted Air Pollution Law. In informal interviews beyond the questionnaire study, we did find more significant uses of legal mechanisms, especially during a field visit in 1999. In rural Anqing this almost always involved directly economic matters rather than the environment. In particular, people are developing a close concern for the many recent regulations intended to protect them from local governments placing undue economic burdens on them.[19] As one local cadre said, "Our motivation for learning the laws comes completely from the peasants, because we are afraid that the peasants will cause us trouble by knowing more than we do." Across China, however, economic cases so far drive this use of the law, not environmental ones.

With environmental issues, people in both Tianjin and Anqing seem much more likely, at least so far, to turn to the media or to older political mechanisms rather than the newer legal ones. Tianjin's environmental report for 2000, for example, listed 7,031 letters of complaint about environmental issues to local government offices.[20] District-level offices had also written 135 letters to the mayor's office in support of some of these complaints. People said they preferred this kind of direct administrative appeal to the environmental bureaucracy because they felt the courts would support entrenched economic interests (generally tied to local government offices, which also appoint judges).

Local judges also complained that the environmental laws and regulations, in spite of the elaboration and publicity, were too general to guide their decisions. Some legal scholars agree that, as the product of a difficult compromise between environmental and economic interests, the law is often ambiguous and occasionally contradictory.[21] Many of these laws and regulations also set a standard so high that local officials responsible for enforcement simply cannot meet the letter of the law. The laws may serve as statements of ideals, or as evidence of meeting treaty obligations, but may be compromised beyond recognition in the implementation process.

Perhaps in the long run the increasing use of the courts for purely economic disputes and protection of farmers' rights will expand into a legal culture where people are comfortable with the idea of using lawyers and courts, and where the legal structure provides a useful mechanism for helping control environmental problems. For now, however, people continue to show a strong preference for strictly political solutions to environmental problems, and only rarely invoke the law. The one legal case involving the environment that we were able to uncover in Anqing was Gao and his dead crabs, as I discussed in chapter 5. Even for him, the economic loss was more important than any general commitment to the environment. And like most people, his use of law was just one of many political channels that he exploited.[22]

A number of causes thus impede environmental policy implementation. China's sophisticated regulatory and legal framework on the environment may be more useful as a statement of ideals than as a practical mechanism for changing environmental behavior. Rural cadres also still lack concrete incentives to promote better environmental performance. This might require, for instance, building environmental indicators into promotion standards, the way economic indicators are now. Finally, regulatory mechanisms often have unintended consequences. Jahiel, for example, shows how a discharge fee system intended to reduce pollution through market mechanisms failed because the fines were lower than the cost of cleaning up polluted factory discharges, and because polluting state-owned enterprises simply added the fees to their budget subsidies. On the other hand, collection of these fees became very important to the fiscal health of Environmental Protection Bureaus – a positive but unintended consequence.[23]

These cases remind us again of the complex dynamics that typify environmental policy on the ground. Environmental Protection Bureaus at county and municipal levels showed differing interests in Gao's dead crabs, for example, with the municipal level much more willing to intervene, and with local economic interests trumping the environment at the county level. His case also had local villagers petitioning in support of this outsider businessman, and a polluting local factory tied to a large urban factory. Hierarchy, in short, is multiple and not singular here.

Taiwan

Power in Taiwan is no more linear than in China, of course. Taiwan's democratization has further complicated the situation. As an example, let me return to Kending National Park, but this time to examine a conflict between local residents and the park administration during the summer of 1993. Nearly 20,000 people lived within the boundaries of the park at the time, and most of their families had been there for generations. Land ownership rights, however, were problematic. The Japanese had nationalized much of the local area, and so many residents had no legal ownership of the land they farmed. When the national park was legally delineated in 1979, some of the land was privately owned, and some was state owned by various branches of the government, but with a long history of use by local people. The particular conflict in 1993 came as the park attempted to exert more control.

When I interviewed the Park Superintendent, Shi Mengxiong, in 1993, he estimated that the park really controls only 10 percent of the land within its boundaries. The rest is private (about 30 percent) or controlled by other government units, especially the Pingdong County government and the national Forestry Bureau. The Anti-Communist Youth League for the Salvation of the Nation, which I discussed earlier, controlled just a little land, but this particularly irked the park because it included some of the most desirable sites for tourists.

Taiwan's national park law, with its eyes on Yosemite, sets very strict limits on land use within the park boundaries, even for people who already lived there. Local people told me they are not allowed to use insecticide on their farm land, for instance. More troublesome as the economy moved toward tourism, though, was the law forbidding any new construction except to replace current housing on the same scale. In practice, however, this law had not been strictly enforced. The result was that people had built roughly ninety hotels within the park, usually by illegally adding upper stories to their houses. In a way very reminiscent of China, the law functioned as a statement of ideals rather than a means of regulating actual behavior on the ground.

This was true, at least, until 1993, when suddenly the park pointed out that all these structures were illegal and razed several of them. At the same time, the park police had opened their own small hotel, and outside capital had been allowed to build several large hotels. In the eyes of local protest organizers, the big commercial hotels must have paid bribes to get special treatment, while the locals were losing their rights to compete. At the time, the GMD still seemed unshakably in control of the national government – including the park service, of course – but the opposition DPP controlled the county government, and was generally strong in this part of Taiwan. They quickly saw an opportunity to help their cause, and led the protest against the park.

I have no way of knowing whether the allegations of bribery were true, but the pattern of allowing outside investors to build "appropriate" resorts instead of allowing locals to profit is common with parks in many parts of the world. The more interesting question in this case is why the park suddenly began to enforce their regulations after a decade of turning a blind eye. The answer lies in the interactions between local and national politics, and between local political factions. Shi Mengxiong was the first superintendent of the park when it opened to the public in 1984. This is an important position in the local political economy because the park is so crucial to them and because it controls so much patronage through direct employment and contracting services from other companies.

When the single-party system finally ended after 1987, elections at the county level and higher became more competitive. Knowing that Shi occupied such an important local position, they had him run for county head. He was elected, but fell victim at the next election as the DPP grew increasingly powerful in this area. The GMD central government reappointed him as head of the park, clearly hoping that by maintaining control of its patronage potential, they could make him a strong candidate again in the future. Shi's interests were fundamentally political, and he was thus unwilling even to attempt to enforce the letter of the national park law; he could not alienate so many potential voters. This hidden agenda was the main reason for the apparently unrestrained private development within the park boundaries – from unregulated jet-skis to all the little hotels.

By 1993, however, the environment had become more important on the national agenda, and the central leadership of the park service had become more dedicated and independent. Perhaps also they realized that the GMD had very little chance of being reelected in the Kending area. For all these reasons, they increased pressure on Shi until he was forced to take some steps toward implementing laws that had been on the books all along.

Many of the locals I spoke to were well aware of these laws, but a decade of ignoring them with the apparent blessing of the park management nevertheless made them feel that their economic rights were being violated. One family I interviewed held a significant amount of land along the waterfront. The nine brothers ran a restaurant, a store, a beach campground that packed in tents like sardines, and a patch of beach where they charged people to swim. Like many in the area, their family had no deeds to this land, although they claimed rights to it. The business at the beach was technically illegal, but the government had not shut it down. Instead, there seemed to be a form of willful ignorance, where the owners did not pay taxes on their business, but the government did not supply running water or electricity. Once the park service began to tear down illegal hotels, however, this whole range of petty entrepreneurial tourism trade felt threatened.

Shi Mengxiong was no happier about it. He felt caught between what he considered the greed of local people and the incomprehension of the central office of the national park administration. He directed most of his ire at other levels of government. This included the county government, controlled by his political enemies in the DPP. The county had given up control of only two of the three most lucrative sites in the park, and that was only in exchange for half the income from ticket sales. Worse still, he found the central administration in Taipei too full of environmental theory and too ignorant of human beings. "They just want to be like Yosemite," he told me. Instead, he thought human beings should be considered part of the park – not so much implying a broader ecological view on his part, but just the pragmatism of an old politician.

Nodes and flows of power

We can certainly see a kind of vertical power hierarchy at work here, with new policies from above, new countermeasures from the local people below, and Shi Mengxiong caught in the middle. To understand the situation in 1993, though, we also need to recall alternative lines of power. In this case, they include first the local electoral competition between the DPP and the GMD. Second, there were the conflicting land claims of the park service, forestry bureau, county government, and local people. Finally, these competing nodes of power each gravitated toward different views of the environment – centered here on acceptance or rejection of the globalized Yosemite ideal of pure wilderness. The Yosemite ideal guided the creation and belated implementation of the park law, but both the superintendent and the local protestors rejected it.

The vertical and unitary images of power – as above and below, state and village, or global and local – are as inadequate for this case as they were for Gao's crabs in Anqing, or the changing neighborhood committee in Tianjin. Power flows through numerous contested and interacting nodes in each of these cases, with competing sources of power sometimes offering people opportunities to manipulate them, as Shi Mengxiong managed for many years. These nodes can sometimes rework the nature of power, much as Tianjin's neighborhood committees reinvented themselves at the very end of the 1990s. All of this is similar to the global flows we have seen in earlier chapters, where ideas about nature flow more strongly in some directions than others, but are reworked and reissued at multiple nodes along the way.

Power, resistance, and slippage

Let me turn more directly to the issue of policies and countermeasures. In part because the metaphor of above and below is inadequate, the idea of policies and opposing countermeasures also makes a complex interplay appear too much like a child's game of tug of war. A simple dichotomy between power and resistance, orthodoxy and opposition, does not leave enough analytic room for hidden resistance, which is safer than open resistance, but harder to organize on any large scale. Nor does it leave room for the ambiguities of silence, irony, or simple difference – it is often impossible to tell if these are meant as resistance, but they are not acquiescence either. Finally, we need to make some room for the unintended consequences and mismatched assumptions – in this case about how humans and the environment should relate – that explain policy failure at least as often as countermeasures. This is not so much resistance as just slippage.

We have already run into a number of such cases in the course of this book. People who take stones from national parks, for instance, are showing their different assumptions about nature, rather than carrying out countermeasures. A comparable mismatch of ideas occurs in the differences between urban elite environmentalists and local protestors over the use of religion. I will elaborate a couple of further examples here, one involving the move away from coal use in Tianjin, and the other a propaganda campaign in Anqing.

One of the most striking cases of apparent environmental policy success in Tianjin, as in many large cities, has been the move from coal to gas for household heating and cooking. A typical family in Tianjin heats for about four months, from mid-November to mid-March, usually in the evening hours. Families with small children or aged parents will heat longer – average use was about ten honeycomb briquettes a day in 1999. Coal has been the primary household fuel because it is cheap and widely available in China, but it causes serious environmental problems. Locally, it produces heavy particulates that cause respiratory problems, in addition to the most obvious effect of filling China's northern cities with dust during the heating season. More broadly, it is a major contributor to global warming.

Unlike the fads for organic vegetables or oxygen bars in the late 1990s, which were driven by market responses to changing environmental attitudes, the fuel change resulted above all from government policy. Piped natural gas requires an appropriate infrastructure, which the government controls, just like the sewers or the electrical system. The natural gas infrastructure in Tianjin began in the 1980s with some luxury apartments for cadres. By the late 1990s it had expanded to the point where the city government now required all new housing to use it. The city's older one-storey housing, however, still burns coal, and the government does not plan to require retrofitting with gas. The idea is that these older stocks of housing will rapidly be replaced, and the city will soon no longer burn coal.

This general transition in fuels has succeeded partly through information campaigns and urban people's greater knowledge of environmental problems, partly through central control over infrastructure, and partly through coercion. For example, the Environmental Protection Bureau in

Tianjin began close inspections of fuel use in the summer of 1999, to make sure people were following a recent law limiting sulfur content of coal, or prohibiting it entirely in some cases. Offenders were punished and exposed in press releases. The immediate inspiration for this was preparation for the International Gymnastic Championships, to be held in October of that year. The city government was also driven by the need to project an image that would help it attract investment capital.

There is, however, a significant gap in this strategy. Like most of China's large cities since the 1980s, Tianjin has experienced two major changes that affect fuel use. One is the enormous increase in sidewalk food vendors, who usually cook on portable, coal-burning stoves. This was one of the early and widely welcomed breakthroughs in urban consumption after the economic reforms. It comes with an environmental cost, though: a typical boiled mutton vendor might consume 25 kilograms of coal a day. The other major change is a massive increase in the "informal" population of Tianjin, just like all the other major coastal cities. The Chinese press usually refers to these people as the "floating population" (*liudong renkou*) even though many of them are in fact long-term residents.[24] These migrants come from the countryside or from other parts of China, and do not have formal residence rights – from access to the public education system to city services. They often work as micro-entrepreneurs (including many of those street vendors) or as laborers in the least desirable jobs. This informal population of Tianjin probably numbers over a million people, fully 10 percent of the population.[25]

Both the vendors and the migrant population represent aspects of the informal economy that have boomed under the economic reforms, but they also show some of the slippage between policy and practice. The press to substitute gas for coal has ignored all of these people and their activities because they are not part of the official understanding of what constitutes the city. Without official city residence registrations, the migrants have no access to gas and must burn coal, just as sidewalk vendors must. The centrally planned network of natural gas has worked well where political control is strong – in state-owned housing and in new housing built by large developers in close cooperation with city or district governments who control the land. It does not work at the margins of political hierarchy – on the relatively unregulated sidewalks and migrant squatter areas of the city.

The result is a massive consumption of coal that has simply slipped out of policy calculations. Part of the explanation for the slippage is the difficulty of central planning (and central coercion) at the margins of the system. It is also a kind of cognitive slippage, though, around the idea of what constitutes a city. For urban planners and policy-makers, Tianjin for most purposes consists of its officially registered population and the social and physical infrastructure to support it. The rest just does not count for some purposes, no matter how much carbon dioxide and how many heavy particulates it releases.

As another example, Earth Day in Anqing also showed significant policy slippage, but of a rather different kind. One reason why environmental policy seems to have had relatively little effect in rural Anqing is that the government does not often make its case through arguments that are locally compelling. Its own understanding of humans and the environment sometimes varies significantly from that of the local farmers, leading to ineffectual campaigns.

Although our sample of Anqing villagers showed little knowledge about or concern for general problems that do not appear as major influences on their own lives – like global warming or acid rain – they are open to arguments that pollution is affecting their own health and wealth. Government campaigns, however, tend to argue from just those global generalities that people find least compelling. We can see this in a brochure that the Anqing Municipal Environmental Protection Bureau put out for Earth Day in 1999, listing the most important environmental crises. These included global warming, the hole in the ozone layer, acid rain, ocean pollution, nuclear waste, deforestation, erosion, and biodiversity loss. This is a perfectly good list of global environmental problems, and it fits well with the sorts of priorities that global NGOs express. They are also the policy priorities that China wants to show to the outside world. Yet, within Anqing – the ostensible audience for the brochure – not a single one of these problems (with the partial exception of erosion) fitted the daily experience of the people we interviewed. Such efforts may have an important effect in letting higher levels of government know that Anqing is following the proper line, and multiplied by hundreds of cities across China it may let the central government claim to be taking action. Such actions, though, have little effect on their intended audience, because they wrongly assume that people will change their behavior out of dedication to universal, global environmental concerns.

In contrast, a strong campaign showing the links between lung disease and cooking with biomass or coal, for example, might convince people to switch to other fuels.[26] This would be consistent with the localist attitudes that have appeared throughout this book, from stone gods to environmental protest movements. To my knowledge, however, this has not yet been tried.

Another possibility, at least in principle, would be to utilize existing understandings of an anthropocosmic relationship between humanity and environment. These ideas, based on a balance of the natural energies of the universe (as I discussed in chapter 2), continue to have a strong daily presence in people's lives through the practice of traditional Chinese medicine, *fengshui*, and diet. They do not, however, mesh well with the government's modernist view of science, and there seems little chance of their being picked up in official discourse.

Urban Tianjin and the rural hinterland of the Anqing metropolitan area differ greatly in environmental awareness, which shows most clearly in the high numbers of environmental complaints in Tianjin and the developing market for "green" products. None of this was happening in rural Anqing. Both cases, however, show a similar kind of slippage between central policy and local conditions. In the rural case, information on the environment was being produced, but it was distant from local concerns with economic and physical welfare, and it did not mesh with existing forms of environmental thinking. In Tianjin, the slippage came instead from the existence of an informal economy that urban planners chose to ignore, since dealing with the fuel issues of street vendors and migrants would have granted them a formal status that China is not now prepared to do.

Implications

This brief survey of various mechanisms to implement environmental policy shows a mix of successes and failures at the intersection of various levels of government, varying understandings of the environment, and competing interests. The idea of policies from above and countermeasures from below captures some important elements of this dynamic. Yet it also simplifies too much by reducing the complex interactions of different political levels and institutions to just a dyad (the state and the people, or the central and the local) and by assuming a level of explicit consciousness that underestimates both unspoken cultural assumptions and unintended consequences.

A distinction between center and local is a useful first cut. The evidence from this and earlier chapters shows a gulf between a national level and a local level. The national-level groups tend to interact closely with global environmental concerns with strong roots in North America and western Europe. Local groups are motivated much more by economic and personal concerns (Mr. Gao's crabs, dust in Tianjin apartments, Houjing's temples); they also have fundamental political limits on their abilities to organize and expand. A similar split shows up in the Anqing Environmental Protection Bureau's concern over the ozone layer and global warming (both promoted by globalizing environmentalism), even though these issues seem to have no appeal to most villagers in the municipality.

It shows up again in the elaborate environmental legal code formulated in Beijing, which is too unwieldy and exotic to implement on the ground in most places. A similar mismatch between law and practice showed up in Kending National Park.

Many of these central initiatives represent a kind of idealism that does not quite mesh with realities on the ground. Unimplemented legal systems are really just statements of ideals, and so are environmental education campaigns that never seem to reach anyone. In a sense, the Tianjin fuel use policy that ignored the unpleasant reality of the migrant population is another way of creating a policy of ideals instead of one that responds to the situation on the ground. County-level Environmental Protection Bureaus are yet another example of a structural change that cannot achieve its ideal, because they are not independent from other county-level needs, especially income generation. Land use in Kending ignored national law for many years because of the rather different dynamics of electoral politics in its local area.

This binary distinction between center and local is too simple, though. Mr. Gao's case already shows a complex interaction between local villagers, various economic interests (the polluting factory, the refinery it did business with, Mr. Gao himself, local farmers), county-level officials, and municipal officials. The changes in environmental behavior of the Tianjin street committee also show multiple levels, with factories, local residents, varying market pressures (for oxygen and organic food, but also for polluting street food), and changing government policies. Taiwan's democracy sometimes puts other mechanisms into play, but they are just as dynamic as the PRC. In each case we have a heterarchy of competing and nested nodes of power, rather than a simple vertical relationship.

Environmental policy (perhaps all policy) anywhere must face unintended consequences – failures of science to predict effects accurately, failures to understand or face up to local social and political dynamics, failures to recognize one's own assumptions. The idea of policies met with countermeasures implies a process of rational confrontation of conflicting ideas, but much of what we have seen involves interests, motives, and assumptions that may never become explicit or conscious. It is not a game of chess.

National NGOs, legal scholars, environmental scientists, county officials, urban neighborhood committees, and local villagers differ in more than just their fuel use strategies. They vary even in how they understand the relationships between humanity and environment, between state and society. By ignoring this, environmental policy on the ground in both China and Taiwan has evolved into a set of mixed messages, with little effective feedback that might lead to more sensitive adjustment of policy to local needs. Democratic competition has helped ease this more in Taiwan than in China – the problems at Kending were remnants of an older patronage system that gave way to national electoral pressures on the central administration. Both places, however, continue to show a significant gap between how nature is understood by political and intellectual elites and by people in villages and urban neighborhoods.

Rather than concentrating our attention on domination and resistance in policy, these environmental cases force us to recall the ambiguities and complexities that create a wide range of interactions with power. These include direct resistance, but also accommodation, collaboration, and alienation. Various actors may interact with direct linear hierarchies of power, but may also manipulate a heterarchy of competing power sources. In much of this chapter, I have concentrated on cases of what might better be called slippage than resistance. Policy failure here comes when different cultural frames and modes of discourse fail to mesh. We saw this in Anqing's uninfluential Earth Day brochure and in continued coal use by Tianjin's migrant population.

The slippage idea can also help reveal some problems in our approach to environmental awareness. One of the main hypotheses about when people begin to show concern about the environment is the "postmaterialism thesis," usually associated with Inglehart's comparative work on value change.[27] He argues that environmentalism, like feminism and other postmaterialist values, only develops after a society achieves a certain level of wealth and more basic needs have been satisfied. At first glance, the data from China and Taiwan seem to support this idea. People in Anqing act less concerned about pollution than the generally wealthier people in Tianjin, who are in turn less concerned than the even wealthier Taiwanese.

Yet the people of Anqing are hardly unconcerned about the environment – they worry about environmental effects on the health of their children and the quality of their crops, they think about the broad interactions of diet and health through traditional Chinese medical categories, and they know their environment (where their water and food come from, for instance) more intimately than people in Tianjin or Taiwan. They lack environmental consciousness only in the sense that they are not concerned with the same issues as national and global elites, or as people who write questionnaires about values. They think about the environment in terms of temples, *fengshui*, medically "hot" and "cold" foods, and personal economic costs and benefits. They tend not, however, to think in terms of current global (and originally Western) discourses about nature for its own sake or about economic effects that they cannot experience directly. The slippage here is in our theoretical idea of "environmental consciousness," by which we usually mean a historically particular global form of such consciousness. Surveys have not picked up environmental thought that is framed in significantly different terms.

Most of what I have discussed in this chapter concerned interactions within state borders, but globalization is always present, especially in its influence on policy formation. From Taiwan's national park law to Anqing's Earth Day brochure, we can see policy-makers either directly accepting some of these global discourses, or at least claiming to for international political purposes. The kinds of dynamic relationships I have been discussing, of heterarchies and slippages, apply as much at the global as at the national level. Globalization, as I have been arguing, is also a matter of multiple and competing nodes of power, and of widely varied ways of dealing with those powers.

NOTES

1. See Andrew Kipnis, "The Anthropology of Power and Maoism," *American Anthropologist* 105, no. 2 (2003): 278–88.
2. See Carole L. Crumley, "Heterarchy and the Analysis of Complex Societies," in *Heterarchy and the Analysis of Complex Societies*, ed. Robert M. Ehrenreich, Carole L. Crumley, and Janet E. Levy (Arlington, VA: American Anthropological Association, 1995), 1–5.
3. Mayfair Mei-hui Yang, *Gifts, Favors and Banquets: The Art of Social Relationships in China* (Ithaca: Cornell University Press, 1994).
4. James L. Watson, "Introduction: Transnationalism, Localization, and Fast Foods in East Asia," in *Golden Arches East: McDonald's in East Asia*, ed. James L. Watson (Stanford: Stanford University Press, 1997), 1–38.
5. Both projects were part of my work with the Harvard University Committee on the Environment China Project. I am grateful to them and to the V. Kann Rasmussen Foundation and the United States Department of Energy for their support. The material from Anhui is based on a collaborative study undertaken with William Alford, Leslyn Hall, Karen Polenske, Yuanyuan Shen, Xiping Xu, and David Zweig. It involved 244 household interviews in rural counties of Anqing City in 1997. See William P. Alford *et al.*, "The Human Dimensions of Pollution Policy Implementation: Air Quality in Rural China," *Journal of Contemporary China* 11 (2002): 495–513. The Tianjin study relied on the research help of Jiansheng Li, whose earlier research experience in Tianjin also proved very valuable. These more informal interviews took place primarily in 1999 and 2001.
6. Susmita Dasgupta and David Wheeler, *Citizen Complaints as Environmental Indicators: Evidence from China*, Report to PRDEI, World Bank (1996), 11.
7. "Environmental Survey," *China Education News*, 1 June 1999. Similar results can also be found in Yuan Fang, "The Environmental Awareness of Chinese Citizens: A Sociological Analysis," in *Environmental Awareness in Developing Countries: The Case of China and Thailand* (Tokyo: Japan/Asia Economic Development Institute, 1997).

8. Zhongguo Huanjing Nianjian Bianji Weiyuanhui, ed., *Zhongguo Huanjing Nianjian (China Environmental Yearbook)* (Beijing: Zhongguo Huanjing Kexue Chubanshe, 1996). For more detail, see Alford *et al.*, "The Human Dimensions of Pollution Policy Implementation."
9. Mark Hertsgaard, "Our Real China Problem," *Atlantic Monthly*, November 1997, 97–114.
10. An even more disheartening 48 percent of women had no education.
11. This is probably not typical of all rural areas. In a more recent study of Panzihua, Sichuan, Bryan Tilt found a much higher awareness of environmental issues. One possible explanation is that awareness in China has increased very rapidly over the few years between the studies. This may well be a factor, but a stronger possibility is that while the rural areas of Anqing we studied had almost no industry, Panzihua had numerous disputes as the central government tried to control local industry on environmental grounds, thus encouraging everyone to use environmental discourse. See Bryan D. Tilt, "Risk, Pollution and Sustainability in Rural Sichuan, China" (PhD diss., University of Washington, 2004).
12. Michael Hsin-Huang Hsiao, Russell A. Stone, and Chun-Chieh Chi, "Taiwan Environmental Consciousness: Indicators of Collective Mind toward Sustainable Development," *Resarch for Sustainable Taiwan* 4, no. 2 (2002): 1–33.
13. For more information on local elections and the environment coming out of our Anqing study, see Alford *et al.*, "The Human Dimensions of Pollution Policy Implementation."
14. For work on neighborhood committees in another context, see Benjamin L. Read, "Democratizing the Neighborhood? New Private Housing and Home-Owner Self-Organization in Urban China," *China Journal* 49 (January 2003): 31–59.
15. Taiwan also showed an extremely fast learning curve when its Environmental Protection Agency changed policy in 1991 and became more responsive to complaints – protests through legal and political means surged almost immediately. See Robert P. Weller, *Alternate Civilities: Democracy and Culture in China and Taiwan* (Boulder, CO: Westview, 1999), 125.
16. For more detail, see Jonathan Unger, *The Transformation of Rural China* (Armonk, NY: M. E. Sharpe, 2002).
17. Abigail R. Jahiel, "The Contradictory Impact of Reform on Environmental Protection in China," *China Quarterly* 151 (1997): 81–103.
18. William P. Alford and Yuanyuan Shen, "The Limits of the Law in Addressing China's Environmental Dilemma," in *Energizing China: Reconciling Environmental Protection and Economic Growth*, ed. Michael B. McElroy, Chris P. Nielsen, and Peter Lydon (Cambridge, MA: Harvard University Committee on the Environment, 1998), 405–30.
19. See Unger, *The Transformation of Rural China*, 213–16.
20. Of these, 41 percent concerned noise pollution, 41 percent concerned air pollution (mostly from coal), and 11 percent concerned water pollution.
21. Alford *et al.*, "The Human Dimensions of Pollution Policy Implementation," 509. Although there were many co-authors, including me, this passage represents the work of William Alford and Yuanyuan Shen.

22. This case is consistent with O'Brien and Li's argument that administrative litigation is best seen as more a political mechanism than a legal one. Kevin J. O'Brien and Lianjiang Li, "Suing the Local State: Administrative Litigation in Rural China," *China Journal* 51 (January 2004): 75–96.
23. Jahiel, "The Contradictory Impact of Reform on Environmental Protection in China."
24. For a study of a migrant community in Beijing, see Li Zhang, "Migration and Privatization of Space and Power in Late Socialist China," *American Ethnologist* 28, no. 1 (2001): 179–205.
25. State Statistical Bureau, People's Republic of China, *China Statistical Yearbook* (Beijing: State Statistical Bureau, 1998), 111. These official numbers are almost certainly too low.
26. These effects can be difficult to sort out because smoking has such a powerful influence on lung function, but they still seem clear from our survey. See Alford *et al.*, "The Human Dimensions of Pollution Policy Implementation." More generally in China, see Xiping Xu *et al.*, "Occupational and Environmental Risk Factors for Asthma in Rural Communities in China," *International Journal of Occupational and Environmental Health* 2 (1996): 172–6.
27. Ronald Inglehart, *Culture Shift in Advanced Industrial Society* (Princeton: Princeton University Press, 1990).

7 Globals and locals

Understandings of nature changed rapidly and radically over the twentieth century in China and Taiwan. Most of these changes added new layers of possibility to existing ideas, rather than substituting for them wholesale. Nevertheless, the new ways of thinking about the environment had a profound effect, above all on the educated elites who became so important in designing policy. We now have national parks and nature reserves, environmental protection bureaucracies and regulations, bird watching societies and environmentalist NGOs. Some of them resonate with earlier Chinese traditions, but all of them look outside that tradition for their direct inspiration. On the other hand, many older ideas remain vibrant, from gods protecting their neighborhood to the anthropocosmic qualities of food. We can also find new creations, for instance in the hands of local nature tourism sites, whose bricolages combine pieces of various traditions into something new.

The usual theoretical stories we tell about globalization seem inadequate for all this. Three such stories have dominated most of the discussion, and I have touched on all of them in earlier chapters. One is the avalanche from Hollywood (or Wall Street, for those who prefer a less entertaining sector), which sees globalization as an unstoppable homogenization that dooms local variation and that makes the nation-state increasingly irrelevant. The second highlights resistance to globalization, instead of the hegemony of the global leviathan. This has been the anthropologist's usual response of finding local agency in the power to negate or rework global pressures. Third, there is a more postmodern view of globalization as an opportunity for creativity. We can see this in Ulf Hannerz's concept of creole cultures, which form, like creole languages, from the creative juncture of different traditions.[1] In a somewhat altered form, this view shows up for the modern Chinese diaspora in Nonini and Ong's claim that this community's mobility "manifests a wildness, danger, and unpredictability that challenges and undermines modern imperial regimes of truth and power."[2]

Each of these views captures some of the changes I have been discussing, but none describes them very fully. There are three areas in particular where, at least to understand changing views of the environment in China and Taiwan, we still need more theoretical elaboration: the continued impact and influence of state structures on how global forces are realized, the multiplicity of both global and local influences, and the different scales of influence and nodes of power that shape the effects of globalization. Let me spell each of these out further, especially considering the ways that these theoretical approaches have important implications for environmental policy construction and implementation.

State power in China and Taiwan

China and Taiwan invite comparison because they offer variants on a shared cultural and social background, but with radically different economic and political histories since 1895, when Taiwan became a colony of Japan. This long century was the crucial period for the development of new ideas about nature and the environment, and so we might expect on principle that the two places would have evolved quite differently. This is especially so because China cut itself off from Western influences for many decades, actively denounced its cultural past for much the same period, and pursued a non-market development strategy. None of this occurred in Taiwan during either the colonial or the Nationalist period. Furthermore, we might expect China to be more effective at implementing its policies because its state was more thoroughly intrusive and organized for mass mobilization. The comparison of two quite different regimes under similar global pressures should reveal the state's ability to enable, resist, rework, or simply give in to the new forces.

Indeed, the form of the state has been important in shaping ideas about nature, and this shows up in some significant differences between China and Taiwan. We saw it, for instance, in the differences between state-run nature reserves in the two places. Taiwan's models draw almost exclusively on American precursors like Yosemite, which attempt to foster a wilderness ideal, preserved against human encroachment. While some of this also occurs in China, they have tended to emulate instead United Nations models, which allow for concentric rings of increasing human interaction with the environment. The disparity comes partly from the different historical attitudes of the two places toward the United States. It also happened because Taiwan entered the world of global environmentalism earlier than China – its national park laws, its environmental protection bureaucracy, and even its public urban noise pollution monitors came in the 1970s, roughly a decade before China. At that point alternatives to the United States nature tourism model were not yet as developed. The two states thus encouraged somewhat different forms of nature tourism.

Environmental protest also takes significantly different forms in the two places, as a direct result of their political differences. While China has increasingly made space for local environmental action – telephone hotlines, petitions, lawsuits, and even some demonstrations – it will not allow any kind of institutionalized environmentalism that argues with government policy. To exist, environmental organizations in China must stay close to official policy, and must tread carefully even when pointing out that practice does not match policy. An organized anti-nuclear movement like Taiwan's, for instance, is impossible. As we would expect, Taiwan has far more room for local protest and national organization. Taiwan's particular political history has also encouraged specific arenas of protest, like the "garbage wars" that have been so common.

In spite of all this, though, the similarities between China and Taiwan are remarkable, especially in light of their very different regime types. Both the United States and the United Nations models of nature preservation share more with each other, after all, than with earlier Chinese traditions of nature appreciation. More market-based nature tourism, which is freer from state-sponsored ideals, has taken a similar mélange form in both places, combining temples, Chinese and Western gardens, water play, nature education, and a host of other indigenous and imported activities. Even environmental protest, in spite of the differences in political space, often takes related forms in China and Taiwan, like the preference for blockades, or the organization through local temples and lineages.

I do not conclude from this that the state became an unimportant factor under late twentieth-century globalization. If that were so, China and Taiwan would look not just like each other, but like every other place in the world. They do not. No one would mistake Chinese or Taiwanese mélange nature tourism, or the social organization of their local demonstrations, for their Indian, European, or American equivalents. One reason for the similarity to each other and not to other places, of course, is their shared cultural and social history. This history has been sometimes denounced and sometimes embraced by various Chinese governments over the twentieth century. It has been thoroughly reworked as people deal with rapid change. Nevertheless, we have seen its influence throughout this book, from Buddhist environmentalism, to attitudes about eating endangered species, to the importance of weird rocks.

A second obvious reason for the similarity is that the global influences in both places are comparable, although Taiwan began responding to them a bit earlier. Nature tourism may be taking unique forms in

Taiwan and China, but no one could confuse it with anything that happened before the twentieth century, and its global inspirations are obvious. The imported idea of bird watching was one of the earliest forms of globalized nature appreciation in both places. Environmental protection bureaucracies, regulatory and legal regimes, appeals to global warming and ozone holes, creation of state-run reserves – all of these draw directly on global currents. Not just environmental NGOs, but the very idea and legal framework for NGOs come from global sources.

A third reason, perhaps not as obvious, is the state itself. The differences between Communist China and capitalist Taiwan, and more recently between authoritarian China and democratic Taiwan, certainly affect environmental attitudes and behavior, but they can also distract us from some fundamental similarities between the two states. Both the Communist and the Nationalist regimes learned their political organization and propaganda techniques together from the Soviets, especially during the 1920s. Thus, while Taiwan never attempted the totalitarian extremes of Cultural Revolution China, it had a domineering apparatus of social and cultural control until its democratization in the 1980s. One result of their shared history of loosely Leninist authoritarian control is that social organizations – including environmental NGOs and protest groups – tended to develop a split between large, subservient, and "modern" groups under central control, and local, less institutionalized, and more "traditional" groups based in communities (see chapter 5).

At an even more fundamental level, both states were the heirs of the unstinting dedication to modernity that characterized the dominant stream of Chinese intellectuals from the early twentieth century on. That is why, in both cases, we see initially an adoption from the West (including the Soviet Union) of a powerfully pro-development discourse that saw nature as a resource to be mined or an obstacle to be conquered. Later, again in both cases, we can see these states taking almost intact foreign models of nature preservation or environmental protection, especially in the creation of legal codes and administrative structures. The reason that the influence of earlier Chinese traditions is so much clearer at local levels, away from state control, is this shared legacy of dedication to modernity that both states have always shown, but that does not always penetrate through all levels of society.

There is little evidence here for shrinking state control under globalization. Both states helped catalyze globalizing change, and environmental behavior would not have taken its current form in either one without the active role of the state. Many of the similarities and differences in the ways ideas about nature have changed in China and Taiwan stem directly from the nature of their states.

Plural globalizations and creative nodes

Much of this argument has been directed against simple top-down approaches to globalization. This is a common sentiment from an anthropologist or anyone who looks at society from the grassroots up. Top-down theories are not completely wrong, of course. Even when we can find successful localization in the face of global forces, there is often a larger context that cannot be explained without some larger top-down globalization. To take an influential Asian example, Watson shows how McDonald's restaurants are reworked in various Asian cities.[3] In some cases, for instance, they have to abandon their fast turnover business model and invest in large floor areas because the restaurants become study areas for groups of teens who spend hours nursing a soda. His argument is convincing, but the broader context also requires us to recognize the powerful influence of global forces that enabled this local variation on fast food – the teen culture, Western-style education, and other features that seem to accompany modernity everywhere.

With Chinese and Taiwanese views of nature over the twentieth century, there is also no escape from a broad global context that encouraged massive industrialization and urbanization – with their formative effects on both the environment itself and attitudes toward nature. At the same time, the outside world offered preformulated solutions to the resulting problems in models of sanitation, conservation, and eventually environmentalism. We have seen these models at work in early industrial policy in both China and Taiwan, and later in national park and nature reserve laws, the structure of environmental protection bureaucracies, and the development of NGOs.

The problem with theories of top-down globalization is thus not that they are utterly wrong, but that they simplify the process to the point where they foster misleading conclusions. Cultural globalization is not just a matter of pouring water down a slope and watching everything get wet. It is a multivocal argument among many people with different interests, different access to the mechanisms of cultural production, and different amounts of power to impose their views.

Rather than just embracing or rejecting the top-down view, it may be more fruitful to ask when top-down influences appear to have been most effective, and when they seem less powerful. The cases I have presented here suggest that top-down effects show up most clearly at the level of national political and intellectual leaders. Chinese and Taiwanese regulatory codes, nature reserve plans, environmental administrations, and NGO mission statements have obvious roots in global models from the West, Japan, or the United Nations. It is not an easy task at all to identify anything uniquely Chinese or Taiwanese about these things, nor did their authors usually strive to be unique.

On the other hand, when we look beyond statements of elite ideals like legal codes and mission statements, the top-down model is far less salient. National park ideals of unsullied nature get compromised by local officials who let people build illegal hotels in Taiwanese national parks, or who serve endangered species for dinner in Chinese nature reserves. NGOs feel undercut when local gods channel protest toward community preservation instead of more universal environmental goals. Planners are frustrated when people take weird rocks as souvenirs from nature reserves, when they ignore environmental propaganda campaigns, or when they consult *fengshui* specialists to improve their anthropocosmic balance. It is at this level of policy implementation rather than formation, law enforcement rather than enactment, practice rather than ideal, that we see the real limits of top-down globalization.

One of the problems with the top-down model is that it usually assumes a straightforward diffusion from a central source – Hollywood, Davos, Wall Street, or just a generic "West." In contrast, even focusing our attention only on the most influential modern Western views of nature forces us to recognize that globalization flows in multiple and interfering currents. It has always been multiple, not singular. All of these currents flowed into China and Taiwan over the twentieth century, arguing with each other the whole time.

As I outlined in chapter 3, at least three different Western views of how people and nature relate to each other influenced China and Taiwan during the twentieth century. The most authoritative by far during the early part of the century was the separation of nature from culture, objectifying nature into a tool for human progress and enrichment. The others – a biocentric valuing of nature for its own sake and a pastoral view of humanity and nature at one – came into China at around the same time, but only grew important later in the century, when both places developed an interest in nature tourism and environmental protection.

Even this metaphor of conflicting currents fails to capture some of the complexity. Globalizing ideas often get reworked at various crucial nodes before being passed along. One early critical such development was the way the United States adapted European Romanticism to develop a wilderness aesthetic that differed from anything in Europe, but that eventually shaped national parks everywhere. For the cases I have been examining, Japan looms especially large as an important node of global remixing. We saw this first in the very word for "nature" (*ziran*) that the Chinese adopted from the West, but only after its reworking in Japan. We also saw it in the ways Taiwan's provincial parks differed from its national parks, because they drew on Japanese instead of American models. I am confident that more detailed study would reveal many more examples, with Japan always playing a key role, but also showing the importance of internal nodes of globalization like Shanghai or Hong Kong.

The most common anthropological response to the top-down model has been to show how local communities resist, rework, or subvert these global forces. I have also looked to such processes throughout this book, but with one important additional observation: the "local" is no more singular than the "global." One of the problems in placing the local in binary opposition to the global is scale. The local that opposes the global can be anything from a tiny and isolated rural group to a nation-state. Each of these scales offers its own opportunities for local/global interaction, and interacts in turn with larger and smaller scales.

Even when the state is brought back in as an independent actor, which anthropology has increasingly done, it tends to be treated as a reified and unitary whole, in contrast to the local community, which we see as diverse and complex. Political science, which generally makes quite sophisticated distinctions among levels of the state and the varying interests among different state actors, tends instead to reduce the local community to a unified whole. This is even clearer in much development work, which has recently developed a strong interest in the "community," but which tends to ignore the differences of power, interests, and even culture within communities. The "social capital" literature in general, which has brought so much favorable attention to local social ties, also tends to imagine communities as solidary and undifferentiated, in a kind of functionalist fantasy.[4]

In Chinese and Taiwanese environmental views we have seen complex interlockings of state and local diversities that will not allow simplifications into a singular, cohesive idea of state or community. The case of Gao's dead crabs, for instance, illustrated different behavior from county and municipal environmental protection authorities, and partially different interests between environmental and other state cadres. In Taiwan, Kending National Park shows differences between central and local levels of park administration, and the consequences of Taiwan's newly democratic politics for park management through the complex interaction of the local and central state, the two main political parties, and the voting constituents. The state – in one guise or another – has been a crucial intermediary in environmental globalization in many of the cases in this book, but never as a singular actor.

Communities themselves are as diverse as the state, especially when we are looking at a society as complex as China has long been. The diverse cultural palette goes beyond the many regional variations – including the variation between Taiwan and the mainland – that characterized imperial China. I have emphasized three of the many views of nature that helped shape China before the twentieth century: Buddhist compassion toward all life and demand for simplicity, the idea of anthropocosmic harmony and resonance, and the particular forms of power of cores and peripheries. For most people these were not philosophical alternatives from which they could choose, nor were they unspoken assumptions of particular regional cultures. Instead, they and other views of nature made up an uneven field of ideas – some consistent with each other, others contradictory, and still others just wandering off in their own direction. These views were available to most people, most of the time, and made up resources from which people would think about the new ideas of the twentieth century.

While such ideas resonated widely with people across China and Taiwan, not everyone is equal in their ability to impose an interpretation. Nodes where ideas get reworked and reissued have been as important locally as globally. These nodes include an urban intellectual like Liang Congjie of Friends of Nature or American-trained technocrats like the people who developed Taiwan's national park policy. They can also be the local village head who decides to close down the town dump (as in Sanxia's garbage dispute), the businessman making villagers aware of environmental legislation while trying to recoup his losses (like Mr. Gao), or just the local *fengshui* specialist trying to explain someone's bad fortune.

Other environmentalisms?

I began this project in the naive hope of finding an alternative Chinese environmentalism, a variation on the theme of local resistance to the global juggernaut. My first superficial look was discouraging, since the most obvious signs of environmental awareness come from NGO leaders, intellectuals, and policy-makers – the very people who speak most clearly in the global discourses of the environment, and show the least interest in the idioms of earlier Chinese ways of thinking about the environment. A deeper look, however, as I have tried to present in this book, reveals a far more complex and interesting situation, for which the very language of "alternative environmentalisms" seems inadequate.

What I found was an interaction of multiple locals and globals, remixed and recreated at various crucial nodes and at different scales. The language of globalization and resistance does not capture these processes very well, although Hannerz comes closer with his idea of global ecumenes – those regions of broad interconnectedness, interaction, and exchange that are reshaping culture.[5] He also uses the term "creole cultures" to get at the creative birth of a new culture out of such interactions, even in situations of inequality, as was typically the case for creole languages.[6] The nodal image of globalization that I have used also owes something to Deleuze and Guattari's writings about rhizomes as an alternative to our usual "arborescent" (tree and branches or root and radicles) images of organizations. Instead of the discrete units and clear hierarchy of the tree metaphor, they offer us potatoes and crabgrass, an "antigenealogy . . . [that] operates by variation, expansion, conquest, capture, offshoots."[7] The rhizomes are fertile clumps of creative possibility.

These images have been helpful in thinking about how understandings of nature have changed in Taiwan and China, and in moving beyond the simplicities of globalization and resistance. On the other hand, such postmodern celebrations of fecund transcendence of boundaries and hierarchies run the risk of downplaying the old-fashioned differences of power that have been just as important.[8] That is why I have sometimes used the language of heterarchy, which attempts to combine the multiplicity of power in both hierarchy and competition.

This book has had many examples of nodes of creative interconnections of globalization, from landscape painting to forms of environmental protest. Not all nodes are created equal, however, and there is little to compete with the dominant global discourses on their own terms. New developments of earlier landscape traditions, mélange tourist sites, or possessed spirit mediums talking about oil refineries have so far been influential only in local contexts. These new creations do not always extend even throughout China and Taiwan, and none of them has been influential beyond national borders.

In addition to having a far more limited sphere of influence than global environmental attitudes, these new creations generally do not compete even as forms of discourse. That is, they have not generated many serious attempts to present themselves as alternate sets of ideas. These local environmentalisms exist in context and in practice, but no one – with the partial exception of some of the new Buddhist movements – has put them into a form where they might compete for the attention of policymakers or intellectuals. Thus while China and Taiwan do offer creative alternatives, they tend not to compete in scale or form of intellectual organization with the global discourses.

Of all the people I have discussed, Chinese and Taiwanese academic and political leaders have been the least likely to voice any of these alternatives, which we find instead mostly in responses to market demand (like mélange tourism) or local community needs (like *fengshui* or the use of religion in protest movements). Instead these elites speak the various global languages of environmentalism. Earlier in the twentieth century they adopted modernist attitudes encouraging the domination of nature.

Later they emulated global models of national parks, recycled foreign legal codes for pollution regulation, and founded branches of Greenpeace. This reminds us that current global environmentalisms, mediated by states and elites, continue to carry much more power and coherence than any of the local alternatives.

We do have alternative environmentalisms, but at least so far they seem unlikely to join any of the global ones, much less displace them. These can be crucially important locally, often shaping real environmental behavior on the ground. They have almost no effect, however, on global nature discourse, and not even much direct effect on Chinese or Taiwanese policy. This is not what I had hoped for when I began this project, but it is not entirely a bad thing either. By remaining local, scattered, and relatively disorganized, these ideas also remain diverse and malleable. They form a pool of different and changing ways of thinking about the environment, always available if we need them. Their localism and disorganization help prevent the kind of homogenization that broader global influence would require.

What are the implications of this for environmental policy today? One is that successful policy must look as much at implementation as at formulation. It is not enough to create rules and agencies to enforce them. The policy slippages I have discussed here – from hotels in Taiwanese national parks to coal use in Tianjin – occurred because not enough attention was paid to the situation on the ground, where policy is not a simple flow from the top down, but a weighing off of divergent interests and assumptions about the world. Many of these interests and assumptions are primarily local in scope, and policy – whether from the state or from NGOs – will have to adjust more flexibly than it has so far.

At a broader level, given the importance of maintaining diverse cultural resources, policy formulation has been too culturally homogenous. I do not mean to refer here only to the Chinese state's infamous penchant for pushing a single policy on everyone, no matter how badly it fits local conditions. The same happens, after all, when international consultants bring cookie-cutter legal codes to new contexts, and when the government in Taiwan or international NGOs in China try to recreate yet another Yosemite. In one form or another, all of this comes as the inheritors of the Enlightenment separation of nature and culture promote policies that universalize their own assumptions, which often remained implicit, unexamined, and unspoken.

The good news is that this universalization appears to have limits, which allow for continued diversity in environmental attitudes. The result is something like the benefit of a diverse gene pool. A completely uniform gene pool may mean that all members of a species are perfectly adapted to some environment, but also spells their doom if conditions change. Maintenance of diversity allows the potential for successful evolution. Culture too must alter and adapt, as our changing views of nature have shown over the last century. China and Taiwan may not offer a grand alternative to global environmentalisms, at least not yet. Nevertheless, they offer us some of the many pools of creative diversity that have survived – even thrived – under the pressures of globalization, and that offer us a source of potential future evolution in our thought.

NOTES

1. Ulf Hannerz, *Transnational Connections: Culture, People, Places* (London: Routledge, 1996).
2. Donald M. Nonini and Aihwa Ong, "Chinese Transnationalism as an Alternative Modernity," in *Ungrounded Empires: The Cultural Politics of Modern Chinese Transnationalism*, ed. Aihwa Ong and Donald Nonini (New York: Routledge, 1997), 19.
3. James L. Watson, "Introduction: Transnationalism, Localization, and Fast Foods in East Asia," in *Golden Arches East: McDonald's in East Asia*, ed. James L. Watson (Stanford: Stanford University Press, 1997), 1–38.
4. The most influential of these neo-communitarian works has probably been Robert D. Putnam, *Bowling Alone: The Collapse and Revival of American Community* (New York: Simon and Schuster, 2000), and the idea runs through the constant calls of agencies like the UNDP or the World Bank to allow for community participation, without examining the community itself very closely.
5. Hannerz, *Transnational Connections*, 7.
6. Hannerz, *Transnational Connections*, 65–77.
7. Gilles Deleuze and Félix Guattari, *A Thousand Plateaus: Capitalism and Schizophrenia*, 1980, trans. Brian Massumi (Minneapolis: University of Minnesota Press, 1987), 21.
8. The best work, of course, still recognizes the importance of inequality. There are "knots of arborescence in rhizomes, and rhizomatic offshoots in roots": Deleuze and Guattari, *A Thousand Plateaus*, 20. The images of rhizomes and ecumenes themselves, however, lend themselves to fantasies on worlds without power.

Chinese characters

Bagua Zushi	八卦祖师
bai	拜
baidou	拜斗
baifang	拜访
bai qin	拜亲
bai shen	拜神
bai zuxian	拜祖先
benxing	本性
bu	补
cai	菜
chaoshan	朝山
chiou-thau kong (H)	石头公
chuanshanjia	穿山甲
Ciji Gongdehui	慈济功德会
Dabangen	大板根
Da Bao Xi	大豹溪
dao	道
da ziran	大自然
difang zhi	地方志
dili	地理
ding (nails)	钉
ding (male descendants)	丁
dizhi	地支
dongchongxiacao	冬虫夏草
fan	饭
fengshui	风水
Gan Wang	甘王
ganying	感应
gezhi	格致

huanjing baohu	环境保护
huoqi	火气
huoyu	活鱼
hutou feng	虎头蜂
jiangyu	疆域
jiashan	假山
jiedao banshi chu	街道办事处
jing	精
jingzhe	惊蛰
Jipu Anuo	吉普阿诺
jumin weiyuanhui	居民委员会
kak-thau (H)	角头
kaozheng	考证
ling	灵
Li Tieguai	李铁拐
liudong renkou	流动人口
mangzhong	芒种
Manyue Yuan Senlin Youlequ	满月圆森林游乐区
Mifeng Shijie	蜜蜂世界
minjian	民间
poe (H)	杯
pufa jiaoyu	普法教育
qi	气
qishi	奇石
re'nao	热闹
ren ding sheng tian	人定胜天
renjian fojiao	人间佛教
senlin yu	森林浴
shang you zhengce, xia you duice	上有政策下有对策
shanshui	山水
shehui tuanti	社会团体
Shenghuo yu Huanjing	生活与环境
shenling	神灵
shitou gong	石头公
Shitou Ji	石头记
Shixian Gong Miao	石仙公庙

shou	瘦
Taiwan Huanjing Baohu Lianmeng	台湾环境保护联盟
teli (H)	地理
tian	天
Tiandi	天帝
tiandi	天地
tian di ren	天地人
tiangan	天干
tianli	天理
tianming	天命
tian ren he yi	天人合一
Tianzhu	天主
tiaoshen	跳神
tou	透
wanshui	玩水
wanwu	万物
wugu	五谷
wuwei	无为
wuxing	五行
xingshi	形势
xingye	星野
xinling huanjing	心灵环境
xinxian	新鲜
xiuxian	休闲
yangqi ba	氧气吧
yumin	愚民
yushui	雨水
yu tian dou, qi le wuqiong	与天斗其乐无穷
zhengfu	政府
Zhongguo Qingnian Fangong Jiuguo Tuan	中国青年反共救国团
zhou	绉
Zhufu Lianmeng Huanjing Baohu Jijinhui	主妇联盟环境保护基金会
ziran	自然
ziran er ran	自然而然
Ziran zhi You	自然之友
Zushi Gong	祖师公

Bibliography

Adams, Jonathon S., and Thomas O. McShane. *The Myth of Wild Africa: Conservation without Illusion*. Berkeley: University of California Press, 1996.

Alford, William P. *et al.* "The Human Dimensions of Pollution Policy Implementation: Air Quality in Rural China." *Journal of Contemporary China* 11 (2002): 495–513.

Alford, William P., and Yuanyuan Shen. "The Limits of the Law in Addressing China's Environmental Dilemma." In *Energizing China: Reconciling Environmental Protection and Economic Growth*, ed. Michael B. McElroy, Chris P. Nielsen, and Peter Lydon, 405–30. Cambridge, MA: Harvard University Committee on the Environment, 1998.

Anderson, Eugene N. *Ecologies of the Heart: Emotion, Belief, and the Environment*. New York: Oxford University Press, 1996.

Appadurai, Arjun. "Global Ethnoscapes: Notes and Queries for a Transnational Anthropology." In *Recapturing Anthropology*, ed. Richard G. Fox, 191–210. Santa Fe: School of American Research, 1991.

Modernity at Large: Cultural Dimensions of Globalization. Minneapolis: University of Minnesota Press, 1996.

Barber, Benjamin R. *Jihad vs. McWorld*. New York: Times Books, 1995.

Bellah, Robert N. *et al. Habits of the Heart: Individualism and Commitment in American Life*. Berkeley: University of California Press, 1996.

Berger, Peter L., and Samuel Huntington, eds. *Many Globalizations: Cultural Diversity in the Contemporary World*. New York: Oxford University Press, 2002.

Berger, Peter, Brigitte Berger, and Hansfried Kellner. *The Homeless Mind: Modernization and Consciousness*. New York: Vintage, 1973.

Blasum, Holger. *Report on Environmental Awareness of Middle School and University Students*. n.d. accessed 21 July 2001, http://www.blasum.net/holger/wri/environ/china/studenv.htm.

Bloch, Maurice. "The Past and the Present in the Present." *Man* (N.S.) 12 (1977): 278–92.

Bloch, Maurice, and Jean H. Bloch. "Women and the Dialectics of Nature in Eighteenth-Century French Thought." In *Nature, Culture and Gender*, ed. Carol MacCormack and Marilyn Strathern, 25–41. Cambridge: Cambridge University Press, 1980.

Bramwell, Anna. *Ecology in the Twentieth Century: A History*. New Haven: Yale University Press, 1989.

Bruun, Ole. "The *Fengshui* Resurgence in China: Conflicting Cosmologies between State and Peasantry." *China Journal* 36 (1996): 47–65.

Chan, Kin-man. "Development of NGOs under a Post-Totalitarian Regime: The Case of China." In *Civil Life, Globalization, and Political Change in Asia: Organizing between Family and State*, ed. Robert P. Weller. London: Routledge, 2005.

Chan, Wing-tsit, compiler. *A Source Book in Chinese Philosophy*. Princeton: Princeton University Press, 1963.

Chang, K. C. *Early Chinese Civilization: Anthropological Perspectives*. Cambridge, MA: Harvard-Yenching Institute, 1976.

Chau, Adam Yuet. *Miraculous Response: Doing Popular Religion in Contemporary China*. Stanford: Stanford University Press, in press.

Clunas, Craig. *Fruitful Sites: Garden Culture in Ming Dynasty China*. Durham, NC: Duke University Press, 1996.

Cockel, Chris. "Tourism as a Development Solution or a Development Disaster: The Case Study of Hainan Island, South China." PhD diss., School of Oriental and African Studies, 1999.

Coggins, Chris. *The Tiger and the Pangolin: Nature, Culture, and Conservation in China*. Honolulu: University of Hawai'i Press, 2003.

The Complete Works of Chuang Tzu, trans. Burton Watson. New York: Columbia University Press, 1970.

Conklin, Beth A. "Shamans versus Pirates in the Amazonian Treasure Chest." *American Anthropologist* 104, no. 4 (2002): 1050–61.

Construction and Planning Administration, Ministry of the Interior. *A Journey through the National Parks of the Republic of China* (*Zhonghua Minguo Taiwan Diqu Guojia Gongyuan Jianjie*). Taipei: Construction and Planning Administration, 1985.

Cronon, William. *Changes in the Land: Indians, Colonists and the Ecology of New England*. New York: Hill and Wang, 1983.

Crumley, Carole L. "Heterarchy and the Analysis of Complex Societies." In *Heterarchy and the Analysis of Complex Societies*, ed. Robert M. Ehrenreich, Carole L. Crumley, and Janet E. Levy, 1–5. Arlington, VA: American Anthropological Association, 1995.

Dai Nihon Pyakka Jisho Benshoshu, ed. *Tetsugaku Daijisho* (*Dictionary of Philosophy*). Fifth edition. Tokyo: Dobunkan, 1924.

Dasgupta, Susmita, and David Wheeler. *Citizen Complaints as Environmental Indicators: Evidence from China*. Report to PRDEI, World Bank, 1996.

Deleuze, Gilles, and Félix Guattari. *A Thousand Plateaus: Capitalism and Schizophrenia*. 1980. Trans. Brian Massumi. Minneapolis: University of Minnesota Press, 1987.

Douglas, Mary. *Purity and Danger: An Analysis of Concepts of Pollution and Taboo*. London: Routledge and Kegan Paul, 1978 [1969].

Elman, Benjamin A. "Jesuit *Scientia* and Natural Studies in Late Imperial China, 1600–1800." *Early Modern History* 6, no. 3 (2002): 209–32.

Elvin, Mark. "The Environmental Legacy of Imperial China." *China Quarterly* 156 (December 1998): 733–56.

"Environmental Survey." *China Education News*, 1 June 1999.

Fang, Yuan. "The Environmental Awareness of Chinese Citizens: A Sociological Analysis." In *Environmental Awareness in Developing Countries: The Case of China and Thailand.* Tokyo: Japan/Asia Economic Development Institute, 1997.

Feng, Hui-t'ien, and Wolfram Eberhard. "On the Folklore of Chekiang: The Tree Temples of Chin-Hua (Chekiang)." In *Studies in Chinese Folklore and Related Essays*, ed. Wolfram Eberhard, 19–24. Indiana University Folklore Institute Monograph Series 23. The Hague: Mouton, 1970.

Friedman, Thomas L. *The Lexus and the Olive Tree: Understanding Globalization.* New York: Anchor Books, 2000.

Friends of Nature. *Environment Education.* 21 June 2002, http://www.fon.org.cn/english/1.htm.

FON's Bird Watching Group. 18 March 2004, http://www.fon.org.cn/index.php?id=255.

García, María Pilar. "The Venezuelan Ecology Movement: Symbolic Effectiveness, Social Practices, and Political Strategies." In *The Making of Social Movements in Latin America: Identity, Strategy and Democracy*, ed. Arturo Escobar and Sonia E. Alvarez, 150–70. Boulder, CO: Westview, 1992.

Gibbons, Felton, and Deborah Strom. *Neighbors to the Birds: A History of Birdwatching in America.* New York: W. W. Norton, 1988.

Giddens, Anthony. *Runaway World: How Globalization Is Reshaping Our Lives.* New York: Routledge, 2000.

Gimello, Robert M. "Chang Shang-Ying on Wu-T'ai Shan." In *Pilgrims and Sacred Sites in China*, ed. Susan Naquin and Yü Chün Fang, 89–149. Berkeley: University of California Press, 1992.

Gluckman, Ron. *Getting to the Top.* 24 February 2003. 3 May 2004, http://www.gluckman.com/Emei.html.

Grove, Richard H. *Green Imperialism: Colonial Expansion, Tropical Island Edens and the Origins of Environmentalism, 1600–1860.* Cambridge: Cambridge University Press, 1995.

Guan, Weihe, and Ray Zhang. "Beijing Residents Protest against Garbage Dump." *China News Digest* GL97-098, 11 July 1997. 11 July 1997, www.cnd.org.

Guangjing Tang Lishu (*Almanac from the Guangjing Hall*). Hong Kong: Hong Ming Brothers Press, 1979.

Guehenno, Jean-Marie. *The End of the Nation-State.* Minneapolis: University of Minnesota Press, 1996.

Guha, Ramachandra. *The Unquiet Woods: Ecological Change and Peasant Resistance in the Himalaya.* Berkeley: University of California Press, 1989.

Guoli Bianyiguan, ed. *Guomin Xiaoxue Changshi Keben* (*Textbook of Common Knowledge for Elementary Schools*). Taipei: Guoli Bianyiguan, 1974.

Hannerz, Ulf. *Transnational Connections: Culture, People, Places.* London: Routledge, 1996.

Harrell, Stevan. "Playing in the Valley: A Metonym of Modernization in Taiwan." In *Cultural Change in Postwar Taiwan*, ed. Stevan Harrell and Chün-chieh Huang, 161–83. Boulder, CO: Westview, 1994.

Hay, John. *Kernels of Energy, Bones of Earth: The Rock in Chinese Art.* New York: China Institute in America, 1985.

Herrold, Melinda. "From Adversary to Partner: The Evolving Role of a Nature Reserve in the Lives of Reserve Residents." Presented at the Annual Meeting, Association for Asian Studies. New York, 2003.

Hertsgaard, Mark. "Our Real China Problem." *Atlantic Monthly*, November 1997, 97–114.

Ho, Ming-Sho. "The Environmental Movements in the Democratic Transition in Taiwan." Presented at the Conference on Civil Society, Social Movements, and Democratization on Both Sides of the Taiwan Strait. Boston University, 24–25 April, 2001.

Ho, Peter. "Mao's War against Nature? The Environmental Impact of the Grain-First Campaign in China." *China Journal* 50 (July 2003): 37–59.

Hsiao, Hsin-Huang Michael. "NGOs, the State, and Democracy under Globalization: The Case of Taiwan." In *Civil Life, Globalization, and Political Change in Asia: Organizing between Family and State*, ed. Robert P. Weller. London: Routledge, 2005.

Hsiao, Michael Hsin-Huang, Russell A. Stone, and Chun-Chieh Chi. "Taiwan Environmental Consciousness: Indicators of Collective Mind toward Sustainable Development." *Research for Sustainable Taiwan* 4, no. 2 (2002): 1–33.

Inglehart, Ronald. *Culture Shift in Advanced Industrial Society*. Princeton: Princeton University Press, 1990.

Island of Diversity: Nature Conservation in Taiwan. Taipei: Council of Agriculture and Department of National Parks, 1992.

Jahiel, Abigail R. "The Contradictory Impact of Reform on Environmental Protection in China." *China Quarterly* 151 (1997): 81–103.

Jing, Jun. "Environmental Protests in Rural China." In *Chinese Society: Change, Conflict and Resistance*, ed. Mark Selden and Elizabeth J. Perry. New York: Routledge, 2000.

Johnson, Todd M., Feng Liu, and Richard Newfarmer. *Clear Water, Blue Skies: China's Environment in the New Century*. Washington, DC: The World Bank, 1997.

Kenting National Park, Republic of China. Taiwan: Kenting National Park Headquarters, n.d.

Kipnis, Andrew. "The Anthropology of Power and Maoism." *American Anthropologist* 105, no. 2 (2003): 278–88.

Latour, Bruno. *We Have Never Been Modern*. Cambridge, MA: Harvard University Press, 1993.

Laungaramsri, Pinkaew. "On the Politics of Nature Conservation in Thailand." *Kyoto Review of Southeast Asia* 2, October 2002. 18 March 2004, http://kyotoreview.cseas.kyoto-u.ac.jp/issue/issue1/.

Lee, Leo Ou-fan. *The Romantic Generation of Modern Chinese Writers*. Cambridge, MA: Harvard University Press, 1973.

Life Away from Home Magazine, ed. *Taiwan Zui Jia Quchu* (*Taiwan's Most Beautiful Places*), 6 vols. Taipei: Huwai Shenghuo Zazhi, 1990.

Litzinger, Ralph. "The Mobilization of 'Nature': Perspectives from Northwest Yunnan." *China Quarterly* 118 (June 2004): 488–505.

Liu, Jianguo *et al.* "A Framework for Evaluating the Effects of Human Factors on Wildlife Habitat: The Case of Giant Pandas." *Conservation Biology* 13, no. 6 (December 1999): 1360–70.

Liu, Xin. *In One's Own Shadow: An Ethnographic Account of the Condition of Post-Reform China*. Berkeley: University of California Press, 2000.

Lu, Hwei-syin. "Women's Self-Growth Groups and Empowerment of the 'Uterine Family' in Taiwan." *Bulletin of the Institute of Ethnology, Academia Sinica* 71 (1991): 29–62.

Lüshi Qunqiu. Sibu Congkan edition. Shanghai: Shangwu Yinshuguan, 1929.

MacKenzie, John M. *The Empire of Nature: Hunting, Conservation and British Imperialism*. Manchester: Manchester University Press, 1988.

Major, John. *Heaven and Earth in Early Han Thought: Chapters Three, Four, and Five of the Huainanzi*. Albany: State University of New York Press, 1993.

Marx, Leo. *The Machine in the Garden: Technology and the Pastoral Ideal in America*. Oxford: Oxford University Press, 2000.

Migdal, Joel S. "Capitalist Penetration in the Nineteenth Century: Creating Conditions for New Patterns of Social Control." In *Power and Protest in the Countryside: Rural Unrest in Asia, Europe and Latin America*, ed. Robert P. Weller and Scott E. Guggenheim, 57–74. Durham, NC: Duke University Press, 1982.

Mitsuda, Hisayoshi, and Charles Geisler. "Imperiled Parks and Imperiled People: Lessons from Japan's Shiretoko National Park." *Environmental History Review* 16 (1992): 23–39.

Muir, John. *Our National Parks*. Boston: Houghton Mifflin, 1901.

Nonini, Donald M., and Aihwa Ong. "Chinese Transnationalism as an Alternative Modernity." In *Ungrounded Empires: The Cultural Politics of Modern Chinese Transnationalism*, ed. Aihwa Ong and Donald Nonini, 3–33. New York: Routledge, 1997.

O'Brien, Kevin J., and Lianjiang Li. "Suing the Local State: Administrative Litigation in Rural China." *China Journal* 51 (January 2004): 75–96.

Ohmae, Kenichi. *The End of the Nation-State: The Rise of Regional Economies*. New York: Free Press, 1995.

Oi, Jean C. "Realms of Freedom in Post-Mao China." In *Realms of Freedom in Modern China*, ed. William C. Kirby, 264–84. Stanford: Stanford University Press, 2004.

Pei, M. "Chinese Intermediate Associations: An Empirical Analysis." *Modern China* 24, no. 3 (July 1998): 285–318.

Perdue, Peter C. *Exhausting the Earth: State and Peasant in Hunan, 1500–1850*. Cambridge, MA: Council on East Asian Studies, Harvard University, 1987.

Potter, Sulamith Heins, and Jack M. Potter. *China's Peasants: The Anthropology of a Revolution*. Cambridge: Cambridge University Press, 1990.

Puett, Michael J. *To Become a God: Cosmology, Sacrifice, and Self-Divinization in Early China*. Cambridge, MA: Harvard University Asia Center, 2002.

Putnam, Robert D. *Bowling Alone: The Collapse and Revival of American Community*. New York: Simon and Schuster, 2000.

Read, Benjamin L. "Democratizing the Neighborhood? New Private Housing and Home-Owner Self-Organization in Urban China." *China Journal* 49 (January 2003): 31–59.

Reardon-Anderson, James. *Pollution, Politics, and Foreign Investment in Taiwan: The Lukang Rebellion*. Armonk, NY: M. E. Sharpe, 1992.

Redclift, Michael. *Sustainable Development: Exploring the Contradictions*. London: Methuen, 1987.

Rostow, Walter W. *The Stages of Economic Growth: A Non-Communist Manifesto*. Cambridge: Cambridge University Press, 1960.

Royal Society for the Protection of Birds. *History of the RSPB*. 2004. 18 March 2004, http://www.rspb.org.uk/about/history/index.asp.

Sangren, P. Steven. *History and Magical Power in a Chinese Community*. Stanford: Stanford University Press, 1987.

Saso, Michael. "Orthodoxy and Heterodoxy in Taoist Ritual." In *Religion and Ritual in Chinese Society*, ed. Arthur P. Wolf, 325–36. Stanford: Stanford University Press, 1974.

Sassen, Saskia. *Globalization and Its Discontents*. New York: New Press, 1998.

Losing Control? Sovereignty in an Age of Globalization. New York: Columbia University Press, 1996.

Schama, Simon. *Landscape and Memory*. New York: A. A. Knopf, 1995.

Schoppa, R. Keith. *Xiang Lake – Nine Centuries of Chinese Life*. New Haven: Yale University Press, 1989.

Schwartz, Benjamin. *In Search of Wealth and Power: Yen Fu and the West*. Cambridge, MA: Harvard University Press, 1964.

Shapiro, Judith. *Mao's War against Nature: Politics and the Environment in Revolutionary China*. New York: Cambridge University Press, 2001.

Smil, Vaclav. *China's Environmental Crisis: An Inquiry into the Limits of National Development*. Armonk, NY: M. E. Sharpe, 1993.

Smith, Joanna F. Handlin. "Gardens in Ch'i Piao-Chia's Social World: Wealth and Values in Late-Ming Kiangnan." *Journal of Asian Studies* 51, no. 1 (1992): 55–81.

Songster, E. Elena. "Reserving Nature for Communist Conservation." Presented at the Annual Meeting of the Association for Asian Studies. New York, 27–30 March, 2003.

State Statistical Bureau, People's Republic of China. *China Statistical Yearbook*. Beijing: State Statistical Bureau, 1998.

Steering Committee, Taiwan 2000 Study. *Taiwan 2000: Balancing Economic Growth and Environmental Protection*. Taipei, 1989.

Stein, Rolf A. *The World in Miniature: Container Gardens and Dwellings in Far Eastern Religious Thought*, trans. Phyllis Brooks. Stanford: Stanford University Press, 1990.

Thomas, Julia Adeney. " 'To Become as One Dead': Nature and the Political Subject in Modern Japan." In *The Moral Authority of Nature*, ed. Lorraine Daston and Fernando Vidal, 308–30. Chicago: University of Chicago Press, 2004.

Thomas, Keith. *Man and the Natural World: A History of the Modern Sensibility*. New York: Pantheon, 1983.

Thompson, Stuart E. "Death, Food, and Fertility." In *Death Ritual in Late Imperial and Modern China*, ed. James L. Watson and Evelyn S. Rawski, 71–108. Berkeley: University of California Press, 1988.

Thoreau, Henry David. *Walden and Civil Disobedience*. New York: Penguin, 1986.

Tilt, Bryan D. "Risk, Pollution and Sustainability in Rural Sichuan, China." PhD diss., University of Washington, 2004.

Totman, Conrad. *The Green Archipelago*. Berkeley: University of California Press, 1989.

Tourism Bureau, Republic of China Ministry of Transportation. *Zhonghua Minguo 77 Nian Taiwan Diqu Guomin Lüyou Zhuangkuang Diaocha Baogao (Investigative Report on the Condition of Citizens' Travel in the Taiwan Region, Republic of China, 1988)*. Taipei, 1989.

Zhonghua Minguo 80 Nian Taiwan Diqu Guomin Lüyou Zhuangkuang Diaocha Baogao (Investigative Report on the Condition of Citizens' Travel in the Taiwan Region, Republic of China, 1991). Taipei, 1991.

Tsai, Lily Lee. "Cadres, Temple and Lineage Institutions, and Governance in Rural China." *The China Journal* 48 (July 2002): 1–27.

Tu, Weiming. "Beyond the Enlightenment Mentality." In *Confucianism and Ecology*, ed. Mary Evelyn Tucker and John Berthrong, 3–21. Cambridge, MA: Harvard University Center for the Study of World Religions, 1998.

Turner, Terence. "Indigenous Rights, Environmental Protection and the Struggle over Forest Resources in the Amazon: The Case of the Brazilian Kayapo." In *Earth, Air, Fire, and Water: The Humanities and the Environment*, ed. Jill Conway, Kenneth Keniston, and Leo Marx. Amherst: University of Massachusetts Press, 2000.

UNESCO. *Biosphere Reserves in a Nutshell*. 19 March 2004. 1 April 2004, http://www.unesco.org/mab/nutshell.htm.

Unger, Jonathan. *The Transformation of Rural China*. Armonk, NY: M. E. Sharpe, 2002.

Wallerstein, Immanuel. *The Modern World-System: Capitalist Agriculture and the Origins of the European World-Economy in the Sixteenth Century*. Studies in Social Discontinuity. New York: Academic Press, 1974.

Watson, James L. "Introduction: Transnationalism, Localization, and Fast Foods in East Asia." In *Golden Arches East: McDonald's in East Asia*, ed. James L. Watson, 1–38. Stanford: Stanford University Press, 1997.

Weller, Robert P. *Alternate Civilities: Democracy and Culture in China and Taiwan*. Boulder, CO: Westview, 1999.

ed. *Civil Life, Globalization, and Political Change in Asia: Organizing between Family and State*. London: Routledge, 2005.

"Matricidal Magistrates and Gambling Gods: Weak States and Strong Spirits in China." *Australian Journal of Chinese Affairs* 33 (1995): 107–24.

"Worship, Teachings, and State Power in China and Taiwan." In *Realms of Freedom in Modern China*, ed. William C. Kirby, 285–314. Stanford: Stanford University Press, 2004.

Weller, Robert P. *et al. Dangdai Huaren Chengshi Shehui de Minjian Zuzhi: Taibei, Xianggang, Guangzhou, Xiamen de Bijiao Fenxi (Civil Associations in Contemporary Chinese Urban Societies: A Comparative Analysis of Taibei, Hong Kong, Guangzhou, and Xiamen)*. Occasional Paper 123. Hong Kong: Chinese University of Hong Kong, Institute of Asia-Pacific Studies, 2002.

Weller, Robert P., and Peter K. Bol. "From Heaven-and-Earth to Nature: Chinese Concepts of the Environment and Their Influence on Policy

Implementation." In *Confucianism and Ecology: The Interrelation of Heaven, Earth, and Humans*, ed. Mary Evelyn Tucker and John Berthrong, 313–41. Cambridge, MA: Harvard University Center for the Study of World Religions, 1998.

Weller, Robert P., and Hsin-Huang Michael Hsiao. "Culture, Gender and Community in Taiwan's Environmental Movement." In *Environmental Movements in Asia*, ed. Arne Kalland and Gerard Persoon, 83–109. Surrey: Curzon, 1998.

White, Lynn. "The Historical Roots of Our Ecological Crisis." *Science* 155 (10 March 1967): 1203–7.

Williams, Raymond. *Keywords: A Vocabulary of Culture and Society*. Revised edition. New York: Oxford University Press, 1983.

Wolf, Margery. *The House of Lim: A Study of a Chinese Farm Family*. New York: Appleton-Century-Crofts, 1968.

World Conservation Union (IUCN). *Guidelines for Protected Area Management Categories*. 29 October 2001. 31 March 2004, www.wcmc.org.uk/protected_areas/categories/eng/c2.htm.

Wu, Pei-yi. "An Ambivalent Pilgrim to T'ai Shan in the Seventeenth Century." In *Pilgrims and Sacred Sites in China*, ed. Susan Naquin and Chün Fang Yü, 65–88. Berkeley: University of California Press, 1992.

Xia, Guang. "An Estimate of the Economic Consequences of Environmental Pollution in China." In *Project on Environmental Scarcities, State Capacity, and Civil Violence*, ed. Vaclav Smil and Yushi Mao, 41–59. Cambridge, MA: Committee on International Security Studies, American Academy of Arts and Sciences, 1997.

Xingzheng Yuan Huanjing Baohu Ju, producer. *Huanbao Xiao Yingxiong* (*Little Heroes of Environmental Protection*). Videotape. Taipei, 1991.

Xi Shan Qing (*Feelings on Streams and Mountains*), ed. Wenqing Huang and Guiyu Zhuang. Taroko: Taroko National Park Administration, 1987.

Xu, Xiping *et al.* "Occupational and Environmental Risk Factors for Asthma in Rural Communities in China." *International Journal of Occupational and Environmental Health* 2 (1996): 172–6.

Yang, Mayfair Mei-hui. *Gifts, Favors and Banquets: The Art of Social Relationships in China*. Ithaca: Cornell University Press, 1994.

Yu, Chien. "Three Types of Chinese Deities – Stone, Tree, and Land." PhD diss., Religious Studies, Lancaster University, 1997.

Zhang, Li. "Migration and Privatization of Space and Power in Late Socialist China." *American Ethnologist* 28, no. 1 (2001): 179–205.

Zhang, Wei'an. "Fuojiao Ciji Gongde Hui Yu Ziyuan Huishou [The Buddhist Compassion Merit Society and Recycling]." Paper presented at the Workshop on Culture, Media and Society in Contemporary Taiwan. Harvard University, 12 June, 1996.

Zhongguo Huanjing Nianjian Bianji Weiyuanhui, ed. *Zhongguo Huanjing Nianjian* (*China Environmental Yearbook*). Beijing: Zhongguo Huanjing Kexue Chubanshe, 1996.

Index